EASY MONEY

"Funny and revealing... This is one of the most readable romps about finance gone mad." —The *Times* (UK)

"If you're looking for a smart, savvy road map through the mayhem of the cryptocurrency madness, *Easy Money* is the guidebook for you. Ben McKenzie has given us a wry and knowing saga of his personal quest to expose the crypto charlatans, and his sleuthing uncovers a world of frauds, true believers, and opportunists that you won't soon forget." —**Ron Chernow, Pulitzer Prize–winning and *New York Times* bestselling author of *Alexander Hamilton* and *The House of Morgan***

"Ben McKenzie takes us on an amazing journey, guiding us through the astounding story of how a bizarre cast of swindlers and scammers persuaded millions of people to take leave of their senses and part with trillions of dollars, only to put them into the surreal and illusory world of so called 'crypto assets' and watch them vanish into thin air. When it is all over, the last couple of years will prove to have been one of the strangest episodes in the history of money." —**Liaquat Ahamed, Pulitzer Prize–winning author of *Lords of Finance***

"Ben McKenzie's *Easy Money* is a perfectly timed page-turner that gets to the heart of the fundamental scam that was (and is) the mania around cryptocurrency. It's a devastatingly well-told story of greed, con men, and endless gullibility. McKenzie goes down the rabbit hole, only to become a full-throated skeptic who then takes us along on his journey of enlightenment and discovery, proving once again that if something seems too good to be true, it probably is." —**William D. Cohan, *New York Times* bestselling author of *Power Failure* and *House of Cards***

"*Easy Money* is the delightful story of how actor Ben McKenzie and journalist Jacob Silverman realized long before most of the rest of us that cryptocurrency was a scam, and set out to take it and all of its promoters down. One part travelogue and one part anatomy of a fraud, it's a must-read for anyone who wants to understand what the hell happened—and how human nature works when there's money to be made." —**Bethany McLean,** *New York Times* **bestselling author of** *The Smartest Guys in the Room* **and** *The Big Fail*

"Superb ... the terrible story of our economic times." —**Julian Zelizer, coeditor of** *Myth America* **and professor of history and public affairs at Princeton University**

"*Easy Money* is a deceptively ambitious project—at once a riveting account of the financial crime of the century, and a thoughtful meditation on the nature of democracy and what we owe each other." —**Zachary Carter, author of** *The Price of Peace: Money, Democracy, and the Life of John Maynard Keynes*

"*Easy Money* is a smart, fast-paced, and timely exposé of corporate greed, fraud, and incompetence masquerading as genius. Simultaneously illuminating and infuriating, authors McKenzie and Silverman's page-turning book goes on a global journey to explain how crypto is the latest Ponzi scheme orchestrated to seduce and defraud the masses while benefitting the very few." —**Wajahat Ali, author of** *Go Back to Where You Came From*

EASY MONEY

CRYPTOCURRENCY, CASINO CAPITALISM, AND THE GOLDEN AGE OF FRAUD

BEN MCKENZIE

with Jacob Silverman

ABRAMS PRESS, NEW YORK

Library of Congress Control Number: 2022950054

Paperback ISBN: 978-1-4197-6640-4
eISBN: 978-1-64700-925-0

Printed and bound in the United States
10 9 8 7 6 5 4 3 2 1

ABRAMS The Art of Books
195 Broadway, New York, NY 10007
abramsbooks.com

To Morena, Julius, Frances, and Arthur
My Home Team

And in memory of Chris Huvane

CONTENTS

AUTHOR'S NOTE

IF YOU CURRENTLY own, or have ever owned, cryptocurrency and have lost money on that investment, rest assured that you are not alone. In fact, you join the ranks of the vast majority of crypto investors, numbering in the tens of millions in America alone, and hundreds of millions worldwide. This book is for you, whether you like it or not. If you want a window into how you may have been swindled, read on.

If you are among the 84 percent of the country that did not indulge, congratulations! But don't get too cocky. Life's a gamble and no one knows the odds.

To be clear, that gamble goes both ways. What follows is my opinion of the events as I perceived them over the nearly two years I spent down the crypto rabbit hole. Throughout the book I use terms like "fraudsters," "conmen," "swindlers," and "scammers" in reference to various actors in the crypto industry. These descriptors are nothing more than shorthand for my opinion. I don't mean to imply that any particular person, in fact, broke a law or violated a regulation. In a similar vein, not everyone who works in cryptocurrency has poor intentions. While we may disagree wildly as to crypto's usefulness, they have not committed fraud. It is my hope they will join me in condemning those who have.

Let the chips fall where they may.

CHAPTER 1

MONEY AND LYING

THIS IS A book about cryptocurrency and fraud: a parable of money and lying, or rather a parable of fake money and lying for money. Thematically, it bears striking resemblance to a popular folktale. Unlike that tale, however, this story is true.

We begin during the wild speculative mania of the Trump years. It was the fleeting era of meme stocks, NFTs, and land sales in the metaverse. While the marketing may have been new, the economics were familiar: These get-rich-quick speculative schemes were merely the latest iteration of casino capitalism. Political economist Susan Strange populated the term in the 1980s, but its roots stretch at least as far back as the 1930s. In *The General Theory of Employment, Interest, and Money*, economist John Maynard Keynes rebuked the boom-and-bust cycles of stocks, where long-shot gambles in unregulated markets—particularly prior to the invention of securities laws—created and destroyed fortunes overnight. Almost a century later, the casino descriptor proves even more apt: Cryptocurrencies and their assorted byproducts are generally regarded by economists as at best zero-sum. One person's gain is another's loss.

You may have noticed something about cryptocurrencies: They don't *do* anything. Sure, you can trade them, betting that one will rise or fall, but they aren't used for anything productive. Cryptos aren't tied to anything of real value, unlike shares in a company or a commodities future. They're computer code uncorrelated with any actual asset. Even the most arcane financial products have some relation to something of use in the material world.

Because they don't actually create any value in and of themselves, investing in cryptocurrency is more akin to gambling—shuffling assets among participants in a game of chance. It's the digital equivalent of playing poker at a casino; you might win, you might not, but there is no increase in overall utility. Nothing of value has been created by playing. Zero-sum games are strictly competitive: For you to win, another player must lose. Much like in a regular casino, the players themselves are required to pay a small amount each hand to keep the game going. In crypto, this comes from the fees charged by the exchanges, as well as the costs associated with validating the transactions. In Las Vegas, it's called *the rake*, the amount the house takes from every pot. This means that, given enough time, the average gambler will lose. It's how casinos keep the lights on. Given a long enough time frame, the house always wins—it has to.

To state the obvious, gambling is not really a valid use case for crypto. You can gamble on literally anything that hasn't happened yet. For example, I could bet that you will finish the sentence you are currently reading. (I win.) Even licensed gambling is not a productive use of capital, and we will delve into its myriad drawbacks throughout this book, but at least when you go to Vegas you know the odds. There's a long list of rules and regulations a casino must follow. There's also entertainment value in the experience. Gamblers may win or lose money at the tables, but at least they're comped a few drinks, they can have a nice dinner and catch a show. Crypto is Vegas without the drinks, the dinner, or the show. At times, I suspected it was even worse than that.

That brings us to the Golden Age of Fraud. Jim Chanos, the legendary short-seller who coined the phrase, knows the subject well. Betting against fraudulent companies like Enron and the German payments company Wirecard made him a fortune. These days, Chanos sees fraud—defined as deception for personal, usually financial, gain—almost everywhere he looks. When I first started paying attention to financial markets in the fall of 2020, I came to a similar conclusion, a troubling sense that graft and deceit had penetrated all aspects of the economy, operating with political and legal impunity. It made me want to scream in anger—and to make a wager of my own.

In 2016, the United States of America elected a con man as president. Millions of Americans from all walks of life cast their votes for Donald Trump over Hillary Clinton. Although Clinton won the popular vote by millions, it didn't matter. Thanks to the peculiar framework of the Electoral College, the world's largest economy elected a man who will lie about anything. Donald Trump wasn't the first liar to occupy the White House, but he may have been the first to exist in a world beyond reason. He helped form a political culture in which truth—factual consensus reality—didn't matter. It was the time of "alternative facts." Fraud and corruption could operate without fear of consequence.

The simultaneous rise in the spread of misinformation has been well-documented, alongside a related trend: the erosion of trust between citizens and their government, and also between one another. In a trustless society, conflict risks becoming all too common, as suspicion and bad faith dominate every interaction. When trust breaks down en masse, when misinformation spreads like a virus, when there are few institutions deserving of our faith or respect, when people view their only way to win as by making someone else lose, we find ourselves in perilous territory.

Easy Money is a work of reportage, culled from hundreds of interviews, too many late nights of brain-melting research, and more than a few bizarre adventures in the world of digital funny money. My colleague Jacob Silverman and I have talked to people inside and outside of crypto, the titans of industry and the average Joes, believers, skeptics, victims, villains, and a few slippery figures who proved difficult to pin down. Although the story starts with me, this book is about them. Over the course of the next thirteen chapters, we will take you on a journey that begins in my tiny office in Brooklyn and rapidly expands to cover the globe. From Texas to Florida, El Salvador to Washington, D.C., and even into the wilds of Manhattan, we will give you an inside look at one of the greatest frauds in history, bigger than Madoff by an order of magnitude.

As a longtime TV actor with a decades-old degree in economics, I might seem like an unlikely casting choice as the author of a book about cryptocurrency. But however strange, my background actually positions me well to pierce the hallucinatory bubble powered by fantasy money. At its core, this is a tale of money and lying. What I know of money I learned in a classroom more than twenty years ago (and from making a little bit of it in Hollywood). What I know of lying I learned from two decades spent in show business. Cryptography, computer science, and finance are not my forte, but I can recognize when they're being used to conjure—to sell—a narrative that might not be true.

I'm a storyteller, too. So let me tell you one.

o o o

In the fall of 2020, the market for so-called cryptocurrencies—cryptographically secured bits of code, transactions for which are often recorded on distributed ledgers known as *blockchains*—exploded. A few thousand cryptos in 2020 grew to 20,000 two years later, and their purported value swelled in tandem, from some $300 billion in the summer of 2020 to $3 trillion by November 2021. An estimated forty million Americans and hundreds of millions worldwide—disproportionately young and male—were drawn into the speculative frenzy. They poured billions of dollars, euros, yuan, and other real monies into digital tokens through the more than 500 crypto exchanges operating worldwide. Most invested for a simple reason—they wanted to make money—and were inspired by tales (and social media rumors) of friends and strangers reaping huge gains by investing in digital tokens. Infected by FOMO—fear of missing out—they now wanted a part of the action.

As more people bought into the hype and saw their investments rise in value (at least on screen), they became de facto evangelists for the fledgling industry, preaching the gospel of crypto to all who would listen. The potential profits seemed unlimited, and the barriers to entry were low. The only thing needed to own a piece of the "future of money" was a willingness to part with the current version of it. The more people invested, the more prices rose, resulting in even more FOMO that drew in yet more people—a self-reinforcing dynamic common to economic bubbles and Ponzi schemes. Quite simply, crypto had gone viral.

In his 2019 book *Narrative Economics*, Nobel Prize–winning economist Robert Shiller examined how economic narratives spread by drawing on decades of research from fields such as history, sociology, anthropology, psychology, marketing, literary criticism, and perhaps most fittingly for our purposes, epidemiology. He defined an economic narrative as "a contagious story that has the potential to change how people make economic decisions, such as the decision to . . . invest in a volatile speculative asset." His first example? Bitcoin.

The stories that resonate with the public don't exist in a vacuum; they're part of the society and culture from which they emerge. Similarly, economic narratives develop in response to actual economic events. Causality runs both ways; an economic narrative that develops in reaction to a particular economic event can precipitate a future one.

Imagine a small bank in a rural town. One year, a drought results in a poor harvest, eliminating whatever profits local farmers might have expected. A rumor starts that farmers could default on their loans. The bank's financial position is in fact healthy and hedged against such a possibility, but these rumors gather steam, and an economic narrative forms that the bank itself may become insolvent. As more and more depositors attempt to take their money out, a bank run ensues, resulting in its financial collapse. The economic event, a drought, didn't directly produce the bank run—the bank was healthy. It was the rapid spread of a distorted economic narrative that led to its downfall. *Narrative Economics* was published in 2019, prior to both the current viral spread of cryptocurrency and the COVID-19 pandemic. Given that, it is remarkable to observe how intertwined these two viruses would become in the following years.

To understand the origins of economic narratives surrounding Bitcoin and other cryptocurrencies, we have to go back to the events that inspired them. Both crypto and the "easy money" policies from which this book derives its title sprang from the same roots: the Global Financial Crisis (GFC), also known as the *subprime crisis*.

o o o

In 2008, an economic earthquake shook the foundation of the global economy. Unbeknownst to most Americans, pressure had been building underneath the surface of the housing market for years. Two of its biggest drivers were financial deregulation and low interest rates—a decades-long, mostly bipartisan political effort to grow the financial sector combined with a policy intended to stimulate the economy in the wake of the first dot-com bubble. Between 2000 and 2003, the Federal Reserve—the Fed, the nation's central bank—lowered interest rates from 6.5 percent to 1 percent. Members of Congress from both parties, as well as the George W. Bush administration, encouraged credit to flow into the housing market. The stated political aspiration was to create an "ownership society" of homeowners.

The economic effect, however, proved far less noble. Lenders issued mortgages with abandon, often to poor and working-class people who had little hope of actually repaying them. Many received so-called subprime mortgages. Because the borrower was more likely to default than a recipient of a prime loan, the loan carried a higher—and often variable—interest rate. The low-quality loans were then bundled by the banks into mortgage-backed securities and collateralized default obligations (CDOs). Those loan packages were then marketed as low-risk and sold off in huge quantities to institutional investors and other large clients. Some of these mortgage-based financial products were chopped up further, reconfigured into ever more complicated financial instruments. Ratings agencies—whose job was to assess risk—bestowed high marks on potentially worthless financial products in order to stay in the good graces of their Wall Street clients. As a result, rigidity, complexity, and leverage seeped into the financial system to an extent that even many people in finance didn't comprehend.

Economists focus on incentive structures, and with subprime loans the incentives were skewed up and down the chain. From the mortgage officer hoping to make a commission to the executive who needed to show ever better sales numbers to the profit-focused corporate boards, few had an incentive to step back and ask if any of it was prudent. The dominant economic thinking of the time was that housing prices would only continue to go up. The idea that there could be a broad decline in the value of US housing seemed far-fetched, even ridiculous. When had that ever happened before? Of course there were warning signs, and some people made a lot of money betting on a crash, as *The Big Short* dramatized so well on the page and on the big screen. But the people holding the purse strings and their allies in power thought that the good times would go on forever, so they enacted self-interested policies and placed risky bets. Such recklessness is easy to come by when you gamble with other people's money, there's little chance of accountability, and you can convince yourself the market only moves in one direction.

As the housing market continued to stall in early 2008 and the economy showed signs of entering a recession, the federal government intervened, trying to stave off a broader disaster. In January, the Fed slashed interest rates by three-fourths of a point, the biggest cut in twenty-five years. It wasn't nearly enough: More decisive action was needed to stem the collapse of the finance industry and, by extension, the overall economy. In March, the government began bailing out bond dealers, the people who had made toxic mortgage-backed securities and credit-default swaps. It was the first in a long list of actions that essentially guaranteed the finance industry's bad debt, but did little to help homeowners and everyday Americans. After Lehman Brothers declared bankruptcy in September 2008, equities and commodities prices crashed, and the world economy appeared on the brink of collapse. Coordinating with other countries' central banks, the US government offered $700 billion in bank bailouts and trillions in loan guarantees, managing to stem the worst of the contagion. Quantitative easing (QE), whereby a central bank purchases financial products on the open market to assure investors, did the rest. By buying longer-dated treasuries and mortgage-backed securities, the Fed encouraged lending and investment. Alongside the bailout and loan guarantees, QE took trillions of dollars of corporate debt off the books of some of the largest (and until recently, most profitable) companies in the country. That debt was absorbed by the balance sheet of the federal government. Before the crisis, the Fed's assets were $900 billion. By early 2010, they were $2.3 trillion.

It didn't end there. Originally intended as a short-term response to an immediate crisis, these policies became entrenched. For both political and economic reasons, the Fed would find it impossible to unwind its backstop of the economy. In fact, it continued to grow. By late 2014, what had been $2.3 trillion of assets on the Fed's books had grown to over $4.4 trillion, a level at which it would more or less remain until March 2020, when COVID-19 hit. At the same time, interest rates stayed historically low as well: effectively 0 percent until 2016, and only rising above 2 percent in 2019.

The government's response to the subprime disaster spawned an era of easy money that benefited deep-pocketed corporations above everyone else, but that was not all it produced. In the wake of the general distrust born of the crisis, a new mutation to the financial system emerged: cryptocurrency.

o o o

The American people had bailed out corporate America, and they were not happy about it. The finance executives who profited from the housing bubble got off scot-free—only one guy, an executive at Credit Suisse, did any jail time. Millions of average folks were saddled with unsustainable debt, contributing to a rise in homelessness, suicide, and depression. The losses were effectively socialized. A powerful narrative developed from the tragedy, that of regular people getting screwed over by the elites. On the left, this helped inspire the Occupy Wall Street movement. On the right, it was the Tea Party. On the internet, through a pseudonymous author (or authors), another story was born.

On Halloween night 2008, someone or some people calling themselves Satoshi Nakamoto published what would come to be known as the Bitcoin white paper. We still don't know who Satoshi was, but their white paper would have a profound impact on financial innovation and the future of digital money. Satoshi had a clear vision: "A purely peer-to-peer version of electronic cash would allow online payments to be sent directly from one party to another without going through a financial institution. . . . The network itself requires minimal structure."

Satoshi's proposal was bold, billed as a new method that would allow people to transact directly with one another, bypassing financial institutions. (In fact, that's not really true; people wouldn't transact directly but rather through a shared database under common or collaborative control.) To replace a centralized authority like a bank was easier said than done, but Satoshi offered a novel solution. It rested on combining two previous developed technologies: public key encryption and blockchain.

Public key encryption plays a vital role in modern life. For example, all https:// websites (nearly all the ones the average person uses) employ public key encryption. It does things like protect users' credit card information from being stolen when making online purchases. Public key encryption has two useful properties: Anyone can verify the legitimacy of a transaction using publicly available information (the public key), but the people/parties conducting those transactions are able to keep their identities hidden (the private key).

Satoshi linked Bitcoin's system of numbered accounts (or addresses) to public keys. Transfers of Bitcoin between accounts are messages signed by the private key corresponding to the originating address, authorizing the transfer to the receiving address or addresses. Addresses are then organized into "wallets," software that handles the bookkeeping and translates it into the equivalent of a single bank balance rather than dozens or hundreds of different addresses. Importantly, Bitcoin ownership is pseudonymous (but not anonymous, as is often mistakenly claimed). Everyone can see which addresses are interacting with one another on a public ledger, but the public is not aware of who owns which address.

This time-stamped, append-only ledger is the blockchain. In 1991, computer scientists Stuart Haber and W. Scott Stornetta, building off the work of cryptographer David Chaum, figured out a way to timestamp documents so they couldn't be altered. Each "block" contains the cryptographic hash (a short, computable summary of all the data in it) of the prior block, linking the two and creating an irreversible record, a ledger composed of blocks of data that can be added to a chain (*blockchain*), but never subtracted from.

So far so good, but one issue remained: what's known as the *double spend problem*. If you remove a centralized authority from the equation, how do you make sure people aren't gaming the system by spending money that's already been sent somewhere else? How do you secure the network against manipulation? "Satoshi" relied on what's called a *consensus algorithm.*

A consensus algorithm is a process by which people with differing views can reach limited agreement about an outcome over time. Bitcoin's innovation is to do this without trusting any clock. Every block in the Bitcoin ledger has to conform with the rules of Bitcoin; for example, you can't spend money you don't have. That's very quickly checkable, but how do you know which blocks are in the ledger?

Each block published references the last block, conforms to all the rules, and has a hash. Many, many, many candidate blocks are calculated to find the next block, but once it is found, the entire network can agree that it was the right next block.

However, they can't reach this agreement worldwide instantly, and so there are additional rules. These rules have the effect of increasing the certainty of the right current block, and its predecessors, over time. The network targets a new block every ten minutes or so, by dynamically adjusting the degree of difficulty required in the winning block; the more participants, the harder the process gets, and the more energy is required to guess the next block correctly. This is the *proof of work* behind Bitcoin: lots and lots of computers ("miners") performing relatively simple mathematical calculations over and over again endlessly. The miner who stumbles upon the right block is rewarded with a Bitcoin for its effort. After about an hour, participants in the network are convinced about history six blocks deep; they know that it is extremely unlikely anyone will rewrite that history.

As you may be able to tell, Satoshi's vision is both immensely clever but also cumbersome, practically speaking. As more competitors enter, the hash rate increases and more energy is expended to agree upon a block of data that remains roughly the same size. This is what's called a Red Queen's race, a reference to Lewis Carroll's *Alice in Wonderland*. As the Queen says to Alice, "Now, here, you see, it takes all the running you can do, to keep in the same place. If you want to get somewhere else, you must run at least twice as fast as that!"

That was the basic technological and philosophical framework for Bitcoin, the original cryptocurrency, from which all others sprang. Ethereum, the second largest cryptocurrency as of this writing, was launched in 2015. It offered an alternative open-source blockchain and became notable for offering what are called *smart contracts*: small computer programs that execute functions automatically on the Ethereum blockchain. A simple example might be to use smart contracts to replicate the escrow process. You could program a transaction that would go through only if two of the three parties said it should, like a buyer, a seller, and a trusted referee. This would let the contract act as something like an escrow agent, with a critical difference: The escrow agent never has to actually hold the money. (That's the idea anyway; in practice these "contracts" often run into problems, both practically and legally.)

Regardless, smart contracts were billed as a way to automate financial markets and to introduce complicated new financial instruments. Out of these emerged DeFi, or decentralized finance, a vast, unregulated ecosystem of crypto exchanges, lending pools, trading protocols (protocol in this context means a set of rules that allow data to be shared between computers), and complex financial products. Ethereum also led to the introduction of NFTs, which are basically links to receipts for JPEGs stored on blockchains (shh, don't tell that to anyone who owns one). The number of cryptos exploded around this time, rising tenfold in five years, from less than one hundred in 2013 to more than a thousand by 2017. There are now an estimated 20,000 cryptos, most of them small and insignificant, their ownership concentrated in the hands of a few "whales," much like penny stocks.

If all this sounds complicated and confusing, don't worry, you're not alone. It's confusing to me even now. If it makes you feel any better, most people who own Bitcoin can't accurately explain it (although they will swear they can). Here's the good news: You are now free to forget everything I just said. The operational details of blockchain technology are not important to understanding cryptocurrency's rise in popular culture. Remember, blockchain is at least thirty years old and barely used by businesses outside of the crypto industry. Since at least 2016, hundreds of enterprises have tried to incorporate it into their business models, only to later scrap it because it didn't work any better than what they were already using. Ask yourself a simple question: If blockchain is so revolutionary, after thirty years, why is its primary use case gambling? Ironically enough, the more important technology is the one that predates it: public key encryption.

What *is* important to understand about cryptocurrency is the economic narrative that developed around it, a constellation of sometimes overlapping stories that built up over the course of its existence. The original story—that Bitcoin represents a response to the devastating failures of the traditional financial system—holds significant power because we all agree on its premise: Our current financial system sucks. But is the story of Bitcoin actually true? Does it do what it purports to do, create a peer-to-peer currency free of intermediaries? Was a trustless currency relying only on computer code even possible?

For Bitcoin's early adopters, those debates still lay ahead. Having stumbled upon a potentially new monetary system, they were focused on one question: Could it go viral?

o o o

Bitcoin may be the most popular digital currency, but it was not the first. In a 1982 paper, cryptographer David Chaum theorized the intellectual scaffolding of blockchain, upon which cryptocurrency would emerge some quarter of a century later. Chaum started his own digital currency company, DigiCash, in the late 1980s. Although it was technically not blockchain based, it possessed cryptographic privacy features that would factor heavily in later iterations of digital money. DigiCash was a legitimate project, without the conflicts of interest and other red flags surrounding many current crypto ventures. Unfortunately, it failed to take off and in the late 1990s the company declared bankruptcy before being sold.

Other attempts at digital cash were similarly unsuccessful. For example, eGold, founded in the late 1990s, allowed its customers to purchase fractional amounts of offshore physical gold holdings. The project was plagued by problems, most significantly that criminals started using it for money laundering and other illicit purposes. It lasted until the mid-2000s before being shut down by the feds for violating money transmitter laws. A similar story involved Liberty Reserve, an anonymous money transmission service run out of Costa Rica. Users could deposit money into a virtual dollar account via wire transfer or credit and then transfer those funds to other Liberty customers. There were no legal restrictions and no effort to validate customers or prevent the flow of illicit money—which was probably the point. In 2013, in an operation involving law enforcement agencies from more than a dozen countries, the FBI raided Liberty Reserve for violating money laundering laws, putting an end to the unlicensed shadow bank. The founder pled guilty and was sentenced to twenty years in jail.

Bitcoin had other important antecedents in areas ranging from online gambling to exchanging items in multiplayer online role-playing games—anywhere people traded value in digital form. Whether it was depositing money into online casinos or paying a dark elf for their sword in *EverQuest*, the issue of how to send someone money—or a digital equivalent—without interference from pesky outside parties had yet to be adequately solved. PayPal and other payment services existed, but they were beholden to annoying gatekeepers like the law, national borders, banks, and terms of service agreements. And while some games, most notably *Second Life* with its Linden dollars, produced thriving online economies that extended beyond the game itself, they had yet to catch on with the broader public.

Bitcoin seemed like a solution, but at first no one outside the small Bitcoin network ascribed any worth to its tokens. In a story that has become memorialized in Bitcoin lore (and etched into the blockchain's permanent record), on March 22, 2010, 10,000 Bitcoins were used to pay for two pizzas, worth forty dollars. For some, that now-absurd expenditure reflected an idyllic time: Sure, the stuff was nearly worthless, but it was open to all, as early adopters could mine Bitcoin with their home computers without racking up enormous hardware and electricity costs. Still, while you could send Bitcoins to fellow dabblers, translating them into actual dollars that could be spent was quite difficult.

That changed with the Silk Road, a dark web drug marketplace, where Bitcoin was finally used as intended: as a peer-to-peer currency operating both free of centralized control and outside the law. Until it was shut down by US law enforcement in October 2013, the Silk Road was the most successful onboarding mechanism in Bitcoin's history. That said, it's worth noting that until 2017, the crypto "market" remained extremely small.

If it didn't work as a currency, perhaps a new story could be told. In the coming years, coiners started talking about Bitcoin as a potential store of value (despite its wild volatility) or as the basis of a new, parallel financial system, free of state control. "Censorship resistance" became a mantra in crypto circles—money that was private, free from any surveillance or control by the state. Free, too, from any public safeguards. Financial freedom came to mean a kind of financial anarchy. Criminals could use crypto to avoid taxes, sanctions, launder money, and collect profits from ransomware.

A deluge of cryptocurrencies appeared, not just Ethereum but hundreds and then thousands of others, with the wave cresting during the so-called Initial Coin Offering (ICO) boom of 2017–18. Much like the dot-com IPO boom of an earlier era, it seemed like every day there was another ICO, with many projects hardly different from their peers except on the level of branding. Billions of dollars, some of it of dubious origin, changed hands, as crypto fortunes were made and lost overnight. The whole thing imploded in a mess of crashing token prices, fraud, and Securities and Exchange Commission (SEC) enforcement actions in the spring of 2018, leading to a prolonged "crypto winter."

The token-mania of 2017 helped show that a different way was possible. Bitcoin and other cryptocurrencies didn't have to be money or a store of long-term value. They could be wildly speculative instruments, pumped via hype, social media, and celebrity endorsements. They didn't really have to *do* anything except rise in price. The entire economic foundation of cryptocurrency quickly became "number go up." With a price tag attached, they could be treated as digital assets unto themselves, capable of being used as collateral for loans or transformed into complex financial products, not unlike the credit-default swaps of the mid-2000s. This was the beginning of DeFi (decentralized finance), in which tokens would be routed through complex, mostly automated protocols that added leverage and risk to the system—and a chance at huge rewards. Turning that magic internet money into fiat, into real dollars that could be spent in the mainstream economy, still presented some challenges. But the promise of turning a few digital tokens into many more—with almost no work involved—would eventually bring billions of fresh dollars into the system, especially from venture capitalists who saw that their money, connections, and insider knowledge would allow them to profit quickly by pumping and dumping hot tokens. They would claim they were building something, even the future of money itself, but all the while they were lining their pockets while regular people—"retail"—were left holding the bag.

From the start, then, Bitcoin, and the larger crypto movement, was a quixotic project, toggling between possible use cases that never quite came together, attempting to redefine conventional notions of value, and operating on the margins of legality. Anytime a private citizen tries to usurp the rights of the state—in this case, to print and manage the money supply—there is bound to be some trouble. Bitcoin was a direct attack on state authority and the shared public good that is our monetary system. For its supporters, that was a thrilling proposition. For someone like me, with a bit of an economics education, an appreciation of democracy, and some familiarity with the troubled history of private money and fraud, it seemed like a formula for disaster.

o o o

In late 2020, I came down with a serious case of FOMO. The entertainment business was on ice thanks to the pandemic, and I was bored and depressed. I saw a bunch of average Joes making money in the stock markets, so I dusted off my long-neglected degree in economics and started paying attention to them for the first time in my life.

It was clear to me from very early on that we were in a bubble hastened by the extraordinary measures taken in response to the pandemic, and that eventually that bubble would burst. While Donald Trump and members of his administration refused to acknowledge the depth of COVID crisis in early 2020, other branches of the federal government panicked. Fearing economic immolation, Congress and the Federal Reserve unleashed a fire hose of money meant to keep the economy from burning to the ground. Remember from earlier that the Fed's balance sheet prior to the pandemic stood at nearly $4 trillion as a result of over a decade of easy money policies. In plain speak, the government never sold back the securities it had bought during the subprime crisis, effectively maintaining a significant asset bubble. It would only inflate further with the government's response to COVID. This is what the Fed's balance sheet looked like at the end of 2021:

Total Assets of the Federal Reserve

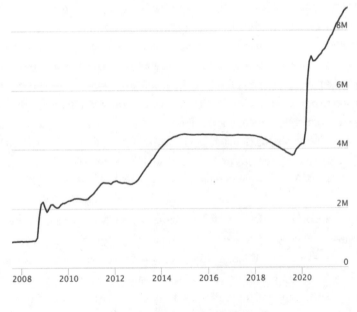

— Total Assets (In millions of dollars)

Source: "Monetary Policy: Credit and Liquidity Programs and the Balance Sheet. Recent Balance Sheet Trends," Board of Governors of the Federal Reserve System, accessed March 3, 2023, https://www.federalreserve.gov/monetarypolicy/bst_recenttrends.htm.

In response to the threat of COVID-19 shutting down the economy, some $5 trillion flooded into the US economy. An unprecedented amount of money was now available for people (as well as institutions) to spend, save, invest, or gamble with. Flush with dough, markets of all kinds went berserk. Home prices, which had steadily climbed back above the 2006 peak, now soared, as did stocks and all manner of speculative investments. Times were good, and on paper it seemed as if almost everyone was richer, or at least a little more secure during some precarious times. But it was already clear that many of the economic gains during the pandemic were going to the ultrarich. And as an armchair economist, I saw far worse storm clouds forming on the horizon.

Surveying the markets in the spring of 2021, I saw all the signs of what Robert Shiller describes as "naturally occurring Ponzi schemes." The premise of a traditional Ponzi scheme is quite simple: A fraudster promises investors he can produce incredible returns if they give him money to invest on their behalf. Instead of legitimately investing that money, the con man pretends to have generated profits and uses that story to lure in more investors. He pays the original investors off with the money from the new ones (See? It works!), while pocketing a good chunk for himself for his trouble. The cycle then repeats itself over and over again, drawing in ever more investors, until ultimately it falls apart. Either the supply of new investors dries up, or worse, the current ones wise up to the fraud and demand their money back, only to discover it isn't there.

Ponzi schemes are traditionally thought of as having a central figure coordinating the fraud. Think of Bernie Madoff, whose Ponzi scheme collapsed during the subprime crisis as investors saw the broader market cratering. By conventional measurements, Madoff's fraud holds the record for the largest Ponzi scheme in history, with some $64 billion lost—at least on paper. But as Shiller describes in *Irrational Exuberance* (2015), a Ponzi scheme does not need to have a central administrator to fit the broader definition of one. Instead, a "naturally occurring Ponzi" can form simply in response to a rise in price. Shiller writes, "Investors, their confidence and expectations buoyed by past price increases, bid up speculative prices further, thereby enticing more investors to do the same, so that the cycle repeats again and again, resulting in an amplified response to the original precipitating factors. The feedback mechanism is widely suggested in popular discourse and is one of the oldest financial theories."

During bubbles, fraud runs rampant. Charles Kindleberger, an economic historian who specialized in the study of manias and bubbles observed: "The implosion of a bubble always leads to the discovery of frauds and swindles that developed in the froth of the mania." When it's easy to access money and credit, people take on more risk in search of higher reward. Separating the truly innovative technologies from those that are instead predicated on hype or fraud is particularly challenging when everything is booming. If market history was any guide, there had to be some fraudulent companies helping pump up this bubble. Armed only with this theory, I decided to join the game and place a few bets of my own.

Sure enough, once I started looking for fraud, I found it in abundance. I began wagering that some particularly suspicious companies would go down. I won a few, lost more than a few, and it became a fun—if slightly addictive—pandemic hobby.

And then I came to crypto.

My buddy Dave is a dear friend from college. He has also given me the worst financial advice of my life. Sometime in the mid-2000s, when I was in my twenties and flush with cash from TV, Dave encouraged me to buy stock in an obscure medical technology company that had purportedly figured out a way to produce synthetic blood. They were going to make a fortune, Dave told me. He had been at a wedding and some random guy assured him so. I was young and dumb and excited by his excitement, so I put $10,000 into it. In less than a year, the stock tanked and I lost almost all of my money.

While losing the money had been painful, at least I had learned from the experience: Never invest in something you don't understand, and always be willing to stay skeptical, even—or especially—if you love your friends.

In early 2021, Dave came over to my house to tell me I should buy Bitcoin.

o o o

The first problem I had with cryptocurrency was the word. They were using the wrong one.

In economics, currencies do things: They are a medium of exchange, a unit of account, and a store of value. Medium of exchange means you use it to buy and sell stuff. Most people, if pressed, will define money this way: You buy shit with it. If we didn't have money, we'd have to rely on bartering for the things we need. As an actor/performer, I'd literally be singing for my supper, which, if you have ever heard me sing, would be a terrible idea. Money simplifies things, creating a quantifiable system of IOUs we Americans call dollars. Unit of account is a way of measuring the market value of goods, services, and other transactions against each other. A stable currency allows an economy to function efficiently; businesses can run their books and monitor their performance over time. The last function of money—store of value—is exactly that: something that holds its value over time. A strong currency has a relatively steady value over time. What good is a dollar if one day my deli bagel costs $1.50, the next $10, and the next $5? I'd rather skip breakfast. The more a currency fluctuates in value, the less useful it is to the public, to businesses, and to the government that issues it.

Cryptocurrencies didn't do any of these things well. You couldn't buy stuff with them—the guys at my deli would look at me like I was nuts if I tried to pay for my bagel and coffee in Bitcoin. Advocates say this is a temporary problem; if more people would just buy Bitcoin, eventually it will become a currency you can actually use. That's wrong for many reasons, but I'll focus on the simplest one for now: The technology behind Bitcoin sucks. It doesn't scale. Satoshi's solution to the double spend problem was innovative, but also clunky. The more miners who entered the competition the more energy was used, but the blocks were the same. Bitcoin is able to handle only five to seven transactions a second; it can never go above that. Visa can process 24,000. To operate, Bitcoin uses an enormous amount of energy, the equivalent in 2021 of Argentina—the entire country. Visa and Mastercard use comparatively miniscule amounts of electricity to serve a customer base orders of magnitude greater. Bitcoin's energy consumption is enormously wasteful, and poses a massive environmental problem for the supposedly cutting-edge technology (and really, for all of us).

When it came to the other two functions of money—store of value and unit of account—Bitcoin also fails miserably. The price jumps up and down like a rabbit on amphetamines, making it impossible to run a business using Bitcoin (or any other crypto) or hold on to it for any period of time with reasonable confidence it would retain its value. Could you use a cryptocurrency as a rudimentary form of money? I mean, sure. You could call a brick a soccer ball, but I wouldn't recommend using it that way.

So if cryptocurrencies weren't currencies, then what were they? How do they actually work in the real world? Well, you put real money into them and hope to make real money off of them through no work of your own. Under American law, that's an investment contract. More precisely, it's a security.

Thanks to a 1946 Supreme Court decision, securities are often defined by what's called the Howey Test. The test has four prongs: (1) an investment of money, (2) in a common enterprise, (3) with the expectation of profit, (4) to be derived from the efforts of others. Check, check, check, and check. Although Bitcoin had somehow come to be classified as a commodity, it was blindingly clear to me that the 20,000 or so other cryptos ought to be classified as securities under American law, and yet they had not been, or at least not clearly enough to stop them from spreading like wildfire.

Prior to the 1930s we did not have federal securities laws in the United States. Securities were regulated at the state level under what were called *blue-sky laws*. They did not work very well. Fraud was commonplace; the stock markets in particular reflected a capitalistic free-for-all with little to no outside oversight. (Recall Keynes and the origin of the term *casino capitalism*.) While everything was going up in price, no one seemed to mind. During the roaring twenties, millions of Americans were lured into booming markets with faulty foundations. It was a bubble, and like all bubbles it eventually burst. The stock market crash of 1929 destroyed the finances of multitudes and ultimately led to the Great Depression. In response to this devastation, and the manipulation and fraud in the markets that contributed to it, Congress passed federal securities laws in 1933 and 1934. In terms of protecting investors, the primary purpose of those laws was to require disclosure on behalf of the issuer; if you were investing money in a particular security, you needed to know what you were investing in (i.e., who you were giving your money to) and what they were doing with that money. Cryptocurrencies have no disclosure requirements, effectively by design; the pseudonymity of the blockchain conceals who owns what. Much like the 1920s, this left the door wide open for deception and scams.

Staring in disbelief at the crypto markets in the spring of 2021, I came to a terrifying conclusion: Slightly less than a century after the crash of 1929, we had come full circle. There were now potentially 20,000 unregistered, unlicensed securities—more than all the publicly listed securities in the major US stock markets—for sale to the general public. Worse, these unregistered, unlicensed securities were primarily traded on crypto exchanges, which often served multiple market functions and, therefore, had massive conflicts of interest. And perhaps most disturbing, most of the volume in crypto ran through overseas exchanges. Rather than being registered in the United States, they were often run through shell corporations in the Caribbean, apparently to avoid falling under any particular regulatory jurisdiction. Private entities were essentially printing their own money and circulating it through offshore markets. In terms of propensity for fraud, what could be more appealing?

Stepping back even further, what did these cryptocurrencies *do*? From where did their value derive? They were bizarre. Imagine a conventional security, such as a share of stock in the company Apple. Where does that stock get its value? Well, Apple makes stuff. (The iPhone is one year older than the Bitcoin white paper.) Apple sells that stuff—phones, computers, watches—as well as services, such as streaming music and video subscriptions. These sales produce a revenue stream—earnings over time that can be projected forward. When you buy a share of Apple, you are effectively a portion of the revenue stream, as well as the brand equity, market share, intellectual property—all of that. But cryptos don't make stuff or do stuff. There are no goods or services produced. It's air, pure securitized air.

o   o   o

After a few months of research, I called my buddy Dave to tell him I would not be buying any Bitcoin. I had decided the cryptocurrency markets were due for a major crash, and warned him he might lose his money. He didn't seem to disagree—he laughed, actually—and to my relief assured me he hadn't invested more than he could afford to lose. Dave argued it this way: *If there's a tiny chance this could be the future of money, why not gamble a little and see if I'm right?* Fair enough. I told him I'd take the under. I mentioned I'd bet some money on other frauds—shorting public companies that seemed suspect—and crypto looked like another slam dunk. Dave laughed again and wished me luck. We came up with a side bet of our own: I bet him dinner at the restaurant of his choosing that Bitcoin would be worth $10,000 a coin or less by the end of 2021. To my mind, it was easy money.

o o o

Unlike the other wagers in this new hobby of mine, however, I couldn't stop thinking about crypto. By the spring of 2021, it was everywhere, the culture besieged with TV ads, billboards, and celebrity endorsements. Social media was rife with crypto promos, often from pseudonymous accounts offering incredible fortunes to be made. I was supposed to be inspired to take an exciting risk but instead I was left cold.

Was I wrong about crypto? Maybe worse, what if I was right?

If these things they called currencies were not in fact currencies but more like the stock that I had bet on with Dave some years prior, wouldn't that mean that millions of regular people were about to lose, collectively, an enormous amount of money? More to the point, if I suspected a massive amount of fraud was occurring in broad daylight, didn't I have an obligation to do something about it? Didn't I need to warn the public?

In his book, *Lying for Money: How Legendary Frauds Reveal the Workings of the World*, author Dan Davies notes his Golden Rule for fraud detection: "Anything that is growing unusually fast, for the type of thing that it is, needs to be checked out. And it needs to be checked out in a way that it hasn't been checked out before." I couldn't get that simple idea out of my head: that this bubble needed to be "checked out" in a way it hadn't been before. I felt an urgent need to do *something*, but what part was mine to play? Should I be tweeting about crypto scams? Posting gambling help line numbers on Instagram? Calling my congressperson? I felt almost guilty, like I could see the iceberg ahead and had to warn the ship's captain. But who the hell was in charge here?

One night, dealing with this mess of feelings, I decided to read my young daughter a folktale, "The Emperor's New Clothes." While I remembered the gist of the plot—an emperor tricked by swindlers ends up parading through town naked—I had forgotten two key points. First, the fraudsters claim only the smartest people and those of the highest station will be able to perceive the beauty of the (imaginary) clothes they weave. In this way, adult after adult is tricked into doubting themselves for the simplest yet most powerful reason of all: They don't want to appear foolish. The con was ingenious in its simplicity. It relied on nothing more than appeal to ego and status worship.

The second part I had forgotten was the ending. At the peak of the story's absurdity, as the emperor galivants naked through the streets and the townspeople pretend not to notice, it is a child who finally calls out the lie. The only one brave enough to speak the simple truth that the emperor has no clothes is a child who does not even know he is being brave. He's simply telling the truth.

I couldn't help but place myself in the role of the child. What did I know? I'm an actor with a barely used undergraduate degree in economics. I earned some money in showbiz but I've never worked on Wall Street or in finance. Who was I to call out a multi-trillion-dollar industry that very fancy people on TV assured us was the future of everything? Then again, I knew about money and lying. And Robert Shiller said something else: "We can think of history as a succession of rare big events in which a story goes viral, often (but not always) with the help of an attractive celebrity (even a minor celebrity or fictional stock figure) whose attachment to the narrative adds human interest."

A dim light clicked inside this middle-aged dad's feeble brain. Perhaps I could be that attractive minor celebrity! Maybe I could help spread an economic counter narrative to the crypto hype shilled by so many of my showbiz colleagues. And leaving my public persona aside for the moment, I was also a bored, mildly depressed, forty-something-year-old man in desperate need of adventure. What exactly did I have to lose?

I decided to do something. I decided to get stoned.

During the pandemic, I received my medical marijuana card from the great state of New York. It was a lifesaver. I've always been prone to depression and anxiety, but they had gone through the roof as COVID hit. I needed to do something other than drink to help me cope. Pot did the trick. While high, I stumbled upon an ingenious notion: I would write a book! It would be a book about crypto, fraud, gambling, and storytelling, as told by a storyteller who was himself gambling on the outcome. To my THC-inspired brain, it all made perfect sense. I had stumbled on something profoundly original! The next day, I woke up a bit groggy and realized the obvious: I don't know how to write a book. Maybe there was someone who could help?

A journalist named Jacob Silverman wrote an article for the *New Republic* that I thoroughly enjoyed: "Even Donald Trump Knows Bitcoin Is a Scam." I looked him up and realized he, too, lived in Brooklyn. I started following him on Twitter. He followed me back. It took me days, and I felt a little silly being nervous, but I finally worked up the courage to DM him, inviting him to drinks at a local Brooklyn bar. For some reason, he agreed.

And that is where our story truly begins.

CHAPTER 2

WHAT COULD POSSIBLY GO WRONG?

"Writing is gambling." —Margaret Atwood

I T WAS AUGUST 13, 2021, and I was perspiring more than I would have liked outside my local bar. It wasn't the sweltering heat of that summer night making me nervous; it was the stupidity of what I was doing. You know how it goes, what had seemed sensible to propose via Twitter DM after some edibles seemed somewhat less so now. I had invited a journalist I'd never met to pitch him on writing a book I didn't know how to write about events that hadn't happened yet. What could possibly go wrong?

Sure enough, Jacob Silverman eventually arrived, albeit a half hour late. It wasn't his fault; I had given him the wrong address. While I had been waiting at a pub called Henry Public, there was another one called Henry Street Ale House just a few blocks away, and I had mistakenly sent him there. Our rom-com meet-cute was off to a textbook awkward start.

Jacob looked more or less like I anticipated from a headshot I found online: a slightly disheveled young Jack Nicholson mixed with a dash of Kiefer Sutherland and a dollop of Carl Bernstein. As he settled into his chair, I apologized profusely for my mistake and made sure to get him a cold beer.

It turned out we had a lot in common. We were both sons of lawyers, both fathers to young children, and both fans of the Los Angeles Dodgers baseball team. Jacob was on staff at the *New Republic*, but was planning on taking parental leave soon. I complimented him on his work, and to my surprise he returned the favor. Turns out he grew up in LA and was a fan of *The O.C.* Eventually, the small talk petered out and Jacob asked the obvious question: *Why am I here?*

I told him about my econ degree and my interest in fraud. I talked about my friend Dave, and about our little bet that a crypto crash was imminent, and that I felt I had a duty to warn others before it was too late. And then I told him I wanted to write a book about it all.

Jacob was silent as another round of beer arrived, either ruminating or planning his graceful escape from the deranged actor with the weird pandemic hobby who had somehow cornered him in a local bar to talk crypto of all godforsaken things. *Oh god,* I realized, *I was one of those guys.*

Nevertheless, I dove in deeper.

I'm worried, I confessed, but I'm also angry. Furious, in fact. If I was correct—and crypto was effectively the biggest Ponzi of all time—then a lot of regular people were gonna get hurt. If I understood the economics correctly, then the crypto industry needed to lure more average folks (retail investors) into the casinos in order to take their cut and keep the scam going. Most people wouldn't risk too much and will avoid the worst of it, but others who went all in on this crypto madness could lose everything. Lives would be destroyed, and for what? So we could all gamble on fake money? So criminals and fraudsters and Silicon Valley venture capital firms and Wall Street hedge funds could make out at the expense of regular folks? What are we even doing anymore?

It's getting to the point that we, as a country, never hold white collar criminals or politicians accountable. Maybe we're still in shock from 2016, I ventured. We were scammed by the biggest con man of them all, and our collective exhaustion was blinding us to an obvious, dangerous fraud happening right then, live on cable TV and Twitter and TikTok for all to see. Apologies if this is melodramatic, I said, but I'm a father and I'm worried about our country and the world we are leaving for our children.

Sitting in the bar, I went on about how trust was breaking down, people were being manipulated in all sorts of ways. It felt like no coincidence that in the era of rampant misinformation, fraud was spreading like a virus. I'd spent too many sleepless nights over the last four years worrying about the state of the world and not being able to do anything about it. Well, as batshit crazy as it may sound, this was something I knew I could do. I could summon my own superpowers as an econ dork and mid-level celebrity and spread the gospel of "crypto is bullshit." I could call out the liars and thieves, write it all down, and put it out there for the people to see.

It was as good a performance as you're gonna get, probably because I believed what I was saying. The more I spoke, the more natural it became. If you'll forgive the triteness, it felt like a part I had been auditioning for all my life. I actually cared about this story in ways I could barely understand at the time. It felt good to talk it out, but like every audition, whether I got the job or not wasn't up to me. Would Jacob Silverman help me write a book on crypto and fraud?

He smiled, and reminded me he was planning to go on paternity leave soon. I ordered a fourth round.

So where do we start, I asked, since I'd never written a book before.

Normally you would come up with a book proposal, Jacob advised. Think of it like a Hollywood pitch deck for book nerds, a literary audition capped off with a deliriously optimistic business plan. While we are working on that, however, why not lay the foundation by writing a few articles on the subject? Establish our bona fides, as it were, before we go to market with the book. Celebrities are endorsing cryptocurrencies left and right. Why not start with your superpower?

o o o

On October 7, 2021, Slate published an article with the unambiguous title "Celebrity Crypto Shilling Is a Moral Disaster," written by yours truly and Jacob Silverman. My first byline! In the piece, we castigated the likes of Kim Kardashian, Tom Brady, Floyd Mayweather Jr., and Lindsay Lohan for their involvement in promoting various crypto projects. Along with former NBA star Paul Pierce, Kim and Floyd had been shilling an obscure cryptocurrency called EthereumMax. Kim's Instagram post from June 2021 read as follows:

> ARE YOU GUYS INTO CRYPTO????
> THIS IS NOT FINANCIAL ADVICE BUT SHARING WHAT
> MY FRIENDS JUST TOLD ME ABOUT THE ETHEREUM
> MAX TOKEN! A FEW MINUTES AGO ETHEREUM MAX
> BURNED 400 TRILLION TOKENS—LITERALLY 50% OF
> THEIR ADMIN WALLET, GIVING BACK TO THE ENTIRE
> E-MAX COMMUNITY. SWIPE UP TO JOIN THE E-MAX
> COMMUNITY.

To borrow from the industry's charming parlance, EthereumMax was a shitcoin. The hastily assembled crypto project seemed purposely designed to be confused with the second biggest cryptocurrency, Ethereum, even though the two were not related. Kim's post, sent out to her then 251 million (!) followers, was an enormous publicity success for the obscure token. A Morning Consult survey found that 21 percent of the American public had seen the ad. Suspiciously, shortly after the ad went viral, the value of the EthereumMax token plummeted. By the time our article was published, it was worth $0.00000002257, meaning that if you had been foolish enough to buy what Kim K. was selling, you had probably lost all of your money. It was unclear at the time what Kardashian had been paid for the ad; we later learned that it was $250,000.

The gambit was so egregious it actually caught the attention of regulators, but not at first in the United States, where the coin's promoters lived and worked. Three months after Kardashian's post, the head of the British Financial Conduct Authority gave a speech in which he discussed EthereumMax and warned the public to consider the risk of buying into such ventures. It was a bit belated, but it was something, a warning to avoid similar scams in the future. In the United States, Kardashian's promotion was initially met with typical regulatory silence. And it wasn't as if any of the other rich and famous people promoting these coins seemed inclined to say anything. Why ruin the party for yourself by calling out someone else's scam? The incentive structure inside the crypto industry reminded me of other bubbles and Ponzis: There was no reason to speak truth to power. Cynicism and selfishness were easily rewarded.

I tried my best to be civil but firm toward my fellow celebrities, some of whom had made a lot more money and had much bigger bills than I did. I get it: Life's a hustle. But let's not be gross about it, or lack any discernment or critical thinking. There's a bridge too far and crypto is past that. You wouldn't want to be responsible, even unwittingly, for convincing your fans to buy into a predatory financial instrument that was just as ethically compromised as a rigged casino or a payday loan vendor. There are better ways to make a little dough.

o o o

As for our Brooklyn dad duo, the paycheck from the Slate article wasn't exactly a game changer financially, but it served its larger purpose. I had emerged from celeb witness protection, where I'd been hiding since the start of the pandemic, to boldly set forth on a new venture. Only this wasn't a TV show or movie. No, it was time to announce exactly what people don't want to hear from famous people: I have thoughts about things other than showbiz.

While I wasn't the only person with doubts about this whole shady crypto thing, I was the only one who was a six-time Teen Choice Award nominee. (One day I will win that damn surfboard.) My pop-cultural bona fides preceded me. Word of my bizarre mission began to spread. The first indication of that was, fittingly enough, Twitter. Several of my blue–check marked journalist colleagues (I was one now, right?) began following me. A few reporters reached out to request interviews, basically to find out what the hell we were up to. Apparently, any willingness to call bull on an industry high on its own supply filled a certain media void. *A celeb who is anti-crypto?* Either that guy from TV is doing something bold and interesting, or he's lighting his career on fire for the world to see. Break out the popcorn! I knew I'd tapped into the zeitgeist when fellow dads at my kids' school complimented me on the article at pickup and drop-off. At long last, I had gotten the intellectual validation I needed in the form of fifteen hundred words in Slate.

The high from the first article dissipated and was replaced by a need to go bigger. While the celeb shilling article had captured some headlines, it felt like low-hanging fruit. The Kardashian shilling was obviously pretty scammy, if not illegal, and calling out my fellow celebs was a juicy bit of provocation, but it was hardly the deep dive exposé of crypto that I initially pitched to Jacob. We had work to do.

CHAPTER 3

MONEY PRINTER GO BRRR

OR SKEPTICS LIKE Jacob and me, there was one corporation that reigned supreme when it came to our suspicions about the cryptocurrency industry: the "stablecoin" company Tether and its assorted entities such as the exchange Bitfinex. Tether was arguably the most important cryptocurrency of them all: At the time, 70 percent of all transactions in cryptocurrency were conducted in it, more than in either Bitcoin or Ethereum. Founded in 2014, Tether claims to be the first stablecoin ever created. (A stablecoin is a cryptocurrency pegged to an actual currency such as the US dollar.) On the crypto exchanges, one Tether (USDT) equals one US dollar.

With their value seemingly stable, Tethers served as the poker chips in the casino. Imagine you're gambling/investing through one of the crypto exchanges and you want to trade one cryptocurrency for another. Do you cash out into real money (US dollars, euros, yuan, whatever) and then go back into the casino with that real money to exchange again for crypto? Of course not! Not only would it be overly cumbersome, it would also cost you money in the form of taxes to be paid on that investment. Crypto investors who wanted to keep their money in the crypto system but not be exposed to the wild volatility associated with any particular coin would instead hold stablecoins like Tether. Theoretically, your money was safe: One USDT was supposed to always be worth one US dollar. And if you were making huge gains or moving money between jurisdictions, Tether helped avoid the imposition of regulated banks with their pesky reporting requirements.

Stablecoins provided the liquidity necessary for the crypto industry to function: As long as there were poker chips to play with, the games could continue. Interestingly enough, Tether's founding in 2014 was just a few years before the crypto market began its rapid rise. But who was behind the mysterious company? How did it operate? For our second journalistic collaboration, Jacob decided on a deep dive into Tether and its murky dealings.

On October 19, 2021, we published "Untethered" in Slate. We hadn't cracked the company's mysteries, but the piece, which built on past investigations by Bloomberg, the *Financial Times*, and writers like Cas Piancey, Bennett Tomlin, and Patrick McKenzie, was consistent with our proselytizing mission. We were here to ring alarm bells and make sure the lay public could hear them.

Just listing some of the incredible but true facts about Tether did half of our work for us. Did you know that the then–$69 billion company had only twelve employees according to LinkedIn, and that even some of those appeared to be fakes? Or that Tether had never been audited, and was run through shell corporations in the Caribbean? Gee, no red flags there. Or that its CFO was a former plastic surgeon who paid $65,000 in a counterfeiting settlement with Microsoft, its CEO hadn't been seen in public in years, and its general counsel used to be the director of compliance for Excapsa, the parent company of Ultimate Bet? Ultimate Bet was an online poker company that fell apart when it was revealed they had a secret "god mode" that allowed insiders to see the other players' cards.

While Tether's absurdities made for good copy, they also hinted at something deeper: fraud. From the outside, determining whether a company is actually committing fraud in the legal sense is extremely difficult. Actually proving fraud in court requires documents and witnesses, and while journalists crave those, we lack the state's power to compel testimony or subpoena documents. Instead, we have to look for clues.

Let's break down five of the biggest red flags for Tether and explain their significance. The first red flag for Tether was the fact that it had never been audited. To state the obvious, an audit would lay bare whether the money received from issuing its coin was backed by real assets, and what those assets were. Tether was a $69 billion company at the time, but two years earlier, there were only $4 billion worth of Tethers in circulation. The fact that it had never been audited—despite years of company promises to do so—was an enormous red flag. After seven years and such tremendous recent growth, couldn't the flourishing company find an auditor? Remember the quote from Dan Davies's *Lying for Money*: "Anything that is growing unusually fast, for the type of thing that it is, needs to be checked out. And it needs to be checked out in a way that it hasn't been checked out before."

The second red flag for Tether was its size relative to its workforce. Twelve employees (maybe even fewer) are running a business that deals in tens of billions of dollars? Forget the absurdity and ask yourself why. If you were running a legitimate, huge business dealing in big-dollar transactions, wouldn't you want, and need, more than a dozen people helping you run it?

Controlling access to information is crucial to running a successful fraud. The fewer the people who know what you are doing, the less the chance that someone accidentally slips up and reveals the con, or worse yet has a crisis of conscience and starts talking to law enforcement. Thieves also tend to turn on one another if it's a matter of self-interest. All fraudsters need people they can trust. Bernie Madoff claimed that he hid the inner workings of his Ponzi from even his children, to protect them. Instead, Madoff had his right-hand man, Frank DiPascali, do his dirty work. Rule number one for fraud: Keep the circle of trust small.

The third red flag was the personal histories of executives running the company. If you want the best predictor of if someone might currently be engaged in a fraud, consider the obvious: Have they committed fraud before? Tether's executives were hilariously well cast in this regard—a CFO who settled with Microsoft on charges of counterfeiting software; a CEO who was once a salesman for a company hawking a product that claimed it could turn nicotine into vitamins; and of course, the lawyer with the ties to the online poker site that was caught swindling its own customers. Classy bunch.

But that was not all. By the time Jacob and I came on the scene in the fall of 2021, Tether had a lengthy, and recent, history with various US law enforcement entities. The Commodity Futures Trading Commission (CFTC), which regulates commodities in the United States, had fined Tether $41 million just four days prior to the publication of our article, to settle allegations that it lied about its digital tokens being fully backed by real money. Earlier that year in February, the New York Attorney General had fined Tether $18.5 million, stating the company and several associated entities (iFinex and Bitfinex) had made false statements about the backing of its stablecoin. In exchange for avoiding prosecution, Tether agreed not to conduct any business activities in the state of New York, the heart of global finance. The company also agreed to pay the fine, as well as submit quarterly attestations showing that it was, at least on paper, fully backed. Attestations are not audits. They're basically a snapshot of a company's accounts, without the rigor of a real audit. In the world of crypto, they're a way of saying, Trust me, bro. I'm good for it.

That was the legal backdrop, but the details of Tether's executive team were also entertaining: Their public spokesperson was their Chief Technology Officer (CTO), a hotheaded Italian guy named Paolo Ardoino. One of Tether's cofounders was a colorful figure named Brock Pierce. A former child actor, Pierce had starred in *The Mighty Ducks* films before segueing into various business ventures in online video and video games. Pierce worked alongside such notable corporate luminaries as Trump strategist Steve Bannon, as well as a guy named Marc Collins-Rector. Pierce was living with Collins-Rector in Spain in 2002, when the two men were arrested in a house that contained guns, machetes, and child pornography. Pierce was eventually released, but Rector pled guilty to charges of child enticement, spent time in Spanish prison, and registered as a sex offender. Pierce left Tether one year after its founding, but his early involvement was another important mark on his very strange résumé.

The fourth red flag for Tether was the redemption process. Regular people gambling on crypto always bought (and sold) Tethers on the exchanges, meaning the poker chips never left the casino. But what would happen if you actually wanted to sell your Tethers back to the company itself and get real money back? Well, if you were a regular Joe, you couldn't. Tether stated on its website that they wouldn't honor redemptions for less than $100,000. And over time, they added other language to their terms of service that practically gave them the right to refuse redemptions for any reason. This is the crimson flag when it comes to fraud, especially Ponzi schemes. Again, from Dan Davies's book *Lying for Money*, "a fraud can be called a Ponzi scheme with greater validity, the greater the extent to which the mechanics of the crime revolve around managing the renewal of its financing and convincing the investor and lender communities to keep their money in the scheme rather than demanding repayment in cash."

Bernie Madoff was a genius when it came to human psychology. Technically, you could withdraw money from his fund at any time with ninety days' notice. But you were only allowed to invest in one of Madoff's funds by invitation (or so went the sales pitch), making investors feel it was a privilege to be allowed access to the incredible returns he produced. If someone asked for their money back, they could get it, but they weren't allowed back in the club. Madoff was so adept in perpetuating a stigma around the redemption process that he was able to run his Ponzi scheme successfully for decades. It was the financial crisis of 2008 that brought him down. With markets crashing, his investors grew nervous and wanted to take their profits off the table. They tried to redeem en masse, only to discover the money wasn't there. But for multiple decades, Madoff was able to maintain the con.

The fifth—but by no means final—red flag was similarly obvious: multiple conflicts of interest. The Tether guys owned the money printer (USDT) as well as an exchange trading that money (Bitfinex). They hid that fact from the general public, only to have it revealed with the release of the Paradise Papers, a trove of confidential financial documents that were leaked to journalists in 2017. Not only that, but stellar reporting from crypto skeptic Bennett Tomlin found that Jean-Louis van der Velde, the CEO of both Tether and Bitfinex, was also the executive director of a Hong Kong–based cryptocurrency venture capital firm, BlueBit Capital. Giancarlo Devasini, the CFO of both Tether and Bitfinex, was a shareholder and director of BlueBit. Paolo Ardoino, the CTO of both Tether and Bitfinex, was formerly a director for Delchain, which was an offshoot of Deltec Bank & Trust, where Tether banks. Claudia Lagorio, the COO for Tether and Bitfinex, is married to Paolo. How these various corporate entities interacted was unclear, but the takeaways were obvious: myriad potential conflicts of interest and a tight circle of trust.

Tether overflowed with surreal details seemingly plucked from a slapstick comedy, and Jacob and I enjoyed parsing the idiosyncrasies of this hilariously inept yet somehow still flourishing company. To pick one more bizarre factoid from an extensive list, their primary bank mentioned above, Deltec, was headquartered in the Bahamas and run by Jean Chalopin, the guy who co-created the *Inspector Gadget* cartoon series. If it wasn't a giant scam, it was at least marvelously entertaining.

o   o   o

Tether's particular situation may have been absurd, but the more I studied its history the more I realized it fit perfectly within the framework auditors use. The "fraud triangle" has three components: need (also termed motivation), opportunity, and rationalization. In 1953, Donald Cressey examined what he called the "social psychology" of financial crime in his iconic study, *Other People's Money*. The foundation of the fraud triangle begins with a simple observation: Most people do not commit fraud because they don't need to do so. Most of us make a living, suffer our lumps, savor our victories, and generally avoid committing serious crimes. We have a sense of ethics and maybe even respect for the social contract. Committing fraud requires a strong need on behalf of the fraudster to compensate for the risk involved. There are many ways people develop such a need: Plain old greed is one of them, but so is pressure from the company or organization they work for, as well as simply making a mistake and finding themselves in a hole that they feel they need to dig out of via financial malfeasance.

In 2016, Tether was hacked. More than 100,000 Bitcoin (worth $71 million at the time) was stolen, and the company was in desperate straits. (In February 2022, Heather Morgan and Ilya Lichtenstein were arrested in New York on charges that they had attempted to launder the coins stolen in the hack, now worth $4.5 billion. Ms. Morgan was an aspiring hip-hop artist, rapping under the stage name Razzlekhan, and a frequent poster on TikTok and YouTube. She was also a contributor to *Forbes*, where she wrote an article on how to protect businesses from cybercriminals.) According to the CFTC and the New York Attorney General, Tether decided to lie about its reserves in order to avoid the equivalent of a bank run. The potential need for Tether to commit fraud clearly existed, and the CFTC and NYAG had, at a minimum, found evidence of false statements as indication of that need.

The opportunity for Tether to commit fraud was as clear as day: They owned an offshore, completely unregulated money printer and casino! In the crypto casinos, Tethers were treated like dollars. What was stopping Tether from simply printing a lot of them, or loaning out huge bunches of them to big buyers who could easily manipulate the prices of cryptocurrencies and would pay them back with their earnings—in real money—later? In a scholarly paper titled "Is Bitcoin Really Untethered?," John M. Griffin and Amin Shams found connections between the printing of Tethers and positive Bitcoin price movements during the 2017–18 bull market. (Griffin's blockchain forensics firm has also had contracts with a number of government agencies, indicating that he is advising on crypto investigations.)

While some disputed Griffin's findings, Tether certainly appeared to provide a piece crucial to a certain type of market manipulation common to crypto: wash trading. *Wash trading* is the practice of buying and selling an asset back and forth among accounts you control in order to give the appearance of demand for that asset. Crypto is perfectly suited for this sort of manipulation. There is no limit to how many addresses an individual or company can own, but their identity is masked by the pseudonymity of the blockchain. What's to stop someone from acquiring a bunch of Tethers (whether at face value or perhaps at a significant discount) and using them to sell a particular coin back and forth among addresses they control? To the outside view it might look like crypto is surging in price; in reality all that's happening is fake money is being transferred from one hand to another to inflate the value of that token. Other investors are drawn in by the surging price and end up buying a coin potentially worth far less than it appears to be.

Or worth nothing at all. In a rug pull, ownership of a coin is concentrated in the hands of just a few owners, or whales, who bid up the price and then suddenly dump the coin in a coordinated fashion, leaving unsuspecting buyers with worthless bits of code. These sorts of scams and frauds are pervasive in crypto. A working paper published by the National Bureau of Economic Research from December 2022 found that 70 percent of trades on unregulated exchanges were fake. For Binance, the biggest exchange in crypto by a country mile in terms of trading volume, that number was 46 percent.

The last piece of the fraud triangle is rationalization. The overwhelming majority of people in the world are not evil. We consider ourselves fundamentally good, if flawed, people. We feel guilt and possess ethics: all that messy emotional stuff that might get in the way of transgressing. If we are committing serious crimes like fraud, it is crucially important that we find ways to justify our behavior not only to others, but also to ourselves.

Tether's executives like to boast of their company's role in boosting financial inclusion, providing financial services to people excluded from the regulated financial system. No doubt some small part of this is true. We had heard of people being forced to use Tether in places like Afghanistan, where the banking system was broken, and Argentina, which experienced an inflation rate as high as 83 percent in 2022. While Tether might have been a last resort for people in need, it carried with it massive costs. Trading in crypto often means incurring heavy fees, and it's difficult to cash out into real dollars via legal means, pushing people into relationships with unsavory characters who are, at a minimum, not motivated by charity. In addition, the use of Tether can be seen to further undermine already weak currencies, contributing further to their downfall. Even if Tether was being used by some good people—if only because they had no better options—Tether could just as easily be used by the bad guys. Once you had gotten your money into the crypto ecosystem, moving it instantaneously and globally at parity to the US dollar was an enormously attractive feature. What was stopping Tether from being used for money laundering, tax evasion, sanctions evasion, or ransomware?

Viewed through the prism of the fraud triangle, all of the requisite pieces seemed to fall into place when it came to Tether. They had the need, the opportunity, and the rationalization. But of course, Jacob and I could not prove they had committed crimes, and that was not our job. We weren't prosecutors. We were journalists. Our article laid out some basics on Tether, and behind the scenes we began to connect the dots. Now we needed to go deeper to find the truth.

○ ○ ○

It was a cool October night, 2021, and I was pacing the deserted streets of my Brooklyn neighborhood like a madman, cell phone glued to my ear, my jaw slack with astonishment. I couldn't believe what I was hearing. On the other end of the line was a male voice I only knew as belonging to a pseudonymous Twitter handle calling himself Bitfinex'ed. He had been on the Tether case for years. Bitfinex'ed had long suspected the company was a fraud, and had paid the price for his obsession with harassment, ridicule, and, he claimed, an attempt to buy him off. On crypto Twitter, some hailed him as a conspiratorial crank while many others, including people in the industry and in mainstream media, had learned to trust his tips.

For Bitfinex'ed, the stakes were too high for him to stay quiet. The shitposting—screenshots from text conversations between Tether executives, recorded admissions of what certainly *sounded* like bank fraud, general insights into crypto industry corruption—would continue until it brought about the desired result, the morally necessary result: exposing the biggest alleged fraud since Bernie Madoff.

Bitfinex'ed, whoever he was, was convinced that Tether's inevitable collapse would bring down the entire crypto house of cards. To hear him tell it, Tether was the ticking time bomb inside a $3 trillion industry. "I'm going to give you a grenade, and this grenade has a random timer. It could be thirty seconds. It could be six months. I'm going to pull the pin. And for every ten seconds you hold that grenade, I'm going to give you a thousand bucks in cash. How long are you going to hold the grenade for?"

Bitfinex'ed and I connected via Twitter. Even his handle implied guilt and deception: Bitfinex is the crypto exchange whose owners are also behind Tether. Bitfinex'ed, whose real identity remained a mystery to us, built up a tremendous following by tracking the shenanigans of the players behind the sister companies. Bitfinex'ed was onto Tether early, spotting a scam when its market cap was in the $70 million range, he said. Outraged by what he saw as a blatant—and growing—fraud being perpetrated on the crypto-buying public, Bitfinex'ed trolled Tether's executives and posted a raft of seemingly incriminating information about the company's game of financial musical chairs.

Despite attempts to dox him—and a temporary Twitter suspension—Bitfinex'ed managed to maintain his anonymity, while developing a growing audience online. His fixation on Tether has bordered on obsession. Even some crypto skeptics thought he was too strident, too focused on this one company that, despite paying hefty fines to numerous regulatory bodies, had yet to collapse or face charges of criminal wrongdoing. Crypto partisans dismissed him as being salty because he hadn't gotten in early enough on Bitcoin. But more sober observers pointed out the fact that Bitfinex'ed *had* been right about many of his claims. Some just took longer to prove. And few people had done more to educate journalists, critics, and the larger public about the perfidy lurking underneath crypto's wildly anarchic market activity. Bitfinex'ed was the angry, roiling conscience of crypto Twitter, always ready to swoop into a conversation and expose the dark underbelly of the latest industry spin. To some that made him a threat.

Jacob and I first spoke with Bitfinex'ed on the night our Slate piece on celeb crypto shilling appeared. Bitfinex'ed wanted to talk late in the evening, and my kids were sleeping, so I decided to get some fresh air and take the call outside. I'll never forget wandering around my eerily quiet Brooklyn neighborhood, talking to some guy I had never met about some company we all suspected, but couldn't prove, was a fraud. Tether's sketchiness was obvious to us all, and we assumed its inevitable undoing would take down the entire crypto industry—if all the chips disappear from the casino, how are you going to keep gambling? Yet Tether seemed unstoppable: Over the first couple years of the pandemic, its market cap went from $4 billion to $65 billion. Eight-figure settlements with the New York Attorney General and the CFTC weren't enough to slow it down. What could a few internet critics do?

On the phone, each of us took turns marveling at the brazenness of the scheme: It was as if a random group of middling ne'er-do-wells had been issued their own money printer. What the hell would you expect to happen? Who do you think would show up at their door? But no one in crypto seemed to care. As long as they were making money, the game would continue until it collapsed under its own weight. As Bitfinex'ed so memorably described, Tether was a grenade set to go off and take all of crypto down with it. If that was true, a few questions naturally followed: What would cause Tether to explode, when might it happen, and who would be caught in the blast radius?

Then again, who was to say if Bitfinex'ed was right? What if he was crazier than I was? I still wasn't sure, but he had a hell of a story to tell. Behind the rosy promises about economic empowerment and frictionless finance were darker echoes of endemic corruption, criminality, deception, and self-dealing. In Bitfinex'ed's accounting, crypto was a cartel run by a dozen or so greedy guys in a group chat, some whose names we knew, some we might never know. It was all rigged.

It was hard to wrap my head around the enormity of his claims and what they might portend for crypto and the larger economy. A dozen guys in a group chat controlled a supposedly multi-trillion-dollar industry? No way that could be true, right? It had been less than two months since I had fallen down the rabbit hole. Things would only get weirder from here.

○ ○ ○

Speaking of holding on to grenades, there was my bet that the crypto markets would crash by the end of the year, and that the broader stock markets would turn south as well, resulting in the collapse of other companies I suspected of fraud. Neither was paying off. Ironically, I had emerged as a crypto critic during the biggest bull run the crypto industry had ever seen, and in the fall of 2021, as Jacob and I began to crank out our jeremiads, the industry's market cap was soaring toward an all-time high of around $3 trillion. According to a Pew study, 16 percent of adult Americans had invested in, traded, or used cryptocurrency, meaning some forty million people had been lured into the crypto casino. A December 2021 study commissioned by Grayscale, a prominent crypto company, found that 55 percent of Bitcoin investors entered the market that year, at the height of the mania. Even the idea of calling crypto a scam was treated as a kind of affront—how dare you, a recent entrant to the scene, call bullshit when it's raining money?

In the abstract, investing in fraud is quite simple: Find the worst companies you can and bet they will collapse. Think of it like the musical *The Producers*, where a theater producer and his accountant must put on the worst musical they can in order to scam investors. Investing in fraud is like that, but for equities; you're trying to find *Springtime for Hitler* in the form of a stock. Sure, during a bubble almost every company may be overvalued, historically speaking, but that's not where the real action is. Economically, a company whose entire business model is predicated on fraud should eventually fall back to earth and settle at a price commensurate with its actual value to society: zero. Of course predicting the timing of a crash was tricky, but if you spread your bets around, you could make a profit by being right on just a few of them. The potential payoffs for each correct call were huge, and inversely related to the price the market believed was correct at the time. The higher the price of a truly fraudulent company, the further it could fall, and the more money was to be made.

Once I started looking for fraud, I found it everywhere. There was Nikola, an electric vehicle company that produced a truck whose engine didn't work, so employees had to push it down a hill for a promotional shoot. (Their CEO would later be convicted of fraud.) Several medical device companies issued products that appeared to have the unfortunate side effect of occasionally killing the patient. SPACs, or Special Purpose Acquisition Companies, were often nothing more than blank checks issued to aggressively self-promoting "investment gurus" who would pocket a huge fee in exchange for gambling with their investors' money. An extraordinary number of Chinese listings seemed nothing more than shell companies with no credible accounting and little real business behind them.

Somehow, despite the rampant fraud, I was still losing money. Distracted by all the excitement of launching a new career as a journalist, I had fallen victim to one of the classic mistakes of retail investors. I refused to acknowledge that I was wrong on the timing. In short selling, being wrong as to when a stock plunges is the same as being wrong. There's no consolation prize for correctly assessing a fraud but betting against it too early. My portfolio of short bets was, to put it generously, in shambles. I started with $250,000 that summer, by November it was down to $38,931. While I had bet on other frauds, the main culprit was simple: I had wagered too much on crypto's collapse too soon, and blinded by my certainty, I nearly lost it all. By the time I got out of my initial crypto positions, they were almost worthless. What had been a lot of money was now very little. To be blunt, it was an unmitigated disaster—the kind of thing that provokes an uncomfortable conversation with your spouse.

As the price of Bitcoin rose to nearly $70,000 in November, as industry leaders like Michael Saylor exhorted people to "go mortgage your house and buy Bitcoin with it," I couldn't believe what I was witnessing. It had the feeling of a generational hallucination that would lead to widespread financial ruin. Tulip mania, the Wall Street Crash of 1929, Albania's Ponzi-inspired civil war—take your pick. But all day, from Twitter to CNBC to the guy running a nearby postal store, I heard how wrong I was. Economic fundamentals didn't matter. The proof was in the charts: Number go up. The financial press was practically in lockstep about the inevitable crypto-fied future of money. Politicians, their pockets brimming with donations from industry moguls like Sam Bankman-Fried of FTX, were preaching the Bitcoin gospel. They were also openly contemplating passing industry-written legislation to further legalize these rigged casinos. Celebrities were pocketing big endorsements, and millions of everyday consumers were ready to roll the dice, because why not? It had been sold to them as practically risk free, and maybe a weirdly named digital token or a cigarette-smoking ape JPEG was worth something now.

Had the high priests of crypto lost their minds, or had I? It was time for one of my regular sanity checks.

"What genre are we working in?" I asked Jacob.

"True crime," he said. "Layered over with as much absurdity as you can handle. This is a Coen brothers movie we're living, man."

"*The Big Lebowski* or *Miller's Crossing*?"

"Who knows? We're still early."

o o o

If there's one rule of thumb in investing that you should always follow, it's never throw good money after bad. That means, no matter what you do, don't double down on an investment that has cratered in value just because you believe, despite all evidence to the contrary, it will somehow turn around in your favor. Listen to the markets. John Maynard Keynes's famous—and somewhat ominous—maxim held true: "Markets can stay irrational longer than you can stay solvent." If you bet wrong, you should cut bait. Take the L. Move on.

I, of course, did the opposite.

My overarching investing thesis had always been based on a simple observation: We were in the midst of a massive speculative "everything bubble" that would soon pop. Because of how much money the Fed and Congress had thrown at the problem, people were gambling in ways they had always done when money was easy to come by. But eventually all that money chasing the roughly same amount of goods and services would lead to inflation. In response, the Fed would have to raise interest rates, piercing the bubble in dramatic fashion. Everything would go down, but the things that were most speculative would fall the fastest. Since in my analysis crypto was only speculation, it would fall like a rock once the Fed raised rates. Unfortunately for me, I had been just a bit early in making that call.

At the same time my crypto bet was crashing, I received some welcome news: A real estate investment I had entered into some years ago had matured, and I received $135,000 as a result. I summoned the courage to call my accountant and had the money transferred into my trading account. While it was borderline insane to put more money into crypto crashing as it reached its all-time high, I did it anyway. This time, however, I spread my bets around a bit more, shorting not just crypto stocks but also several other unrelated companies that I suspected of fraud based on published research.

In the interests of objectivity—and not wishing to be a participant in the kind of market manipulation I've denounced—I've never written about the companies I've shorted. You don't have to trust me on this; you can look at my work. I've never written about publicly traded companies, only privately held ones. I've never traded or owned any cryptocurrency. My bet on crypto was simpler, and bigger than any one company: I thought the whole thing—all $3 trillion of it—was a speculative bubble. That part was obvious to me. The thing I couldn't prove yet was that it was a bubble predicated on fraud. Hence, my journey with Jacob.

I still strongly believed the markets were going to turn south. Historically speaking, there was a lot of evidence to back up this claim. During bubble times, markets tended to go parabolic, rising steeply right before crashing down just as dramatically. This bit of knowledge was what I decided to hang my hat on, even though in November 2021, there was scant evidence in mainstream media to support my thesis. Beneath the surface though, there were signs things were about to change: rumblings about rising inflation, China's teetering real estate market (itself rife with suspected fraud), the Fed stepping away from its easy money policies, and tensions rising between Russia and Ukraine. I still felt crypto, and the broader stock market in general, was about to experience a rude correction. Maybe I had to believe it. Regardless, I decided to put my money where my mouth was.

○ ○ ○

Thankfully, Jacob and I still had our beloved Dodgers to fall back on when times were tough. We met up in a Brooklyn sports bar to get a few hours respite from the responsibilities of fatherhood and crypto-skeptic journalism. Over some cold ones and a disappointing batch of nachos, we settled in to watch the Dodgers against the Braves in the National League Championship Series and to celebrate our new partnership. Given the mixed record of that partnership thus far—we seemed to be broadcasting the right message, but to an audience that mostly didn't want to hear it—a little R & R was a relief. I might have just lost a ton of money irresponsibly gambling on fraud while the crypto virus had continued on its glide path toward infecting the global economy, but at least I had baseball and friendship and purpose. Life was good.

And then Matt Damon appeared. As the baseball game cut to commercial, the unmistakable voice of one of the country's most beloved movie stars filled a cavernous, and clearly digitally enhanced, corridor as the man himself appeared in the far distance. Clad in a tight black T-shirt, striding with confidence, gesturing randomly toward CGI constructions of heroic historical stuff, he speechified in the way only a movie star or politician could:

> *History is filled with almosts. With those who almost adventured, who almost achieved, but ultimately, for them it proved to be too much.*
>> *Then, there are others.*
>> *The ones who embrace the moment, and commit.*
>
> *And in these moments of truth, these men and women, these mere mortals, just like you and me, as they peer over the edge, they calm their minds and steel their nerves, with four simple words that have been whispered by the intrepid since the time of the Romans.*
>> *Fortune favors the brave.*

Goddammit, I thought. *Goddammit*, Matt Damon, not you! I've seen *Good Will Hunting* dozens of times. He was great in the *Oceans* movies. *Rounders* was maybe the only good thing to come out of the mid-2000s poker boom. He even made *Stuck on You* mildly entertaining. Why did he need to promote an exchange for unregistered, unlicensed securities on national TV when all any of us wanted to do was watch baseball? And why was he effectively shaming dudes for being wimps if they weren't man enough to gamble on crypto? WTF, man. There was only one solution to the problem: I ordered another round.

The Dodgers ultimately lost the NLCS to the Braves four games to two. Just as I had struck out with the bet, so had our Dodgers' season ended in defeat. A valiant effort was made, but there was no sense arguing with the umps (who bore patches on their uniforms for another crypto exchange called FTX). It was over, time to wait out the long winter before spring training.

I consoled myself with the fact that at least I wouldn't have to watch the World Series and see Matt Damon's ridiculous Crypto.com ad during every commercial break.

○ ○ ○

It was cold and dark in Brooklyn over the holidays. Snow filled the streets. As I nursed my wounds from the money lost and pondered a book project that might turn out to be just another celebrity's misguided indulgence, a text lit up my phone. It was from my good friend Dave, with whom I had made the Bitcoin at $10,000 by the end of the year bet. It was a GIF of Garfield the cat, a checkered napkin around his neck, grinning while waggling a knife and fork.

I owed my good friend a dinner at the restaurant of his choosing. To be honest, I was happy to pay.

CHAPTER 4

COMMUNITY

"Le doute rend fou, la certitude rend con." —Jean-François Marmion

(Doubt makes you crazy, certainty makes you stupid.)

BY EARLY 2022, I was down bad and feeling it. My short bet showed little signs of paying off, whereas crypto was everywhere. Tens of millions of Americans had entered the crypto casinos, drawn in by tales of friends, family, and others they knew who had witnessed the value of their tokens soar, at least on screen. More and more regular people—as well as a few institutional players—decided to roll the dice with crypto in search of fabulous returns. The industry, flush with cash from those investors, unleashed a fire hose of marketing dollars aimed at drawing in even more.

Bitcoin maximalists proudly boast that "Bitcoin has no marketing department," which is technically true, but in practice dead wrong. Multibillion-dollar corporations—at least on paper—spent real dough to convince people to buy crypto. Sometimes the appeals were explicitly about Bitcoin, leveraging the brand awareness of the best-known cryptocurrency.

But what were everyday consumers buying? Just a story, a myth about magical blocks of computer code. And if crypto is only a story, or rather a constellation of stories that coalesce around an economic narrative, as Robert Shiller points out, *then crypto is only marketing*. There is no product, only dollars flowing from you, dear retail investor, to the casino owners.

To grow their investor/gambler base, crypto corporations employed a time-honored mass marketing device: celebrities. In addition to Matt Damon, other movie stars got in on hawking various forms of digital "assets." Gwyneth Paltrow and Reese Witherspoon shilled NFTs, as did musicians Justin Bieber and Steve Aoki. Sports stars LeBron James, Tom Brady, Steph Curry, and Aaron Rodgers pitched crypto exchanges and apps as the future of personal finance, with some taking equity stakes in companies like FTX. (It was later revealed Tom Brady received 1.1 million common shares in FTX; his soon-to-be ex-wife Gisele Bündchen held 686,000. She served as the exchange's ESG—environmental, social, and governance—advisor.) The torrent of interest crested with the pinnacle of American marketing and consumerism: the Super Bowl.

One of the perks of being married to a successful actress is getting to be her plus one at fancy shindigs without having to do any actual work. My wife Morena had a new show, *The Endgame*, premiering that spring on NBC, the network that happened to be airing the Super Bowl. The promotional opportunity was obvious, and when my charming better half asked whether I wanted to accompany her to Los Angeles to witness the biggest sporting event of the year, I did my best not to shriek with delight. Would I like a free ticket near the fifty-yard line to the Super Bowl? Yes, yes I would. As a proud Texas boy and former high school football player myself, I was in pigskin heaven.

But I also had another agenda. While laser-eyed Tom Brady was battling it out on the gridiron and celebrities preached the gospel of crypto via slick multimillion-dollar ad campaigns, my trip to Los Angeles marked my first trip outside the wire on a mission to deconstruct the lies surrounding digital funny money. It seemed fitting to start in Hollywood, a town built on myth. It also felt appropriate that I found myself on the opposite side of the proverbial line of scrimmage from the Hollywood consensus, but seemingly without a squad of my own. To counter the feelings of isolation and depression in my quest for truth in crypto, I needed to finally meet some fellow skeptics in the flesh. I needed a team of my own. Crypto-skeptic nerds assemble!

o o o

If you are new to crypto, you might be surprised by its mangled use of the English language. A lot of the industry jargon is boilerplate Silicon Valley nonsense. Crypto CEOs refer to the "ecosystem" or the "space" as though crypto were a fragile, but vital, thing or a cool place where you could chill and soak up vibes instead of a morass of competing businesses only bonded by the same goal: to make as much real money as possible out of the fake stuff. The original linguistic sin may have been to call these speculative, ephemeral digital "assets" money, but it would hardly be the last.

Crypto has its own lexicon, with many words representing the opposite of what they claim to be. Many stablecoins ultimately proved to be not so stable. Smart contracts were neither smart, nor contracts in any familiar sense. Decentralized invariably meant centralized, only in private hands. You could even combine nonsensical crypto words to form meaningless new phrases, like some absurdist German language exercise. DAOs, or decentralized autonomous organizations, were neither decentralized, autonomous, nor particularly organized.

For the uninitiated, crypto's obscure jokes and clunky buzzwords can be hard to parse. GM is *good morning*. WAGMI is *we are all gonna make it*, conveying a sense of shared purpose. NGMI is *not gonna make it*, used to deride someone or something as destined to fail, often because they don't exhibit enough faith in the future of crypto. HODL is *hold on for dear life*, meaning that you should cling to your crypto no matter the price. After all, it's not a loss until you sell. (Or at least that's how some gamblers console themselves.) Between the contortions—or outright abuse—of the English language and the acronyms, it was hard for a forty-four-year-old dad to keep up. Don't even get me started on the memes. You can DYOR—*do your own research*—on those.

Yet the silliness of crypto-speak belies the important role it plays, and the most pernicious language abuse in crypto is crucial to understanding its economic structure. The near-constant invocation of the word *community* is impossible to miss. From day one in the cryptosphere, I don't think there was a word I heard more. People weren't customers or investors or clients (or suckers); they were part of a community, you see. The word became the clarion call to otherwise atomized crypto owners—largely young men trading alone from their phones or computer screens, some of them steeped in trollish internet subcultures or libertarian political forums. According to the Pew study, some 42 percent of men ages eighteen to twenty-nine had bought or traded crypto, a huge number in my mind, but perhaps understandable given the trends in social media usage and the isolation wrought from the COVID pandemic.

They gathered on Telegram, Twitter, Discord, and other forms of social media to talk about which token was hot at the moment and ripe for quick gains. Many of them used pseudonyms, masking their identities, but also their motivations. Did they honestly believe in the coin they were shilling or were they trying to pump their bags? (*Pump your bags* means to get others to invest in cryptocurrencies you own so that you can sell out of them before the price crashes.) While online communities have existed for decades, these crypto communities differed from ones that became popular in the infancy of the internet in that they involved an investment of money. However passionate these supposed believers were about their pet crypto project, they almost always stood to benefit financially from hawking it, and all incentives pointed in that direction.

Linguistically, the use of community bears a striking resemblance to the verbiage of a multi-level marketing scheme. An MLM—also known as *networking marketing* or *relationship marketing*—is a business model predicated on existing members recruiting new ones in order to sell them stuff. Someone comes up with a product, then recruits others to sell it to even more people. It's important to understand that in an MLM, if you join as a member, you are required to purchase the product to demonstrate its usefulness to others. You therefore have skin in the game. Not only that, but for every new member you recruit, you receive a percentage of their sales, as does the person above you. The person who recruited you is known as your *upline*, the people below you are your *downline*. Multi-level marketing companies have flourished during the age of social media. Through Facebook, Instagram, and other platforms, MLM members are able to expand their reach and engage with a wider social circle more efficiently than in the past. The hours-long Tupperware party of the 1950s has been replaced by a sixty-second TikTok video.

When viewed through that lens, many crypto influencers appear uncannily similar to someone pushing an old-fashioned MLM. Crypto-world celebrities employ a number of social media channels, hawking this or that cryptocurrency based on technobabble "fundamentals," rumors, misinformation, or just a sense of optimism. Twitter, YouTube, Discord, Telegram, and TikTok were essential platforms for crypto influencers, but there was almost no scrap of web real estate they didn't touch. Every app or platform was an opportunity to build one's audience, to find more suckers to become part of their downline.

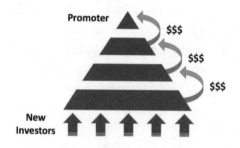

As if the shape weren't obvious, the hierarchical structure of MLMs closely resembles that of a pyramid scheme. The main distinction is that one is legal and the other is not. As Amanda Montell points out in *Cultish: The Language of Fanaticism*, "In theory, the difference seems to be that members of MLMs like Avon and Amway chiefly earn compensation from selling a particular good or service, while pyramid schemes primarily compensate members for recruiting new sellers as quickly as possible. But in practice, a pyramid scheme is essentially just an MLM that was run poorly and got caught."

Surveying the landscape in 2022, it was hard not to notice the myriad similarities between crypto and pyramid schemes. Both depended on recruiting new believers rather than buying anything with an actual use case. Social media was awash with accounts (often pseudonymous or automated bots) encouraging people to buy this or that crypto. Yet there was no actual product being offered: What did these tokens actually do in the real world? Nothing, except offer the hope that "number go up." So what were you buying when you bought a particular cryptocurrency?

This was where storytelling and use of language played a key role. To convince investors that they weren't buying some essentially useless piece of code, they were instead told they were entering a shared social space. The most ardent believers even argued that the existence of the community was more important than the token's price. The irony—or perhaps the warped perception—of this attitude became clear pretty quickly. Of course it was about money; that's the whole ballgame. Crypto is a highly individualistic, adversarial, zero-sum, get-rich-quick scheme in which for me to win, someone else has to lose. Contrary to the WAGMI meme—*we're all going to make it*—in actuality, crypto is divided into a few winners and a vast number of losers. Bitcoin ownership is highly concentrated in an extremely small number of whales who wield enormous power in the highly illiquid market. According to an October 2021 study conducted by finance professors Antoinette Schoar at the MIT Sloan School of Management and Igor Makarov at the London School of Economics, .01 percent of Bitcoin holders control 27 percent of all the coins in circulation. Some community.

If there's any common bond when it comes to crypto, it's that most people will eventually lose real money investing in it. Perhaps that's why some of the strongest, most authentic communities I've encountered in crypto have been among scam victims bonding over their experience, trading information, comforting one another, and organizing to seek legal restitution. The eccentric community of crypto skeptics also fits in that category, and I was proud to call myself a member.

A few win, most lose, while everyone thinks they can scale the mountain. The overall structure is designed to funnel money from a large group of ordinary people upward to a few people at the top, who occupy privileged positions of control. Jon M. Taylor studies MLMs, and is the founder of the Consumer Awareness Institute. His 2011 paper "The Case (for and) against Multi-level Marketing" analyzed more than 400 such companies. He observed that the vast majority of commissions paid by MLM companies go to a tiny percentage of TOPPs (top-of-the-pyramid promoters) at the expense of a revolving door of recruits, 99 percent of whom lose money. In the case of crypto, the TOPPs are influencers, celebrities, VCs, crypto company executives, and other insiders. They are the industry's 1 percent, and everyone else is overwhelmingly likely to lose, often through no fault of their own.

The top 1 percent are the beneficiaries of the information asymmetries that abound in crypto—and the discounts sometimes offered to friends, family, and investors. How do you know if a certain coin is about to go "to the moon" or crash catastrophically? You need to be connected to the people controlling its supply (and its overhyped marketing). In this kind of arrangement, a large group of people, some of them financially desperate, are competing for limited, volatile, and risky rewards. It's hardly a recipe for bonhomie, much less a tight-knit community. It's a recipe for fraud, and notions of "community" play an important sociological role.

In fraud, there's a concept called *cooling out the mark*. A mark is a victim of illegal exploitation, the one who loses money to a con artist. The less charitable term is sucker. When a person gets scammed or defrauded, they're not happy about it. The mark may accept it as the cost of doing business and move on, comforting themselves with the notion that they at least learned a valuable lesson. But if they don't, they may seek vengeance against those who wronged them, perhaps turning to law enforcement. This is a bad outcome for the scammers. The fraudster wants to redirect the mark's anger and frustration away from holding them accountable and toward basically anyone else. To cool out a mark, fraudsters employ many tactics, but one of them is false sympathy. They acknowledge the feelings, sympathize with the mark, maybe even claim to have been scammed themselves. It's a bad-faith attempt at kindness, performed in the service of getting the mark to chill out, to keep his mouth shut.

This is where the community comes in again: If everyone says they have been scammed and defrauded, it becomes the accepted cost of doing business, a rite of passage. Oh man, you got scammed?! Me too, dude. It sucks, but you learned a valuable lesson: DYOR next time. You've also earned the respect and sympathy of other members of the group. In that way, "community" can be seen as just another way of turning a mark's outward anger at getting scammed inward, so the sucker blames himself/herself rather than the con men who perpetrated the scheme. The victim finds (misplaced) comfort in the deceptively sympathetic remarks of the very people who perpetrated the fraud. It's a time-honored con man tactic updated for our pseudonymous digital age.

The contortions involved in such verbal cosplay can be impressive, but they are predicated on a familiar psychological foundation. Responding to feelings of alienation and disaffection from traditional finance, government institutions, and a rigged economy, many coiners really do feel that they are part of a like-minded community, albeit one that reflects a certain strain of libertarian, escapist politics. Their community is one that enables their freedom to exist outside of mainstream economic institutions, which they think have irreparably fallen apart. It also commits them to a shared purpose with broad appeal: getting rich.

In this, let's face it, cultish world, being scammed is a necessary educational experience in order to be reborn in the community of the free. I'm not kidding: Practically everyone I spoke to at crypto conferences and other public events both admitted to being scammed and accepted it as if it was almost obligatory, a character-building exercise and bonding agent. Few spoke about stopping scammers in general. If they did, it was usually to say that while it was regrettable that fraud occurred, fraud is everywhere. Just look at our regulated markets—what a mess! I agreed with them on that point, though I feared they missed the fraud forest for the blockchain trees.

This hollow use of community was unnerving, and it spoke to how crypto apostles misunderstood the nature of money. While speculation and gambling were central to the operations of crypto, true believers still had their original vision in mind: creating a new form of trustless money where people were free to transact directly without any need for a trusted third party, whether a bank, a government, or even just another person. Instead, all they must do is "trust the code."

Unfortunately, this was nonsense. Code does not fall from the sky. People write it—sometimes badly, sometimes making mistakes, sometimes implanting backdoors or other subtle forms of trickery. In the case of the 20,000 cryptos other than Bitcoin, it should be simple to categorize them under the law. Most were securities made by real companies with real employees. Some tried to blur this essentially corporate dynamic by paying lip service to decentralization, or developing a foundation, or describing developers as volunteers. But these were still business ventures pushing what looked like digital securities. The goal was to make these companies and digital assets rise in value, like any business enterprise.

As for Bitcoin, it's true we don't know who Satoshi Nakamoto is, but it was *someone* or *some people*. The Bitcoin white paper was not brought down a mountain by Moses. And despite the high-minded goals of its authors, over time, Bitcoin, or at least the economy surrounding it, has proven highly centralized, dependent on whales, major exchanges, and other institutional gatekeepers.

For crypto's true believers, it wasn't supposed to be this way. Bitcoin was going to be a way to transact directly, with no intermediaries, a peer-to-peer currency. Adoption was extremely low and few people trusted each other, although it was somewhat useful for buying drugs and pizza (both things I like, FWIW). As late as the summer of 2016, its global market cap was less than $10 billion, absolutely tiny by global trade standards. By the end of January 2018, it would be $666 billion. What happened to cause so much growth? First, there was competition. The second major cryptocurrency, Ethereum, launched in 2015, and the floodgates opened for all sorts of coin projects built off its open-source code. (Ethereum also used proof of work to mine its cryptocurrency, until turning to proof of stake in September 2022. In *proof of stake*, owners of the crypto validate the blocks, making the system far less energy intensive, but incentivizing even more centralized ownership.) Centralized exchanges appeared to manage transactions, provide a measure of security (in theory), and offer novel financial products. What started as simple speculation and peer-to-peer exchange became a web of derivatives markets, DeFi protocols (a set of rules governing a particular asset, often using so-called smart contracts, run on blockchains), lending pools, and other newfangled features of digital finance.

For most investors, exchanges became the main entry point into crypto markets. It's simply too hard to transact easily and at scale without them. Tether was also founded in 2014, and it quickly became the most popular gambling chip to facilitate crypto trades without the benefit of a fiat bank account. Yet the fairy tale of Bitcoin and cryptocurrency as a decentralized grassroots movement continued to thrive, because it was more romantic than the reality: A lot of projects, many of them funded by venture capitalists or traditional titans of finance, competing against one another to take your bets.

Under this arrangement, buying Dogecoin on a crypto exchange like Binance was indeed an act of trustlessness, but only in the sense that it was hard to trust any offshore crypto entity. Most crypto investors were effectively putting their trust in the people running FTX, Binance, Bitfinex, or any one of the more than 500 exchanges in existence by 2022. While it was possible to hold the cryptocurrencies you owned off an exchange (referred to as *self-custody*), practically speaking this could be complicated and, therefore, was not done by the vast majority of crypto investors. "Not your keys, not your coins," was the mantra thrown around by die-hard crypto fanatics, meaning you should keep your crypto in a "cold wallet" that didn't touch an exchange—or even the internet. But that kind of advice did not reflect the reality of the markets. It defeated the primary purpose of money, which is to make buying and selling stuff convenient and fluid. And it was diametrically opposed to crypto's promises of community. If you could only trust code, if one of the industry's core principles was that trust between people and institutions was not only unnecessary but also bad—an unnecessary risk—then how could there possibly be a sense of community?

In the abstract, the fantasy of a trustless money might be compelling. The horrors of corrupt governments and dictatorships are well-documented, and there's an alluring simplicity in the idea that open-source computer code could free humanity of oppression. Unfortunately, creating money that's trustless is impossible in practice, for it goes against the very nature of money itself. Adopting it as a mission can only lead to disappointment. To explain why, let's begin at the beginning, with money.

∘ ∘ ∘

Money is not real; we made it up. It's a social construct, like government or religion. Like all social constructs, money relies on consensus. For money, this means a critical mass of people in a society agree to its value in order to transact with one another, stimulating economic activity and, at least aspirationally in a democratic society, providing economic benefit to all. When we accept pieces of paper with funny markings on them (or numbers on computer screens connected to databases run by credit card companies and banks) in exchange for goods or services, that's what we are doing: relying on a shared social consensus. In the United States, the nation with the largest economy in the world—as well as the issuer of the world's reserve currency since 1944, the US dollar—we often take this consensus for granted. Everyone wants dollars, especially in times of crisis.

Consensus and faith—as well as the trust built off that consensus and faith—lie at the heart of our modern economic system. Think of the close historical link between a society's faith in their government and in their nation's currency. When we witness a foreign government collapse, we often find the currency collapses as well, cratering the economy. When enough members of a society no longer trust each other or the government that purportedly represents their interests, its economy and its currency, which similarly depend on trust, may be soon to follow.

In that sense, the stated goal of cryptocurrency—to create a trustless form of money—is literal nonsense. You cannot create a trustless form of money because *money is trust*, forged through social consensus. As Jacob Goldstein writes in *Money: The True Story of a Made-Up Thing*, "The thing that makes money money is trust." Saying you want to create trustless money is like saying you want to create a governmentless government or a religionless religion. I think the words you are searching for are anarchy and cult. The bartender should cut you off and make sure you get a ride home.

Any currency backstopped by governments (as all real currencies at the moment are) is predicated on trust, in both a democratic government and its enduring institutions. Obviously governments are imperfect, politicians can be greedy and corrupt and fail their constituents, and money isn't always subject to the fairest form of political governance. Political and social consensus are fragile things, but an effective currency should actually enhance trust in a society by reliably promoting economic activity, encouraging the free exchange of goods and services that ideally redound to the benefit of all that nation's citizens.

The failures of our current system to do so have no doubt lent the story of cryptocurrency much of its power. A severe, and very understandable, lack of trust in the financial system reflects a wider loss of faith in democratic governance. Wealth inequality is at near record highs and many working people feel that the economy is rigged against them. But that doesn't mean the story of cryptocurrency is true, or offers a better alternative to the present situation. You cannot replace people and flawed institutions with magical bits of computer code.

That code was written by human beings who themselves are far from perfect. What seemed strange was that, by invoking community, trustlessness, and the supposed solidity of code, coiners thought that they had created a new system deserving of their faith. In a society whose financial and political institutions could generously be described as moribund, they placed their hope in the work of programmers who had entangled financial interests and who often worked for corporations that existed beyond typical regulatory and legal structures. More importantly, these programmers made mistakes. Some acted with malice: Insider trading and theft are commonplace in crypto.

Trustless was supposed to be achieved through the alchemy of decentralization—the notion that power and decision-making can be dispersed, made more democratic, via systems that lack a centralized authority. Decentralization has been treated as a good unto itself, and while it can sound promising in theory, what I often found was that, like many concepts in crypto, decentralization was basically the opposite in practice. There was almost always a centralized entity—a company, a crypto exchange, a lender, a team of developers—exerting authority or mediating transactions, sometimes for good reason. Decentralization served as a mask for how power and influence really operated. Instead of dispersing or democratizing power, I found that crypto's version of decentralization instead redistributed power, promoting new classes of experts, decision-makers, and intermediaries. Their roles might be hidden, or they might be overt, but the decentralized utopia promised by crypto leaders seemed not only unachievable, but in many cases a deliberate deception. A decentralized financial system seemed less like an inherently noble pursuit than an alternative structure that, just like TradFi, further enriched those at the top.

I will inevitably be attacked by crypto promoters as advocating for nation-state supremacy or excusing the myriad failings of this or that government, but that is missing the point entirely. To say that money has only really worked at scale when countries themselves issue it and guarantee its use is to state a historical and social fact. You need that trusted third party to provide a bridge.

Consider a familiar example: our banking system. Why do you trust that the money you put in a licensed US bank is going to be there when you want to use it? Because the federal government guarantees it in the form of the FDIC (Federal Deposit Insurance Corporation). Since it was created in 1933, no depositor has ever lost a penny of insured deposits in an FDIC bank, despite hundreds of banks failing—more than 500 since 2001. The system works, and people trust it because it works. Here's how: The US government effectively franchises licensed banks, allowing them to take deposits from customers and create more money in the form of credit by issuing loans to other customers. The government backstops those banks so that people know their money is good; they cannot lose it. In order to receive FDIC insurance, US banks must comply with a litany of regulations designed to keep them from taking on too much risk and going under. Is our financial system perfect? Of course not! In fact, it is deeply, deeply flawed. It cries out for more reform and democratic accountability. But it at least includes guardrails that protect consumers and a legal framework that acknowledges the role of trust in binding people together, whether in social life or commerce.

In the past, we have tried what cryptocurrency purports to be: private money. It did not work very well. When crypto advocates claim they want to replace state-issued money with something else, the obvious question is where this magical new money will come from. They don't like to admit it, but the answer is corporations and other private actors. (*Private* here means privately owned, rather than government issued/backstopped.)

We tried private money in the United States in the nineteenth century during the free banking era. Between 1837 and 1864, before the National Banking Act of 1864, each state was allowed to grant charters to local banks who could issue their own notes (private money). To receive that charter, a bank would have to agree to hold a certain amount of bonds issued by the state. The system did not work very well. In Michigan, Minnesota, Indiana, Illinois, and Wisconsin, banks failed at alarming rates. Sometimes this was due to poor risk management by the bank or the poor performance of the state bonds themselves, which were prone to wild swings in value, but there was also a lot of fraud.

The banks were called *wildcat banks*, a term derived from the fact that they only had one location, and the owners often chose a purposefully remote one in the wilderness among the wildcats to keep depositors from being able to withdraw their money too easily. Once you had people's money, and had set up shop somewhere in the boonies, what was stopping you from taking off with the loot? Admittedly, fraud didn't occur quite as often as you might expect. There were actual physical communities back then and defrauding your neighbor was a bad idea, especially when he had a gun. But nonetheless, the private banking era was not a success, and eventually central banks were created to better manage the franchisee banks and ensure the safety of customer deposits.

Among the many butcherings of language in cryptocurrency, historians may find this the cruelest cut of all. The purported "future of money" is in fact the past of money, a failed experiment and one we revisit at our collective peril.

o o o

I have to address one last false story that Bitcoin maxis—the people with the laser eyes who aren't Tom Brady—have been spreading. You may have heard that Bitcoin is "digital gold," which was a popular story when people were buying it for over $60,000 per coin but less so when its price fell dramatically. What hardcore Bitcoiners mean by this is that Bitcoin's strictly limited supply—only twenty-one million Bitcoins can ever be mined, according to the code—make it scarce, impossible to manipulate, and therefore valuable, the same way gold functioned in the economy of the nineteenth century. But they are making a fundamental error.

In economics, supply does not determine scarcity. Supply is simply the amount of something available to be bought or sold. Scarcity occurs only when *the demand* for that thing exceeds the supply at the price of zero. If you remember anything from Econ 101, it's probably that where supply meets demand (recall those two lines crossing?) you get a price. Here's a refresher:

Supply and Demand

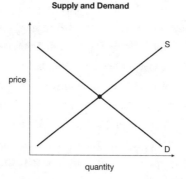

Something can have limited supply and be valuable, but only because there is demand for it—oil, for example—or it can be limited in supply but not valuable. Consider, if you will, a hypothetical. Imagine I own the rights to all the dogshit in Brooklyn. I have approached each and every dog owner in the fair borough, and they have agreed to sell me their dog's poop. I do not own the dogs, mind you, merely the rights to their fecal matter. Now, there are only so many dogs in Brooklyn, and there is only so much they can defecate. The supply fluctuates by the number of dogs—despite how it may appear, there is an upper limit here on the number of dogs, certainly lower than twenty-one million—and the amount of times they poo. But is dogshit scarce? Are people clamoring for it because it is prized and useful? Will my cornering the market make me a rich man? Unfortunately for my empire of shit, the answer to all those questions is no.

Remember what drives demand for Bitcoin, along with other tokens: "Number go up." Most people buying Bitcoin in 2020–21 were drawn in by speculation, observing the meteoric rise in price, which happens to be the key ingredient in Shiller's naturally occurring Ponzi. But what if that price was, say, manipulated by a company with a fake money printer loaning a bunch of fake money to other companies to drive market action? What would happen to the demand for Bitcoin if this manipulation spilled out into the daylight and people realized they couldn't get their real money back? Tens of millions of Americans might collectively realize that the thing they were told was "digital gold" is instead dogshit.

The point is that just because a lot of people *think* that bits of computer code are valuable doesn't mean that they actually *are* valuable. During bubbles, folks often speculate wildly, hoping to sell a thing they see rising in price to someone else for even more money. In economics, this is called the *greater fool theory*. The price of an asset becomes uncorrelated with its actual value, and it ends up only being worth what you can convince the next person, the person more foolish than you, to pay for it. The first speculative bubble in history was also one of the most absurd: tulip mania. Between 1634 and 1637, citizens of the Dutch Republic became obsessed with the flower. Tulips were briefly sold for astronomical amounts. In *Extraordinary Popular Delusions and the Madness of Crowds*, Charles MacKay recounts how, at the peak of the mania, a single tulip bulb was exchanged for twelve acres of land. But a tulip, no matter how pretty, is just a flower, and eventually the market for them crashed back down to earth.

By now, more than 90 percent of the Bitcoins that can ever exist have already been mined. That makes Bitcoin's supply almost perfectly *inelastic*, a fancy word meaning it can't grow or shrink in response to changes in price. It's basically fixed. This makes the price of Bitcoin even more susceptible to changes in demand. Let's compare the supply and demand chart I mentioned before with Bitcoin's:

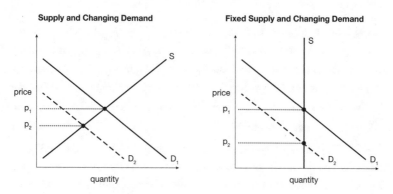

Supply and Changing Demand   Fixed Supply and Changing Demand

Notice anything? Look at the differences in price between the two models in response to the same change in demand. Because supply of Bitcoin is more or less fixed, a change in demand for it has severe consequences for its price.

The problem with the Bitcoin-as-digital-gold argument runs even deeper when we examine economic history. Bitcoin maxis are often "gold bugs," meaning they want us to return to the gold standard, when you could exchange paper money for a certain amount of gold. Technically, the gold standard was a thing until 1971, when Nixon officially abandoned it, but we'd been moving away from it for decades, in part because most economists realized it was an idea that had outlived its usefulness.

The gold standard was meant to keep the supply of money limited, tightly controlled by how much physical gold a country held in its reserves. Because extracting gold from the ground is expensive and there is a finite supply of it in the world, actual gold also has a significantly inelastic supply. But elasticity is crucially important in times of crisis. In response to some unanticipated calamity (such as COVID, for example), the public's first reaction is often paralysis, followed by panic. Fearing worse times to come, people hoard rather than spend. Economic activity nosedives, and less spending leads to less production, which causes unemployment to surge, resulting in even less spending and thus less production. The dynamic quickly becomes self-reinforcing, capable of plunging an economy into a downward spiral that can last years, as it did during the Great Depression.

As Liaquat Ahamed chronicled in *Lords of Finance*, the Pulitzer Prize–winning book on the central bankers of the 1920s and '30s, commitment to the gold standard exacerbated an already fraught situation. As paralysis turned to market panic, the financial contraction that started in America morphed into an economic contagion that spread to cover most of the globe. The narrative that worse times lay ahead became the reality. Eventually the powers that be in the United States realized their mistake. In 1932, Congress belatedly passed the Glass-Steagall Act, injecting $1 billion of cash into the banks by designating government securities as assets eligible to back the US dollar in addition to gold. But by then it was too late; credit kept shrinking at a rate of 20 percent a year. As Ahamed notes, "A similar measure in late 1930 or in 1931 might have changed the course of history. In 1932 it was like pushing on a string."

The economy continued in its tailspin, bottoming out in March 1933 as the commercial banking system collapsed. It would take years for the American economic engine to restart. Commitment to the gold standard did not cause the Great Depression, but adherence to it prolonged the extraordinary pain that ensued. At its worst, nearly one in four Americans were unable to find work; poverty and hunger were endemic.

A counterexample is the American economic response to COVID. Because the United States wasn't tied to the gold standard, Congress and the Fed were able to effectively inject enormous amounts of money into the economy to keep it from crashing. Without that ability, another Great Depression was certainly possible. Of course, the current system is far from perfect; it places enormous power in the hands of politicians and unelected members of the Federal Reserve. These people make mistakes, and sometimes even abuse their power. I am well aware of its deficiencies; the title of this book was partially inspired by the easy money policies born of that system. But that does not mean returning to the gold standard would be any better. Mainstream economists consider the gold standard a relic of a bygone era. It served a use to build trust centuries ago, but as money has evolved it's no longer useful. There are no countries in the world that are currently on the gold standard.

All social constructs are only as strong as the social consensus that under-lies them. This includes a thing called money that we made up and are continu-ing to make up as we go along. As societies evolve and progress, they discard the things that never worked or no longer work—such as private money and the gold standard. It's important to remember why they were discarded. If we don't learn, we will keep trying them, no matter how many times they fail us. We are doing that right now with cryptocurrency.

◦ ◦ ◦

The day after the Super Bowl, I finally met in the flesh my first fellow crypto skeptic not named Jacob Silverman. Cas Piancey and Bennett Tomlin host a podcast called *Crypto Critics' Corner* that proved a lifeline when I first stumbled into the seemingly lonely world of crypto skepticism in the spring of 2021. Sensing something was off about the industry but hoping to educate myself, I searched for decent podcasts on the subject. Instead, I got a lot of shows with dudes—really loud dudes—hawking this or that cryptocurrency while waxing philosophically on freedom and privacy and displaying a garbage under-standing of economics. It was annoying, tedious, and a tad suspect: If these investments were so great, why did they need hype men? For the pro-crypto podcasts, it seemed to be about showing off newfound wealth to spur FOMO in the minds of the listeners, while then selling ad time encouraging them to invest in this or that crypto scheme. And the referral codes—there were always referral codes—allowed crypto podcasters/influencers to profit off of every new customer they sent to an exchange. If you thought of crypto as naturally occurring Ponzi or multi-level marketing scheme, it all made perfect sense.

Crypto Critics' Corner was different. Cas and Bennett knew their stuff. They had both owned crypto, understood the operational intricacies of var-ious blockchains, and originally believed in crypto's promise of producing a censorship-resistant, privacy-respecting new form of currency. Ultimately though, both became disenchanted by the failures of the industry to live up to its initial promise as it descended into fraud, greed, and scams.

The Lyft dropped me off in front of a recording studio in East Los Ange-les. I felt the same tingling sensation of a first friend date that had come with meeting Jacob the previous summer. What would Cas be like in the flesh? Would he and Bennett look down on a new entrant to the crypto-skepticism beat? Maybe they'd see me, like some others did, as a celebrity dilettante chasing some kind of intellectual prestige or internet fame or whatever the hell it was that I was doing. After all, I was still finding my footing, honing lines of argument. Appearing on *Crypto Critics' Corner* alongside Jacob, who joined remotely from Brooklyn, would mark my first long-form interview in my bizarre career pivot.

Cas, a sideways-baseball-cap-wearing SoCal native, welcomed me generously, showing me around the studio owned by an artist friend whose elaborate wood carvings decorated the walls. In a courtyard garden filled with succulents, we performed our version of a crypto icebreaker, chatting about frauds and eccentric characters plucked from industry lore. Eventually it was time to get down to business. Jacob jumped online, as did Bennett from his home in Illinois. It was a wonderful experience. While our discussion covered some fairly esoteric ground, to me it felt like home; just some obsessive dudes nerding out over how the cryptocurrency markets appeared rife with fraud. As one does.

The episode was nominally about celebrities shilling cryptocurrencies and the insanity of the Super Bowl ad campaigns. I pointed out something I had been mulling over internally for weeks: If you acknowledged that cryptocurrency markets resembled a Ponzi, then everything about the massive marketing campaigns made sense. If the entire crypto market was predicated on getting more regular folks to gamble via exchanges like eToro, Crypto. com, FTX, and Coinbase, then the exchanges had to go all out for the biggest TV audience of the year to reach the most potential customers. The Super Bowl was the natural culmination of the grift. Celebrities were a tool, the megaphone necessary to get the most folks into the casinos. It didn't absolve them of responsibility for their endorsements, but it said something about their role in a very exploitative economic structure. I even ventured a silver lining. Perhaps the celebs and the Super Bowl madness might mark the peak of the madness? After all, no matter how big the con, eventually you run out of suckers.

Cas and Bennett entertained my ideas, and the four of us had the kind of back-and-forth—spirited, funny, insightful—that makes a guy remember college dorm life, when every late-night conversation seemed laden with meaning and discovery. Leaving Cas's studio, I realized I had found my community. It had nothing to do with a coin we were pumping, a company we believed in, or some utopian technological vision that, in practice, came with a heavy side of dystopia. We wanted to understand this crazy new financial system, especially its dark side. And it helped that we liked each other.

We were all fascinated by fraud and shared a desire to protect people from exploitation. People who gambled and lost were often told that they should have known better. I was beginning to learn that everyone—including those who might once have shown an obnoxious certitude in the crypto-fied future of money ("Have Fun Staying Poor!")—deserved sympathy when they lost it all. Almost anyone could be a scam victim, especially those who should know better. Sometimes they were the ones who thought they could game the system, and the comedown from that high could be brutal.

It was important to heap blame on the powerful, but it became equally important to not indulge too deeply in cynicism. People bought crypto for all kinds of reasons, and some knowingly risked more money than they could afford to lose. That was probably a mistake. But blaming individuals—and not the systems or forces that put them in that position—didn't get us very far.

The crypto skeptic community that Bitfinex'ed, Cas, Bennett, Jacob, and others brought me into became my team, friends, and trusted colleagues. A few of them I regarded as heroes—or at least the closest thing to it in an industry in which it seemed most people would sell a Ponzi scheme to their mother if it would help pump their bags. Bitfinex'ed—whoever he was!—was our initial ambassador to this new community, but he was soon joined by other pseudonymous online sleuths, as well as economists, computer scientists, indie journalists, cynical former bankers, straight-laced former regulators, stoner podcasters, Scandinavian businessmen, and a few untrustworthy cranks.

To say I learned a lot from them would be a vast understatement, and it quickly became apparent to me why a community like this was valuable. The world didn't need just one crypto critic, it needed a thousand of them, of diverse backgrounds, interests, and motivations, spelunking through the industry's darker corners and sharing what they found. When everyone was selling something, we needed a few people to say, "I'm not buying, but I'm curious how you do it."

There were many more leads to follow and sources we would uncover in the months ahead. I left the recording of *Crypto Critics' Corner* and returned home to Brooklyn from the city of make believe feeling less alone and more sure of the story I was telling. The day before at the Super Bowl, surrounded by the extraordinary hype fueled by multimillion-dollar crypto marketing campaigns, it was hard not to feel outmatched in the ring. Anyone speaking out against crypto in the press and on social media was routinely bloodied by the most outspoken of the crypto faithful, who mocked and jeered at us with surprising ferociousness. At least now, with Cas, Bennett, and a delightful crew of eccentrics behind me, I had a corner of my own to retreat to in between rounds. Admittedly, it was a David and Goliath battle—a random group of skeptics up against a multi-trillion-dollar industry. But I came back from Los Angeles with more pep in my step. Maybe it was just the gambler in me, but I liked my chances.

o o o

Two weeks after the Super Bowl, the headline in *Variety* blared: *'The O.C.' Star Ben McKenzie, Journalist Jacob Silverman Sell 'Easy Money,' Book About Cryptocurrency, to Abrams Press*. After a few setbacks, Jacob and I had managed to convince Abrams Press, an imprint of the storied New York publisher initially known for its lavish art books, to join us in our quixotic quest to unravel what we suspected amounted to one of the largest frauds in history. I have to say I admired their bravery. The crypto market was still flush with real as well as fake money, the buzz rising to the level of pop culture ubiquity. But I wasn't intimidated by that. I had a team of my own. Our goal—to find the truth, no matter what it might be—was clear. Now Jacob and I needed to go into the field and get to work.

CHAPTER 5

SXSW, THE CIA,
AND THE $1.5 TRILLION
THAT WASN'T THERE

T HERE'S A COUNTRY song in here somewhere, but my journey from pretend journalist to pretend author started as it should have, at the beginning. In early 2022, South by Southwest (SXSW), a big tech and music conference in my hometown of Austin, Texas, invited me to organize a panel of crypto skeptics. I was pretty fired up. SXSW would mark our first venture into the real world; everything Jacob and I had done thus far was online or remote. We recruited Edward Ongweso Jr., a razor-sharp journalist for Motherboard, Vice's technology site, to join us on stage. I decided to record the whole thing, hiring a local director of photography, Ryan Youngblood, to film whatever hijinks might transpire. Maybe I'd stumble into something newsworthy.

My parents still lived in Austin, and the allure of free babysitting was strong. I decided to take my six-year-old daughter, Frances, along for the ride. She'd been hearing a lot about Daddy's weird foray into cryptocurrency; now she would have the opportunity to see me in action. And with that, our motley crew SXSW dream team had been assembled: three journalists, a cameraman, and a six-year-old who couldn't care less about cryptocurrency.

In typical Austin fashion, we were ready for things to get weird. But we couldn't anticipate quite how weird they would get.

o o o

Our first ever in-person journalist outing—a SXSW blockchain schmooze-fest—turned out to be one of the strangest. Having just picked up our press passes, Jacob, Ryan, and I strolled into a bar that had been converted into a demo space for Blockchain Creative Labs, the new crypto venture from Fox Entertainment. Immediately a few ironies presented themselves. Blockchain was supposed to overthrow the old techno-economic order and yet here was one of the country's most powerful media conglomerates leading the supposed revolution. The decentralized and democratized future of finance, brought to you by Lachlan Murdoch. Interestingly, much of my TV career was spent under the Fox umbrella (*The O.C.* and *Gotham* ran on their channel in the United States), so I knew some of the publicity people at the event. But this time, we weren't necessarily working toward the same ends.

We were greeted by eight-foot-tall animations of the wrestler "Stone Cold" Steve Austin, which, through the miracles of corporate branding partnerships, were now available as NFTs. The place was littered with massive screens tuned to maximum brightness, strobing through various NFTs of Fox-owned intellectual property—wrestling and cartoons were heavily featured—that were being monetized under the Blockchain Creative Labs brand.

The plain absurdity of the situation was immediately clear. Could this garish display of crypto novelties really be the next frontier of entertainment? Would consumers really want to buy and sell their own unique receipts for individual episodes of sitcoms stored on blockchains?

The crowd was a mix of techie true believers, digital artists in search of a business model, and corporate profiteers. We tried to approach people where they were at, asking why they believed in this stuff so much, and why some of them were willing to take such extreme financial risks. One man told us that he belonged to at least four DAOs—decentralized autonomous organizations—from which he earned several different cryptocurrencies. A DAO starts with a loose group of people who share a common goal. They build (or attempt to build) an organization without a central authority, instead relying on a set of rules, otherwise known as a *protocol*, run through automated computer programs called smart contracts and stored on ledgers called blockchains. Membership in the organization is denoted in a governance token, aka a cryptocurrency, which is sort of like a voting share of a stock. If it all sounds painfully complicated, it's not you. DAOs are notoriously unorganized, and prone to hacks and scams. Again, someone has to write the code on which they are based, and this exposes the members of DAOs to a lot of risk. We mentioned this to the gentleman we were interviewing; it seemed more than a touch reckless to have nearly all of one's income and net worth in volatile crypto tokens. We asked how he juggled all of the different digital currencies.

"Well, there's another DAO that helps with that," he said. His dream was to move to Portugal, a burgeoning crypto tax haven.

Nearly everyone we interviewed had been scammed. When asked, most admitted it quite readily. It was, if not a rite of passage, then an accepted cost of entry to an unfettered market defined by financial freedom. Bad actors are everywhere—certainly in so-called TradFi, or traditional finance—so why should crypto be different? The rationalizations piled on top of one another until it was, at times, hard to see what was so appealing about a new monetary system in which having something stolen from you, with no insurance, no possibility of restitution, much less accountability, was expected. Worse, folks tended to blame themselves for being scammed. They hadn't educated themselves about security, they said, or they clicked something they shouldn't have, or their greed got the better of them and they were convinced to hand over a small piece of information that they didn't realize would leave their digital assets exposed.

It had all become so deeply internalized, forming a fundamental part of crypto culture. There was rarely anger directed toward the scammers themselves. (Occasionally there was admiration for their skill and boldness.) DYOR. It doesn't matter if crypto, from the executive-level bloviating to the bullshit hype on social media, was riven with misinformation and outright lies. You got scammed? You fucked up. DYOR next time, man. And welcome to the club.

It sounded like a cult, I said to the DAO guy. There was a certain shared form of understanding, a sense of value, that appealed only to people in the in-group. He laughed and shrugged. *Well, yeah.*

Later we met a sweet, earnest man in his thirties named Marcel, a digital artist and UX designer whose colorful asymmetric haircut and fluency in the economics of web3 made him far hipper than me. Asked if he worked at SXSW, he shook his head. "I just like helping onboard people to blockchain stuff." Marcel traded NFTs of his own art with friends he met online and was increasingly excited by the possibilities of NFTs in gaming, where elaborate NFT- and token-based economies would allow someone to, say, make small bits of digital money by flying an F-16 in a video game. It seemed like a rather banal and not very tech-forward future—something that would inevitably be dominated by veritable sweatshops of poorly paid Southeast Asian laborers tapping away on apps for distant western clients. (At the time, the big player in this growing "play-to-earn" space was Axie Infinity, which was made by a Vietnamese gaming company whose player base was concentrated in the Philippines. It would get hacked on March 23, the week after SXSW ended, for $620 million worth of crypto.)

We excused ourselves from Marcel and the strobing NFT displays and sought refuge at the bar. Refreshing ourselves with cold beers, we took a few deep breaths and contemplated our next move. I felt eyes on the back of my head. I turned to find a tall, broad-chested man in his late forties standing just a few feet away, staring at me in the awkward way I had grown somewhat accustomed to as a celebrity. I braced myself for the "Do I know you from somewhere?" or "Are you that guy from TV?" but what actually came out of his mouth was:

"I'm with the government. Can we talk for a moment?"

Sure, we said, immediately thrown.

"Are you all American citizens?"

Yes, we said.

"I'm with the CIA. Sometimes we work with prominent people and celebrities, like you."

The guy who had approached us, whom I will call Charles, led us over to a group of six people with SXSW name tags that read USG in the spot reserved for their employer. Most of them were unassuming: close-cropped hair, dress shirts, fleece vests—the typical uniform of law enforcement people playing at casual dress. We made a peculiar form of small talk. Just one of the supposed CIA officers had long unkempt hair; he claimed to work on cartels. He said that while crypto was being used by the bad guys for money laundering, he had also found it useful to pay informants. Easy to move across borders. All of them claimed to have some reason to be at the conference—an interest in new technologies or to keep an eye on important political or tech figures with the usual suspect associations: Russia, China, Iran, North Korea. In 2022, Ukraine was also on the list.

Someone handed Jacob a business card that identified himself as part of an interagency task force based in Austin. Other cards and affiliations passed back and forth. We had no idea if any of it was real. Charles said we should continue the conversation. He asked what we were up to that night.

We stumbled out of the party and back into daylight.

"What the fuck was that?" asked Jacob.

"The CIA wants to take us to dinner," I said.

"Are we? Are they?"

"Of course."

I was pretty new to the profession, but I was fairly sure a cardinal rule of journalism was that whenever the CIA invited you to dinner, you said yes. Not because you were susceptible to their pitch, mind you, but isn't your primary job as a reporter to seek the truth, to wheedle it out of sources and then fashion it into a compelling story? My moonlighting gig as a member of the fourth estate had already brought me into some strange rooms with some decidedly strange people. To that point, most of it had come virtually, in the form of Zoom calls with off-the-record sources, private exchanges with self-proclaimed whistleblowers, various social media DM groupings, and chat rooms with people posting under pseudonyms. Its many charms aside, the digital world of crypto gossip and information-trading couldn't hold a candle to the meatspace environment we had somehow found ourselves in. Reporting from our very first in-person event, we had been approached by intelligence operatives with some bizarre interest in us. It was clear there was no choice in the matter. We were going to dinner.

Forget the metaverse; the physical world was a trip, man.

o o o

That night we sat down with Charles and his friend Paul at one of the city's better steak houses. Martinis appeared with regularity. No one mentioned the evening being off-the-record, but when Jacob made reference to his work, Charles cut him off. "No, no. If I'm meeting with a journalist I have to report it. Be something else."

Jacob told him he was shopping a novel to publishers.

"Great! You're a novelist tonight."

There was no debate over what I was to be classified as. I tried not to take it personally.

The exchange practically repeated itself verbatim later in the evening, but somehow we contorted facts to obscure what was obvious: Jacob was a journalist, I was at least playing one, and we, of course, were going to write about all of this.

It was all really weird. Charles and Paul seemed far too solicitous and far too revealing in what they said and how they acted. They also seemed to know almost nothing about crypto. Every story we told them, even the most well-established tales of corporate malfeasance, was greeted with what might have been mock astonishment. They had no idea it was so bad, they said. Perhaps we should talk to some of their colleagues at the FBI?

Gee, guys. Sure.

Charles was a couple years from early retirement. "I can't wait to smoke weed!" he said.

"It's great," we assured him.

All evening, Charles cited regulations—no dinners with journalists being among the most obvious—while also flouting them. He made a joke about his next polygraph, maybe his last, being a ways off.

Two-pound lamb chops, bathed in sweet marinade, were slapped down on the table. Thick creamy potatoes au gratin, a polite helping of asparagus, more martinis to wash it down.

Charles and Paul sketched out their résumés. Charles claimed to be a case officer who worked in various global hotspots and world capitals recruiting covert sources. Paul appeared more polished, at least at first, ticking off stints at West Point, Delta Force, NSA, then onto the private sector, working for major tech and consulting firms. He spoke three languages and saw action in an equal number of undeclared wars. Asked if he was still in the intelligence world, Paul laughed. "There's a dotted line," he said.

After initially coming across as more reserved, Paul was soon talking about his divorce and his kids and the personal trainer he had recently broken up with. He flashed us a photo of a pretty blonde on his phone. "I couldn't deal with her anymore."

I had been waiting all night for a specific ask and never quite got one. Charles elaborated on what he had said when he approached me that afternoon. Sometimes the intelligence community works with famous or prominent people to broker introductions to people of interest. Imagine if I were at some rich person's soiree talking to a Chinese tech CEO. Suddenly, my friend Charles walks by, and I do the "Have you two met?" routine. Or so it went in theory.

Would that actually happen? And why would I want to do it? It sounded, quite frankly, insane—something out of a movie that I had no interest in starring in. Charles asked if I had ties to the area. I said I was from Austin. No, some way I could prove a connection there, he said. I told him I owned a piece of real estate in a nearby city. Perfect! Since he was based in Austin, he could be, well, my handler, checking on me when I passed through town. This was not the sort of check-in I wanted when I brought the kids to visit their grandparents.

Charles and Paul couldn't help themselves and were breaking their own rules all night. Or perhaps that was part of the game. It was hard to know what to attribute to incompetence plus male bravado plus alcohol and what to attribute to the clever dissembling of trained liars, as most spies are (but perhaps not these two).

"You need to be a borderline sociopath to do this work," Charles said. "Ryan is probably too normal," he added, referring to our local cameraman, who said he had been rejected years earlier from the CIA. Ryan smiled uncomfortably.

More than one story shared that night involved either Charles or Paul saying something like, "Well should I . . ." or, "Maybe I've gone too far, shit how do I say this part . . ."—before inevitably continuing to dish. There were a couple allusions to a "home run," some recruitment or inroad made with someone visiting for the festival. For someone now ostensibly working in the private sector, Paul was clearly wired into what Charles and his team were doing. They shared a familiar shorthand—the nicknames for old colleagues, two-word references to past glories.

They had the typical geopolitical concerns of intelligence professionals: Russia and China. We had to win 5G. We had to win AI. We had to win quantum computing. Paul bragged, after another "Well should I . . . ," that Michael Dell had met with then-CIA Director Gina Haspel about the importance of securing 5G networks against Chinese companies like Huawei. Dell left Langley a convert.

It went like this all night, Jacob and I exchanging occasional looks that indicated our mutual disbelief. At one point, Jacob gawked as Charles explained that the NSA had found "a small bug" in Signal—the encrypted messaging app used by journalists, activists, and millions of other people, including the spies at our dinner table—but if you restart your phone once a week or so, it wasn't a problem. It was hardly a sophisticated technical explanation, and maybe it was all bullshit braggadocio, but a Signal exploit would be incredibly valuable—easily seven figures on the open market—and a closely held secret by any intelligence agency.

None of it made much sense. They seemed to know nothing about crypto, blockchain, or the fraudulence and criminality that we claimed undergirded the industry. Why were two guys who expressed such ignorance about our core concerns recruiting us? Were we being had?

Charles said he would be my main contact, but he also wanted us to meet with a local FBI cyber guy and talk about what we knew. Could we do it the next day? Jacob and I looked at each other, a flash of panic passing between us. It was an easy no. We were journalists, not FBI informants, or confidential human sources, as Charles said we'd become (our names couldn't be FOIA'd, he promised, protecting our identities). I told him we had too much scheduled. Maybe a phone call later in the week. Sure, Charles said. We'd hear from him.

It didn't feel right. We had some decent sources, perhaps, but what could we possibly tell the FBI about crime in the crypto world that they didn't already know? And not for the first or last time: Why the hell would we want to?

As the bill for our lavish, boozy dinner came—paid for by Charles, which is to say, by you and me, fellow taxpayer—it was clear that our new friends weren't ready to go home. They asked us what was next. More drinking was the obvious answer.

At a bar on Rainey Street that had been converted to a branded garish party house for CNN+, the lavishly advertised streaming venture that would shut down six weeks later after having squandered $300 million, a chipper young woman greeted me as soon as our group entered. "Ben, so glad you're here! Please come with me."

Our group of six-plus dudes, most of them not quite the smooth club-going type, was escorted through the bar, a former single-family home, into the backyard, where we sat on couches behind a gray velvet rope. It was a bit of a flashback to my twenties, when I shamelessly surfed the Hollywood club scene like other suddenly famous teen idols. Now, cowed by experience and happily domesticated in my forties, I wasn't sure what to make of it, the pageantry and the looks from other partygoers. We eyed the open bar—those being two of the deadliest words in the English language—with short-lived suspicion, then thirst.

We all drank more, toasting to . . . something? Maybe blockchain. Ironically. At a certain point, Charles got up and said, "I want to give you guys something." Then, in a series of too obvious exchanges, again like we were parodying a spy flick, he shook hands with me, Jacob, and Ryan, giving each of us a CIA challenge coin, a marker of accomplishment for law enforcement officers and sometimes a kitschy souvenir for people they're trying to flatter. In our case, it was obviously the latter. On one side of the thick coin was the CIA emblem and on the other a U-2 spy plane with the words "In God We Trust, All Others We Monitor." We put them in our pockets.

Things deteriorated from there. Other friends and colleagues, uninitiated to the fact that we were in the midst of a possible clumsy CIA recruitment effort, joined us. "Tell them we're in private equity," said Charles. Sure, okay. We took advantage of free drinks, free food, and the overwrought and oh-so-friendly service provided to people who are at least a little bit famous. At some point, we were joined by Katie, a publicist who had quickly become a friend and indispensable guide to the internal politics (and parties) of SXSW. Charles took an early opportunity to grope her butt.

Katie took us to a TikTok-sponsored party at a fancy hotel. In line, Charles and Paul started worrying, a bit histrionically, that they would have to install TikTok, or a TikTok-related app, on their phones to enter the party. TikTok, of course, was Chinese. Charles asked Jacob if he had ever had TikTok on his phone.

"I'm not sure. Maybe once," said Jacob.

"Well, then you're fucked, even if you deleted it."

Eventually, through the alchemy of TV celebrity and Katie's connections, we bypassed the line and headed upstairs. We were eventually deposited in a private cabana where more people came and went, idly discussing their startup ideas or asking questions about season 3 of *The O.C.* Charles continued making crude—and legally actionable—passes at the publicist, who insisted in a whisper she could handle herself. Strangers pontificated about stablecoins and big tech and the next cool party they would attend. Eventually, I realized that I was maybe a decade too old to be doing what I was subjecting myself to and announced my exit. We all decided to use the opportunity to escape Charles. Jacob, who handled a lot of our communications, told our intelligence friends that we would surely talk to them soon. We bid the CIA bros a hasty farewell and ordered an Uber.

o o o

The next morning, my head reeling from our night with the spooks, I stumbled out of bed and managed to make my way to the Austin Convention Center to meet Jacob and Ryan. The day before, when sober, we had made a loose plan to meet up before our panel later that afternoon, figuring we could fill time by conducting a few impromptu interviews with average crypto enthusiasts before the main event. Jacob was running late, so Ryan and I decided to head to the convention floor to check out the various companies shilling their digital wares.

As we entered the exhibition hall, the first corporate booth I saw made me laugh with disbelief. I knew the company, and not in a good way. Turning around, I recognized a man I was deeply familiar with from our online sleuthing. My pulse quickened. As I stared in disbelief, Jacob arrived.

"We need to talk to a lawyer," he said. He was thinking about the CIA and that weird approach, but my mind was elsewhere.

"Yes, but never mind that now," I said. "First—and don't look—I need to tell you who's sitting on a couch about twenty feet behind you. Alex Mashinsky."

In the last few years, the crypto economy has become much more complicated than enthusiasts buying and selling a handful of popular cryptocurrencies.

There are more than 20,000 cryptocurrencies out there, sophisticated exchanges, decentralized finance protocols that allow billions of dollars of crypto to change hands without human intermediaries, and financial products that resemble less regulated, riskier versions of their Wall Street equivalents. At least in the gambling-like realm of financial speculation, there's a lot you can do with crypto. With few guardrails in place, it's easy to borrow money and add leverage in order to increase one's odds of winning big or losing everything. Many of these financial products and transactions are extremely complicated, and difficult for the average investor to navigate. Nearly all of them are extraordinarily risky.

To guide consumers through this world of high leverage and wild speculation, a new generation of supposedly bank-like entities appeared. They took your crypto and managed it, with a typical offering allowing customers to "stake" their tokens for extraordinarily high interest returns—think 10 percent or more, sometimes much more. And with your crypto, they made their own bets and loans and investments, acting at once like a bank and a hedge fund. The problem was that crypto was extraordinarily volatile, with no inherent value, and that these banks (or bank-ish entities) might have been engaging in the kind of Ponzi economics that seemed to animate much of the crypto world. Many of these companies had also received scrutiny from the SEC and other regulators.

So it was a bit of a surprise for me to walk into the main convention hall at SXSW and find myself staring at a booth for Celsius, one of the biggest crypto "banks" out there, at one time claiming somewhere around $20 billion of crypto assets under management. By some measures, Celsius was a successful going concern, but with investment backing from Tether (they loaned Celsius over $1 billion), strange lending activities, sky-high interest rates on offer, and some murky movement of its tokens, it was an object of extreme speculation and rumor within the crypto-skeptic world. Many people suspected that it was yet another Ponzi scheme. Some government agencies shared those suspicions, with Celsius facing legal action in multiple states: New Jersey, Alabama, and even Texas. To set up a promo stand in a state where your company was currently embroiled in litigation against that state took a certain kind of gall.

But gall was in abundant supply in the risk-tolerant world of crypto. Alex Mashinsky, the CEO of Celsius, wasn't immune to this kind of hubris. Celsius's chief financial officer had been arrested in Israel in November 2021 on charges of fraud, but Mashinsky refused to even discuss the issue publicly. Instead, he continued to tout the Celsius brand on Twitter, at conventions, and across crypto media. Angrily denying the rumors swirling through crypto Twitter, Mashinsky held regular Ask Me Anything sessions on Twitter Spaces—events celebrating the Celsius "community" and its growing wealth.

At SXSW, Mashinsky was in his element. His booth, a garish mix of off-white and purple paneling, touted the company as the obvious partner for consumers looking to escape the tyranny of TradFi banking. The typically voluble Mashinsky sat kibitzing with cofounder and Chief Technology Officer Nuke Goldstein and Chief Growth and Product Officer Tushar Nadkarni on some white leather couches nearby.

Despite my nerves, I had to talk to him. I felt the same performance jitters I'd felt before going onstage on Broadway just two years prior.

I wired up and quickly rehearsed some points of inquiry with Jacob— Celsius's relationship with Tether, its legal problems, its improbably high yield rates, its executives' apparent connections to Israeli money launderers, and maybe whether it all was a giant Ponzi scheme. Jacob and our friend, the journalist Ed Ongweso Jr., slunk off to the corner, sitting in a couple chairs obscured by large plants from where they could monitor the scene and take some cell phone videos. It was comically cloak-and-dagger, more *Pink Panther* than *All the President's Men*, but that was becoming the dominant tone of our investigation.

I took a breath, told myself that I wasn't hungover from a night of drinking with CIA operatives, and, trailed by my cameraman, did my most confident walk over to Mashinsky and his confederates.

"Hi, Alex. My name's Ben."

"Hey! Didn't I meet you in Vegas?"

I hadn't been to Vegas in at least a decade.

"Sure, yeah! Must have been. Anyway, I'm an actor and I'm writing a book about cryptocurrency now. I've got my buddy Ryan here and I was just wondering if we could do a little interview on camera about crypto and your company."

For reasons that can only be attributed to ego, Alex Mashinsky said yes.

So we talked: about an industry rife with speculation, about Celsius's relationship with Tether (he downplayed it), about risk, about the supposed promise of crypto. As the conversation went on, several Celsius staffers, all of them young women, circled the couches, alternating between punching away at their phones and staring at their free-talking CEO with growing concern. At one point, Mashinsky's wife Krissy, decked out in a pink Juicy Couture velour jumpsuit, stood directly across from him, giving him a death stare. The point was clear: *End the fucking interview!* But Mashinsky brushed her off with a wave of his hand.

We got it on camera. There were moments that astonished me. Talking about scams, he took the usual tack and said people needed to educate themselves. Alas, there are a lot of scammers out there, but always DYOR. I asked him, didn't that really mean it's the customer's fault? Most crypto CEOs duck that question, or pretend to be offended. Instead, Mashinsky leaned back and said, with a "Who me?" kind of mock innocence, "If you left money on the street, you['d] expect it to be there in the morning?"

Toward the end of our conversation, when the video was off but with audio still rolling, Mashinsky told me something that made my blood run cold. I asked him how much "real money" he thought was in the crypto system. I didn't think he would actually answer the question, but he did.

"Ten to fifteen percent," Mashinsky said. That's real money—genuine government-backed currency—that's entered the system. "Everything else is just bubble."

The number seemed straightforward and eminently believable. But it was still shocking to hear it from a high-level crypto executive, who seemed totally unconcerned about it all. Mashinsky acknowledged that a huge speculative bubble had formed. If the overall crypto market cap was about $1.8 trillion at the time we spoke, that meant that one and a half trillion or more of that supposed value didn't exist. And given the general lack of liquidity in crypto markets—that a billion dollars' worth of Ethereum isn't redeemable for a billion dollars of cash without tanking the market—that meant that the crypto economy was dancing on a knife's edge. One bad move by a major player might tip the industry into freefall. An illiquid market based on irrational speculation, it was all essentially vapor. Crypto critics call it "hopium," and it's a powerful drug. People thought they had money, something of value, and yet they didn't. They would never get their money back, because it wasn't there. It existed in the form of rapidly depreciating tokens or had already been shuffled between a dozen offshore corporations. As OG crypto critic David Gerard would say, "You lost your money when you bought the tokens."

Alex Mashinsky didn't have to ask what I meant when I talked about "real money" in the system. He had an answer ready. Was he that deeply cynical about the industry, or was he just another profiteer squeezing out whatever value he could before the crypto market fell back to earth, leaving behind a crater filled with ruined investors?

o o o

Speaking of thuds, there was our crypto-skeptic panel. Delusions of grandeur had driven me to encourage SXSW to put us in a huge ballroom to accommodate what would surely be the droves of Texans desperate to hear that crypto was bullshit. Peeking out from behind the curtain backstage, I saw what appeared to be approximately 576 empty seats in the cavernous convention ballroom and flinched in embarrassment. Oh well, at least the stakes were low. Between my parents, their friends, some *O.C.* fans, and a couple people just enjoying the air conditioning, it was a sympathetic crowd.

The panel somehow proceeded without any major embarrassment. We opened with a satirical video we'd commissioned highlighting some of crypto's bizarre characters—the messianic, mortgage-your-house-to-buy-Bitcoin types. I triumphantly scaled the dais, ripped through a quick intro on incentives (bad), marketing (bad), and markets in crypto (also bad), before introducing Jacob and Ed Ongweso Jr. We had a good chat, took a few questions from the audience, and called it a day.

After it was over, I walked over to where my parents were sitting.

Touchingly, they had compelled my six-year-old daughter to bear witness to her father's shining moment of glory. Frankie was lying on my mom's lap, half asleep. "I know it was boring," I said. "Are you mad at me?"

Thankfully, there was an ice cream truck outside the convention center. All was forgiven.

o o o

If you drive for about an hour northeast from Austin, past the scrub brush and the quota-driven traffic cops, you reach a former Alcoa aluminum smelting plant on the outskirts of the tiny town of Rockdale (pop 5,323). It was the kind of old-school corporate holding that's so big they built a lake to service it (Alcoa Lake). The facility, sold in 2021 for $240 million to an obscure real estate firm, had mostly gone fallow. But its mere existence—the mothballed warehouses, silent smokestacks, miles of fencing, the power substation on site—was a reminder of a not-so-bygone era when large industries operated in the United States and factories, perhaps even staffed by decently compensated union workers, actually made stuff.

One company—and its gregarious front man—had a plan to change that, albeit with a crypto twist. The abandoned Alcoa aluminum plant had been transformed into the Whinstone Bitcoin facility, the largest crypto mine in the United States and part of a growing portfolio owned by Riot Blockchain, a publicly traded multibillion-dollar firm (rebranded in January 2023 as Riot Platforms). Suddenly, the site, and especially its robust connection to Texas' often-stressed power grid, was important again. Money was coming in, ambitious building projects were planned, people were getting steady construction work—all the supposed hallmarks of basic economic progress. But to what end and at what cost? I had come to Whinstone to find out, accompanied by Jacob and David Yaffe-Bellany, a reporter from the *New York Times* who wanted to write a piece on me.

We loitered outside a massive industrial site that would have worked as a set for a Bond movie, or maybe a place worth destroying in yet another *Jurassic Park* sequel. Armed security guards sat in a small office-turned-command center, checking our bona fides. Beyond a large white gate, trucks, forklifts, and other heavy machinery moved about, transforming a dilapidated old aluminum plant into a cutting-edge Bitcoin mining facility.

"You're not Bill McKlensley?" a guard asked.

I assured him I wasn't. Someone had confused us with a CNBC crew scheduled for later in the day. For now, we just cared about getting in and touring the place before they decided, like Alex Mashinsky's PR team, that we were the enemy. It was a genuinely great opportunity to tour a major mining facility and experience the scale of things, the enormity, up close. We wanted to hear their pitch: how Bitcoin mining brought jobs, stimulated development, and would be an asset for the whole community. To hear that pitch, they asked us to sign what amounted to nondisclosure agreements. David, the *Times* reporter, assured us that he couldn't, his job wouldn't allow it. None of us felt comfortable. What was the point of signing something that might limit our ability to write and report on what we might see? It made no sense to do so when we were going in with cameras—if they were going to let us in with cameras.

Eventually we confronted a more urgent reality: Jacob really had to pee. Standing practically cross-legged outside the car, his face radiated the barely withheld anxiety that comes after a long car ride *after* a morning guzzling coffee. I was a bit out of sorts, too. We were supposed to be featured in the *New York Times* as intrepid crypto critics, and here we were unable to get into our featured location while self-urination seemed to be a non-zero possibility. Unfortunately, the surroundings—a brand-new industrial facility guarded by armed men and surveillance cameras, perched on the kind of flat Texas landscape where you could watch your dog run away all day—didn't seem suited to clandestine acts of hygiene.

In my chummiest voice, I communicated to a clipboard- and gun-equipped guard that we'd driven a while and could use a restroom. Soon we were rotating through the bathroom in their office. Despite the initial resistance, the Bitcoin mine cops' daily routine appeared rather boring and uneventful in practice, largely confined to chaperoning the occasional visitors through the gates. (We'd met a lot of strident Bitcoin critics but not anyone interested in attacking a Bitcoin mine.)

We chopped it up for a few more minutes, and then, after the typical alchemy of bureaucratic authority parceling out permissions, we were told that we could go in the gates and drive to the main office.

"I left my NDA in the bathroom," said David as soon as we piled into the car.

Jacob announced his paper was under his foot. Others had disposed of theirs quietly in their pockets. Either some Whinstone official had forgotten about the agreement during our time in the office or perhaps had been overruled. It didn't matter. We weren't signing anything. They waved us through the gate and we drove in.

We were met by CEO Chad Harris in a large trailer that doubled as Whinstone executive offices. At least a half dozen dogs, left to their own devices, ran and lumbered and lazed around. Chad, a serial entrepreneur who once owned a landscaping business in Louisiana, began cycling through anecdotes in the practiced cadence of an experienced salesman. At one point he casually mentioned something about having a "disagreement"—he implied it was a good-faith disagreement—with a local bank. Eventually, he got into warehousing, which led to him hosting some Bitcoin mining machines, and well, things took off from there. Now he was an executive at the biggest Bitcoin mine in the United States, and being in Texas, he was also a potential participant in the battles over Bitcoin's energy usage and the lucrative politics of Bitcoin, which were distinctly right wing. For Chad, Bitcoin itself was at times an afterthought—an accidentally valuable byproduct, like ambergris. Chad was foremost excited about the physical infrastructure he was building and the opportunity he was creating in a small community that had seen thousands of jobs evaporate. Or that was the story being sold. We piled into his pickup truck—the dogs stayed behind—and let him show the way.

The featured attractions were two large warehouses that, from the outside, betrayed no sense of their purpose. These mines were filled with thousands of Bitmain Antminer Bitcoin mining machines, which typically have a lifespan of about five years and can cost several thousand dollars. The company had plans to purchase thousands more. It couldn't hire fast enough to fill some positions.

Inside the first warehouse, the machines created an otherworldly buzz—eerie, alien, their hum filling the cavernous structure. Thousands of them were stacked fifty feet high. Lined up together, they formed rectangular walls of hot whirring metal. Chad opened a door in the wall of mining rigs and waved us in. We stepped through and found ourselves surrounded on all sides by high-powered computers emitting that unsettling alien sound—and their heat.

"It's about 125 degrees in here," Chad said. "It gets up to 150 sometimes."

The room acted like a funnel, allowing hot air to flow upward toward the ceiling where it could escape through openings at the top. I stood in the middle of it and looked up. It was something from a dystopian science fiction novel: the heat, the surrounding wall of steel and plastic and other metals, the fans that produced that strange mechanical sound, like a million digital locusts humming in unison.

In another warehouse a short drive over, we found the opposite: near silence. Hundreds of Antminer machines were immersed in mineral oil, which acted as a coolant. The noise was faint, murmuring beneath the viscous liquid. There was no miasma of heat rising from the machines, no otherworldly noises. But there was a sense of experimentation and vague horror, with the shimmer of the oil and the tubes that emerged to connect to other machines, lights flashing dimly beneath the oil in a way that seemed unnatural, like none of it should work.

As we toured the facility, Harris, our host, made one point over and over again: This was about jobs. Harris, who was from out of state, claimed that Whinstone was providing exactly what the people of Rockdale and the surrounding area needed: good paying jobs in a growing industry. While I agreed that, everything else being equal, employment was a good thing, I couldn't help but notice the flimsy underpinnings of this otherwise sturdy mining operation. This company was using enormous amounts of electricity to mine speculative digital assets to keep a zero-sum game of chance going. Texas' notoriously over-worked electric grid, also known as ERCOT, had gone down after a winter storm in February 2021, contributing to the deaths of 246 people. Mining Bitcoin hardly seemed worth the potential harm to the population.

What benefit did any of this produce for the rest of us? Was it worth the cost? In 2021, the greenhouse gasses released to produce the energy consumed by Bitcoin and fellow networks more than offset the amount saved by electric vehicles globally.

It was all ridiculous, but I kept coming back to the same thing. Economically, the parabolic rise and fall of bubbles was well established. But what would crypto's downfall do to this community? How long could the speculative fervor possibly last before it invariably came crashing down, resulting in all of the Riot Blockchain employees Chad claimed to care so much about losing their jobs? Little of the experience felt real, much less sustainable.

o o o

On the plane ride back to New York, slumped in a window seat with my daughter beside me and Jacob on the aisle, I reflected on what had been a whirlwind of seventy-two hours back home. I was disoriented, but adrenalized. This was only my first venture into the wilds of crypto, and it proved to be more eventfully surreal than I ever could have imagined. I noticed a peculiar feeling welling up inside me, one this cynical middle-aged man hadn't experienced in a long time. Was I . . . having fun?

I looked over at my daughter. Engrossed in her iPad with her headphones on, she was blissfully oblivious to her dad's quiet, sentimental moment. I leaned over and gave her a kiss on the head. She punched me hard on the shoulder and I smiled.

CHAPTER 6

THE BUSINESS OF SHOW

"Nobody knows anything." —William Goldman, *Adventures in the Screen Trade*

N APRIL 1, 2022, OUR months-long investigation into the world's largest crypto exchange, Binance, was published in the *Washington Post*. By now we had heard from multiple sources that the number of meaningful players in crypto was actually extremely small. At or near the top of that list was the founder and CEO of Binance, Changpeng Zhao. Born in China but raised in Canada, CZ, as he preferred to call himself, graduated from college with a degree in computer science. After school, he relocated to Tokyo, working for the Tokyo Stock Exchange and then Bloomberg Tradebook, where he developed futures trading software. In the mid-2000s he moved again to Shanghai to start his own firm developing software for high-frequency trading, Fusion Systems. CZ claims to have stumbled upon cryptocurrency in 2013 during a poker game in Hong Kong. With his CS degree and extensive knowledge of the inner workings of financial markets, CZ and crypto were a match made in heaven.

In 2017, in the midst of a crypto bull run, he founded Binance. Within months the Shanghai-based crypto exchange had become the largest in the world by trading volume. There were several reasons for this, but two are worth noting here. The first is that while gambling is technically illegal under

Chinese law, ever since the Communist Party took power in 1949, it is an immensely popular pastime in the country. Gambling centers in Hong Kong and Macau provide citizens outlets for their interest, but crypto offered a more accessible alternative. The second, and perhaps more important, reason crypto took off in China was to avoid capital controls. The official limit of $50,000 in overseas foreign exchange per year is an attempt by the state to restrict wealthy Chinese from moving their money out of the country. If you are a Chinese billionaire, there are numerous ways to get around this, but one of the less expensive ones is crypto. Either buy crypto with yuan and cash out into dollars or other currencies overseas, or perhaps better yet, invest in Bitcoin mines (often using electricity stolen from the grid) and then move the mined Bitcoin via crypto trading elsewhere. Mining exploded in China in 2016 and 2017, and as the value of Bitcoin and other cryptos rose, the country quickly became the dominant player in the industry, accounting for approximately 75 percent of global mining capacity.

The success of crypto in China garnered increased scrutiny from government regulators. In September 2017, just months after CZ founded Binance, Chinese authorities prohibited exchanges from turning fiat into crypto and banned initial coin offerings. CZ responded by moving his operation to Japan, only to have to move it again the following year when Japanese authorities warned against selling cryptocurrencies to the public without a license. Since 2018, Binance has refused to give a location for its global operations, claiming it has no headquarters.

The murky dealings of CZ and Binance fascinated Jacob and me, as well as the fact that the exchange periodically shut down. We decided to focus our piece in the *Post* on some bilked traders who were trying to hold the stateless company accountable.

o o o

On May 19, 2021, Francis Kim thought he had hit it big. The Australia-based entrepreneur had been dabbling in derivatives trading in regulated markets, and he was used to their relative volatility. Now, however, he was trying his hand in the Wild West of finance: cryptocurrency futures. He had begun trading on Binance only a month prior with less than $20,000, when Bitcoin and Ethereum were at then-all-time highs. Kim thought their prices would fall, and using leverage—essentially borrowing from the exchange to risk more on a trade—he put his money on the line. What he would soon find out is how, in the topsy-turvy world of crypto trading, a person can be right about the market and still lose it all.

Perhaps the most remarkable characteristic of Binance is its size: In terms of volume, Binance is the largest crypto exchange in the world by a wide margin, regularly processing tens of billions of dollars in transactions per day. (There is a Binance US exchange, but in terms of activity, it's dwarfed by what's sometimes referred to as *Binance global*.) Binance has four times the spot trading volume of its nearest competitor on a typical day, and its activities potentially have wide influence across this globally interconnected industry.

Binance allows its customers to employ enormous leverage—at one point up to 125-to-1 (now down to 20-to-1 for most customers, comparable to other exchanges). That means retail traders can gamble with far more chips than they actually bought. The upside is large, but so is the downside: At 125-to-1, for every 1 percent move, your one-hundred-dollar bet could net you a fortune, or wipe you out instantaneously. Kim was trading with 30-to-1 leverage.

In mainstream financial markets, offering extreme amounts of leverage to retail traders—not accredited investors who must prove they have the funds to withstand a margin call—is not allowed, a rule meant primarily to protect inexperienced traders from themselves. (The popular online brokerage Robinhood, for instance, offers loans to customers to buy stock, but nowhere near the amount that Binance once offered.) So why would Binance, along with some competing exchanges, allow such sky-high leverage? According to experts such as Carol Alexander, a professor of finance at University of Sussex Business School, it may be because, like some of its competitors, Binance plays a number of roles that may pose conflicts of interest.

As Alexander pointed out, Binance is not just an exchange where people can buy and sell crypto. The company, whose valuation some employees once claimed may be as high as $300 billion, is practically its own vertically integrated crypto economy, offering crypto loans and the widest selection of tokens. If that weren't enough, Binance itself trades on its own exchange. In traditional markets, this kind of arrangement would never be allowed, as the conflicts of interest—and potential for market manipulation—are glaring. Imagine the New York Stock Exchange or Nasdaq taking positions on different sides of trades it facilitates. No financial regulator would allow it, for obvious reasons. ("Market-making activities are standard in both traditional finance and crypto," a Binance representative said in response to a question about whether the company trades on its own platform. "They ensure liquidity and directly support a healthy, vibrant, and efficient marketplace to the benefit of end users.")

For crypto, this is how the whole market works, especially since much of it is based in offshore jurisdictions and operates in legal and regulatory gray areas. "It's not just Binance," said Alexander. Practically all crypto exchanges occupy these varied, potentially conflicting roles, which in conventional markets are divided up between different entities. "And they're completely unregulated," she said. Even relatively savvy investors stand to lose everything on risks they could never take in another circumstance.

This was the situation Francis Kim had put himself into when he took out a Bitcoin short position on Binance. Whether by luck or skill, his bet soon proved right—or seemed to. In the first few weeks of May 2021, the price of Bitcoin fell from $58,000 per coin to $40,000. On May 19, it collapsed. As Kim watched on his phone screen, the price per Bitcoin fell in minutes from $38,000 to $30,000. And as the market tanked, his short position exploded, its value growing from $30,000 to $171,000. Time to cash out. All Kim had to do was click a button on the Binance app to lock in his gains.

But the app wouldn't respond. Experienced in online trading, Kim switched to the two other internet connections he had installed as backups in his house. None of them got the app to work. "So I'm just going there, going crazy, going *click click click*, you know, trying to close out of that position, to lock in the profits," he told us. "And you know, I jump on Twitter. Other people are having similar issues."

Flash crashes in crypto markets tend to be accompanied by technical snafus or unexplained outages, including an inability to withdraw funds. On September 7, 2021, for example, when El Salvador introduced Bitcoin as a form of legal tender, a market-wide slide led to a number of exchanges reporting transaction delays and other problems. Similarly, Binance users have reported regular technical issues, with Tesla chief executive Elon Musk publicly criticizing the exchange for an issue that prevented traders from withdrawing Dogecoin for at least two weeks in November of 2021. (A Binance representative said that "the Dogecoin withdrawal issue was an unlikely and unfortunate coincidence for Binance and the DOGE network," and pointed out that "the technical issue was resolved.")

On the other side of the world, in Toronto, Fawaz Ahmed, a thirty-three-year-old trader, was having the same experience as Kim, but from the opposite end of the gamble. Over the past year, also using leverage, Ahmed had ridden the crypto wave up, turning an initial stake of 1,250 Ethereum tokens into 3,300 that were eventually worth more than $13 million. (He said he started trading in 2017 with about $25,000.) Ahmed was betting that the crypto market would continue its overall rise, though he said he planned to cash out if the price of Ethereum reached $4,100. Like Kim, Ahmed expected some volatility along the way, but it was only on May 19, when Ethereum plunged dramatically alongside Bitcoin and other currencies, that Ahmed realized the gravity of his situation. He needed to close his position, and fast.

For an hour he frantically tried to get out, but just as for Kim, the app wouldn't work. "I saw my position get liquidated," said Ahmed. Rather than allowing Ahmed time to rectify the situation by providing more funds, in what's referred to as a margin call, Binance's liquidation engine was triggered and Ahmed's money disappeared instantaneously. "It was right in front of my eyes." Just like that, Ahmed's eight-figure crypto fortune was gone.

By the time the Binance app was back up and running some hours later, it was too late for both Kim and Ahmed. While Ahmed's position had been liquidated because the app wasn't working and the price was plunging, destroying the value of his holdings, for Kim, something even stranger happened. Although he was correct in his bet, and his short position was worth $171,000 when Bitcoin hit its lowest price that day, by the time the Binance app was usable again, the price had bounced back to near its original level. Rather than being up nearly $150,000, all his profits had evaporated. Hoping for the market to turn in his favor again, Kim held on to his original position, only to see his short position liquidated when the price continued to rise.

The response from Binance was of little help to users. It nevertheless revealed something fundamental about how cryptocurrency exchanges exist as murkily operated casinos that are essentially unaccountable to their customers. Instead of acknowledging the full scale of the problem, the official Binance Twitter account simply said that Ethereum withdrawals were "temporarily disabled due to network congestion," before announcing them "resumed" less than ninety minutes later. Aaron Gong, a company executive, tweeted a vague apology, urging "affected users" to fill out a "derivatives compensation claim form," which has since been taken offline. Then Gong deleted the tweet. No announcement appeared on the official Binance blog. Two months later, Binance announced that it had "recently learnt of a few users who publicly claimed to have been impacted during a market-wide outage on May 19," but that it had investigated and "could not identify any relevant technical or system issues that impacted their trading." (In the course of reporting this book, we were never offered an official accounting from Binance PR of what happened in the May 19 crash, although more than once we were told that one was forthcoming.)

Thanks to social media, Kim and Ahmed soon learned that they weren't alone—and that strange outages like this one weren't atypical for Binance. On Twitter and Reddit, horror stories abounded, with at least one individual claiming a loss of $30 million. On Discord, an ad hoc support group swelled to more than 700 people. Some of the traders, including Kim, had dealt fruitlessly with Binance's customer service, which offered them a small percentage of their losses. At one point, according to a screenshot of a chat with a Binance customer service representative that Kim shared, he was offered a voucher for $60,000 in Tether and another $60,000 in trading credits as an inducement to keep him on the very platform that he felt had robbed him. (Binance said that it does not discuss individual cases, but is "always happy to assist any user who has a concern.")

With Binance failing to make them whole, the Discord group began to plan a class-action lawsuit, which has the potential to win relief for a broad swath of aggrieved customers. Kim and Ahmed connected with Liti Capital, a Switzerland-based blockchain private equity firm—essentially a litigation finance firm that issues its own cryptocurrency and tries to incorporate public decision-making into which cases it takes on. Liti staked $5 million to support the suit, which was being led by international law firm White & Case.

Binance's user agreement requires litigious customers to submit to arbitration at the Hong Kong International Arbitration Centre. With a minimum cost of $50,000 for the services of the court and a qualified arbiter, this clause in the agreement creates a prohibitive barrier for traders who lost a few hundred or thousand dollars seeking restitution. By pooling millionaire day traders with mom-and-pop claimants, and using the backing of Liti Capital, White & Case got around that hurdle.

Binance declined to comment on "potential legal proceedings."

First the Binance claimants have to win, but if they do, then they would have to collect, and no one seemed sure how much money Binance might have in the bank—or which bank. There was a lot about Binance that seemed strange, even in the freewheeling world of crypto. Just as exchanges like Binance have helped "decentralize" finance, the company had essentially decentralized its workforce and had no central headquarters. Nominally headquartered in the Cayman Islands, Binance's employees are scattered across the world, with growing hubs in Paris and the UAE. Binance's crypto-nerd-celebrity chief executive, Changpeng Zhao, or CZ, serves as the company's face via Twitter while jetting among various global tech and financial capitals. He now appears to be based in Abu Dhabi. Binance is a company dealing with billions of dollars in daily transactions. A Binance representative said of its structure that the company "is a remote-first organization, and as such does not have traditional buildings or campuses like Apple or Google."

The company's hazy operations and lack of regulatory oversight have spurred investigations in a number of countries, including in the United States, where the Commodity Futures Trading Commission is reportedly investigating possible market manipulation, and the Justice Department and Internal Revenue Service are examining whether Binance facilitates money laundering and tax evasion. The *Wall Street Journal* reported that the Securities and Exchange Commission was investigating relationships between crypto trading firms and Binance's US division.

Binance declined to comment on these investigations but said that it aims to work "collaboratively with regulators and share information with them when requested." A representative said that the company "has always welcomed increasing regulatory and government involvement in the crypto space. We believe regulation and compliance is necessary for the growth of the industry. We are committed to being fully licensed and regulated around the world, and we were recently awarded virtual assets service provider licenses in Bahrain and Dubai."

Binance's best defense may be to claim basic technical incompetence—perhaps network congestion really did lead to malfunctions in the company's app. What actually happened on May 19 remains a mystery. But people like Carol Alexander and Matt Ranger, a data scientist and former professional poker player, propose that the platform's problems may go beyond simple technical outages. In blog posts, academic papers, and conversations with journalists, they have argued that Binance has been outplayed in its own casino. According to their analysis, Binance has become the perfect playground for professional trading firms to clean up against unsophisticated retail traders. Using state-of-the-art algorithmic trading programs and access to the latest market-moving information, these firms are both faster and more powerful than the regular Joes they compete against.

Ranger compared what was happening on crypto exchanges to the online poker craze of the mid-2000s. Back then, you had a sense of the stakes and could see who was beating you at the virtual table. "At least poker's kind of honest," said Ranger. "You're losing to this guy named, like, Penis420, and he bluffed you out of your cash, and you're here." But for average crypto investors/gamblers trading on Binance, there was no such clarity. Across the table could sit an advanced computer trading program. Regular traders don't stand a chance; when the professional firms easily outmaneuver them, they can get wiped out in seconds.

Under these circumstances, the litigants argued, it's impossible to have anything resembling a fair market. In their view, Binance was so compromised—dependent on a constant stream of suckers coming through the door while also keeping an eye on the savvy trading firms picking novice traders' pockets—that its problems may be existential. (Zhao himself said that Binance may eventually lose out to more nimble and harder-to-regulate DeFi, or decentralized finance, exchanges.) Along with its proliferating legal troubles across the United States, Europe, and Asia, Binance had thousands of newly alienated customers and one of the world's top law firms ready to use it as an example of what happened when an unregulated crypto exchange was put under the microscope.

Binance probably faced significant legal headwinds, but it had developed a distributed—and mostly unaccountable—corporate structure that would be the envy of any offshore financial concern.

It was hard to see how this "democratization of finance" was going to lead to a fairer economy rather than a more chaotic one, with a vast gulf between winners and losers. The liberatory rhetoric and experimental economics of crypto could be alluring, but they amplified many of the worst qualities of our existing capitalist system while privileging a minority group of early adopters and well-connected insiders.

Binance exemplified the worst of these excesses. It was a premiere operator in an industry that prided itself in risk-taking and constantly "building," although it seemed to be building little more than a better mousetrap.

o o o

Getting our work published in the *Post* offered validation, but there was more work to be done. Before leaving for SXSW, Jacob and I applied for press passes to the annual Bitcoin Conference in Miami, being held April 6–9.

(Given crypto's puerile culture, this date range was almost certainly not a coincidence.) The largest Bitcoin gathering in the world (50,000 people were expected to attend) seemed like the logical next step in our deepening voyage through the bowels of the crypto industry. Surprisingly, the press passes actually came through. We received an official invitation to make a pilgrimage with the true believers.

Buoyed by our success in Austin, I decided to go bigger in terms of getting it all down on film. I reached out to Jeremy, a director of photography I knew, and threw together a three-man crew: two cameras plus a sound guy. The plan was to assemble in Miami on April 6 to film my interactions with the ringmasters of the crypto set, along with some average conference attendees. The general attitude was that anything could end up being good material, so keep filming.

o o o

Peter Thiel, the arch-capitalist fifty-four-year-old cofounder of PayPal, was throwing one-hundred-dollar bills from the main stage, trying to signify their unimportance. When members of the crowd rushed to grab them, Thiel appeared shocked. "I thought you guys were supposed to be Bitcoin maximalists!" Raging against the "finance gerontocracy"—which, of course, had helped to make him very rich—Thiel derided legendary investor Warren Buffett as the "sociopathic grandpa from Omaha." (Tell us about your childhood, Peter). Also on the dais were luminaries like Jordan Peterson, the Canadian psychologist who found his true, and truly lucrative, calling as an alt-right provocateur who encouraged young men to clean their rooms.

In the hall backstage, we passed Tucker Carlson, deep in expository discourse to some trailing microphones and cameras. On the conference floor, picking up on the trend, Bitcoin influencer Max Keiser, a vocal supporter of Salvadoran president Nayib Bukele, tore up some dollar bills with another attendee—caught on smartphone video, of course. They immediately posted the video, cackling at their own daring, their ultimate, performative disregard for real money.

All these histrionics felt choreographed and banal. For me, the conference was less about experiencing loud, overwrought paeans to the glory of Bitcoin than studying some of the industry's leading personalities in their seemingly candid moments (which admittedly could be rare). It was also about retail investors, the average folks who had committed their lives to this stuff. I wanted to understand what attracted people to the Bitcoin story.

But first, I wanted some merch. Across the sprawling Miami Beach Convention Center, the product and sales pitches ranged from free NFTs to getting in on the ground floor of the next ICO that seemed a lot like the last ICOs. A DAO promised an investment scheme to "democratize yachting." Crypto mining machines sold for thousands of dollars each. There was a surprising amount of art, loosely defined. One painter was selling a knockoff of a Jeff Koons–style balloon Bitcoin dog fucking—doggystyle, naturally—another dog representing the US dollar. We passed Panties for Bitcoin, a father-son undergarments business that was mostly an exercise in enthusiastic branding. Bars sold overpriced drinks matched by concession stands that sold overpriced stadium food. A mechanical bull, booth babes, endless giveaways, all of it filmed and tweeted and Instagrammed from every angle. In front of a small crowd, I did some push-ups for the Lord and received a "Jesus for Bitcoin" T-shirt.

If you ignored the formal hysterics and instead talked to regular folks milling about the conference, Bitcoin Miami sometimes felt like just another trade show. Big and energetic, full of boozy salesmen talking about how Bitcoin had changed their lives, with sponsorships adorning every surface, it was a Potemkin village of American consumerism and gambling addiction masquerading, in typically humble crypto fashion, as the future of the entire financial system. Eight-dollar Budweisers were offered for sale underneath the fifty-foot-tall Bitcoin volcano that burped out steam with all the grandeur of a high school science fair project. The volcano was meant to celebrate the issuance of El Salvador's Bitcoin Bonds and tee up President Nayib Bukele's keynote address. Sadly for the attendees, on the first day of the conference, Bukele canceled his trip to the United States to deal with the growing unrest in his country.

At the conference, the featured speaker was in the wind, but the featured volcano still spewed smoke and the bar remained well stocked. I ordered a Budweiser and asked if I could pay in Bitcoin. Unfortunately, their Bitcoin-into-real-money machine was down, but they accepted my American dollars that conference notables seemed eager to rip up in protest. Maybe TradFi still had its uses.

Outside the convention center, all eyes were drawn to an imposing sculpture of a swaggering creature known as the Bitcoin Bull, an homage to the Wall Street original. Fashioned from thick glossy plates of material that seemed like an unholy amalgam of metal and plastic, this creature was no joke. Replete with laser eyes and a fierce stare, the bull was slick: a gleaming, furious testament to capitalist America's macho brand of innovation. "In Miami we have big balls," said Francis Suarez, Miami's Bitcoin bro mayor, who has toyed with the idea of abolishing taxes and funding the city through a nearly worthless token known as MiamiCoin.

There was just one problem: Contra Suarez, the bull did not have big balls. Yes, the ferocious Bitcoin bull was apparently of the castrated variety. I gently asked a few folks posing for pictures beside him if they had ever heard of incels. The confused responses were reassuring.

The local faithful, while zealous, were peaceful. No one yelled at me at the Bitcoin Conference or denounced me as a nonbeliever. Some people overflowed with solicitous generosity—there was at least one strip club invitation that I believe wasn't a covert marketing stunt. The lack of open conflict was almost a letdown—and an indicator of my own latent narcissism, perhaps. Everyone was just excited to talk to some guy from TV that had cameras following him around.

I can't say that the conversations were always coherent or that my interlocutors and I existed on the same metaphysical plane, but I learned some things about what it meant to devote one's life to Bitcoin. After talking to folks such as Mear One—an artist and former Occupy Wall Street participant whose signature oil painting, apparently well known among crypto heads, envisioned a cabal of Jewish bankers against the ascendant righteous forces of Bitcoin—it was clear I needed to broaden my view of what constituted the "community."

There are many different ways one could define the crypto community, but the cynic in me would say there were none, not really. The majority of the people in Miami seemed only loosely tied to one another through commerce. They had few other bonds to speak of besides a utopian vision of financial freedom. To me, they were a projection of the timeless American fantasy: getting rich for free as quickly as possible. They flew to Miami to perform the rituals of multi-level marketing-style salesmanship and gladhanding. Also, there were parties.

o o o

On the second floor of the cavernous Miami Convention Center, tucked into a windowless room, was the Bitcoin conference's press area. It was a standard soulless box with rows of plastic benches and chairs, and with the requisite coffee stand, a caffeinated oasis humbly situated near the middle of the room. Around the edges, about a dozen or so interview stations had been set up to accommodate film crews, many of which were from the crypto industry itself, performing acts of self-mythology. We arrived late and were forced to scramble. We set up a makeshift interview station with two stools deliberately set uncomfortably close to one another. If we were gonna get some Bitcoin bigwigs on camera, I planned to make the conditions just right.

Much as with SXSW, we benefited from luck and, it turned out, from our slapdash sense of organization. In the hall outside the media room, I saw a gaggle of people walking our way, trailed by a cameraman. A reporter held a microphone out desperately trying to keep up with a little man in a red, white, and blue Bitcoin trucker hat whose legs were pumping almost as fast as his mouth. It was Brock Pierce, the former child actor of *Mighty Ducks* fame and cofounder of the stablecoin company Tether. From his home base in tax-friendly Puerto Rico, Brock maintained numerous crypto business interests and had become one of the industry's most colorful spokespeople. I hadn't expected to stumble upon him like that, but Brock—an insider with a sketchy past—was an ideal interview subject.

I lurked around the press room waiting for my opportunity as Brock gave interview after interview. Having become determined to query the guy, I was now worried that he would evade me, so I spent close to an hour tracking him around the room, hoping for an opportunity to insert myself. It was a bit ridiculous, but eventually Brock came up for air and I jumped into action. I introduced myself and reminded him we met briefly many years ago in Hollywood. Surprisingly, he agreed to an interview with little hesitation. And as easy as that, I was sitting down to talk shop with one of the strangest characters in a decidedly strange industry.

o o o

The goal of interviewing Brock was to talk about Tether, the company he cofounded in 2014. While Brock had no current involvement with the company, we had heard from a source that he had at one point tried to buy back into Tether's ownership group for the laughably low amount of $50,000. A source had also told us Brock dangled his political connections to the Trump White House in the hopes of getting back into the good graces of Tether executives like CFO Giancarlo Devasini. Brock had some Trump-world associations, having run a company, Internet Gaming Entertainment, with Steve Bannon, who succeeded Brock as CEO. That spring, people close to Bannon were now reportedly advising Brock on his Senate bid in Vermont. Some of these gambits were successful, others ended ignominiously. (The improbable run for Senate followed an unsuccessful 2020 presidential run in which he received a grand total of 49,764 votes.) But they added to the picture of who Brock was: He was a hustler and a survivor. He helped create Tether, and he operated within the same business networks.

Brock signed a release form and sat down across from me. I started the interview off gently, playing the role of a moonlighting actor passing through a buzzy world I found interesting. We talked about Mr. Pierce's previous companies, his relationship with Bannon, his abiding love of "innovation," and his supposed deep ties to major players in the crypto industry. Brock talked up his friendship with CZ, the CEO of Binance, with whom he had been spotted in El Salvador recently. Brock claimed to have helped CZ meet with Salvadoran President Nayib Bukele.

"I talk to more world leaders, probably, than our secretary of state," he said. "I'm talking to forty-plus governments."

These statements seemed absurd, the kinds of exaggerations told by a particularly imaginative friend in grade school, but I smiled and nodded. It would take a little forbearance to eventually steer the conversation toward Tether. "Why hasn't Tether been audited?" I asked.

His response was telling: He simultaneously claimed that they "probably" were working with a major accounting firm while bemoaning that they had tried and failed "hundreds" of times to get an audit. His reasoning was that no firm would touch them because of the lack of "regulatory clarity" around crypto, invoking a common industry complaint. For us crypto skeptics, this didn't even rise to the level of cliché. There was plenty of clarity. It was just that companies like Tether tended to operate offshore and outside the ambit of American law. Tether's executives, who never stepped foot in the United States, were reportedly being investigated by the Department of Justice for bank fraud.

Given their role as essentially crypto's unacknowledged central bank, with a few multimillion-dollar settlements already behind them, the company's behavior potentially violated all manner of security, banking, and financial laws and regulations. Some even argued that by minting a dollar-denominated digital token, Tether was engaged in counterfeiting. As Jacob liked to joke, one sign that Tether was a fraud was that the company had never sued anyone for calling it a fraud. (As Tether's leadership surely knows, the discovery process goes both ways.)

Brock didn't acknowledge the innumerable red flags, at least not directly. Instead, he used the example of Arthur Andersen, the accounting firm that fell apart after they took on Enron as a client. When Enron imploded, in part because they had been cooking the books, the accounting firm auditing those books—Arthur Andersen—cratered as well. See, said Brock. You have to be careful who you audit, or you could suffer as a result. The crypto sector was seen as too "high risk."

That finally set me off. "You are saying 'high risk,' [but] Enron was a fraud."

"Yeah, banks wouldn't take on crypto companies as clients for many, many years." Brock replied. "And why is that?"

"Because . . . they might be running frauds?"

"No."

"Oh."

What else could I say? We went around and around to little satisfaction, but it was interesting to watch him squirm. Like so many people I interviewed in Miami, Brock appeared to became uncomfortable when asked basic questions. Clearly most folks were only used to the softballs thrown at them by the fawning crypto industry press. Throw them off their script and they began fumbling their lines.

We moved on from Tether's history to the present day. We both marveled at the fact that crypto's explosion since late 2020 had gotten the attention of the big Wall Street firms. They may not have wanted to play in the crypto waters before, I pointed out, but now it's making so much money.

"Correct, which is why the J.P. Morgans and the Goldman Sachs and everybody works with this (crypto) now," he agreed. "It's become a big enough business."

"Interesting." I hazarded a comparison, "Sort of like the financial crisis, right? All the companies were taking on CDO and credit-default swaps. They saw a lot of money to be made, right?"

Brock shifted on the stool. "Clearly large markets attract large businesses."

There was an awkward pause. The interview appeared to be over. But as we got up from our stools, he kept talking, despite the fact that the cameras were still rolling. I saw my opportunity to ask him about his ties to politics, and specifically to politicians like recently elected New York City Mayor Eric Adams. Adams had reportedly flown on Brock's private jet to Puerto Rico in November 2021, where he engaged in a publicity tour to promote the Big Apple as a future crypto hub. He proudly announced that he would accept his first three paychecks as an elected official in the form of Bitcoin. It was a ridiculous exercise in showmanship, so of course Jacob and I had written an article in Slate about it. There was no proof he had actually done this, but it was a clever, if unseemly, marketing ploy. I asked Brock about his ties to Mayor Adams. He offered a rambling response about being "pro-innovation." I then asked him about what prompted his Senate bid in Vermont.

"Conversations I've had with our government at the highest levels. And they are very alarming, their lack of understanding."

"Of crypto?"

"Of innovation in general. I can't really share the conversations I've had ... National Security Council and things ..."

I may have involuntarily laughed at that point. Obviously Brock Pierce would not have attended an NSC meeting! The whole ruse was absurd, a flashback to my Hollywood days. Here was a bullshitter practicing a craft he'd honed for years. Then again, Pierce was connected to former Trump aide Steve Bannon, and the Trump administration wasn't exactly known for discretion or choosing the highest caliber of people. So who was to say? Could the source who told us Pierce dangled his relationship to the Trump White House to get back in business with the Tether guys actually be right? Had Brock Pierce, the former-child-actor-turned-crypto-insider, who was trailed by a disturbing list of easily googleable rumors and accusations, made inroads with the office of the Fraudster-in-Chief? It no longer seemed like such a stretch. It actually made perfect sense, albeit in an incredibly depressing way. The Golden Age of Fraud, indeed. My head hurt.

Stepping back, I felt a growing civic concern after I started to see too many similarities between the unregulated crypto markets and the subprime crisis of 2007/08 that had nearly brought down the entire economy. My hunch was that crypto, which was born out of the ashes of the Global Financial Crisis, was now, ironically, recreating the circumstances that had led to the previous crisis. Risk-tolerant crypto traders and exchanges owners were stacking leverage on leverage (or fake dollars on top of fake dollars) to extract returns—in real dollars—on their investments. Tethers were being printed by the billions and issued to a very small group of important players like crypto mogul Justin Sun, who issued a token called TRON, along with sophisticated trading firms like Cumberland and Alameda Research, the Bahamas-based outfit owned by Sam Bankman-Fried, known in the crypto world (and now beyond) as SBF.

Those players then gambled with the Tethers. The supposedly democratizing, decentralizing currency of the future had come full circle: a way to enrich the few at the expense of the many, in opaque games of chance the public couldn't hope to understand.

The problem with these financial games was that they were ultimately unsustainable, and when they collapsed, the impact crater could extend far beyond a few devoted crypto obsessives. My fear was that the primary difference between a potential collapse in the price of crypto and what we had seen in the subprime crisis is that a crash in crypto would fall even more heavily on average folks. If it all came apart, the casino doors would shut—much as they had on May 19, 2021, for Fawaz Ahmed, Francis Kim, and many other Binance customers—and retail would be the ones left holding the bag. At least in the years leading up to the GFC, some people got to live in houses. And even after the crash, the houses didn't disappear, even if they were foreclosed on. After a major crypto crash, regular people would be left with nothing. Vapor.

o o o

The physical and symbolic centerpiece of the conference—the Bitcoin volcano—was meant to represent the issuance of El Salvador's Bitcoin Bond. The idea was that the Bitcoin true believers would invest in bonds that would finance the mining of Bitcoin by harnessing geothermal energy from a volcano (Volcán de Conchagua) on the eastern edge of the country. A gleaming Bitcoin City would be built, along with another international airport to service the new metropolis. Nayib Bukele, the marketing-pro-turned-crypto-bro president of the small Central American country, had announced the bond scheme in November 2021 alongside slick digital renderings of what Bitcoin City might one day look like. There was a lot of gold. Bukele, a devotee of Twitter who had more than a little in common with Trump, seemed to share the former US president's Gaddafi-esque aesthetic.

Bukele clearly tried to time the volcano bond's issuance to coincide with the conference in Miami for maximum publicity value, but unfortunately, by the time the conference was actually held only a few months later, the domestic situation in El Salvador had deteriorated significantly. Gang violence was on the rise—a result of a breakdown in a secret agreement between the government and the major gangs—and Bukele declared martial law. The bond issuance seemed to be indefinitely postponed. Bukele bailed as the conference's headliner and recast himself as a field marshal leading a war against gangs.

Despite their political figurehead being suddenly absent, the conference attendees appeared to pay no mind. The other speakers—Thiel, Peterson, Kevin O'Leary of *Shark Tank* fame, NFL quarterback Aaron Rodgers, and tennis star Serena Williams, among others—filled the Bukele void and issued the requisite bits of crypto enthusiasm. O'Leary was particularly bullish, claiming that as soon as regulatory clarity arrived, crypto would explode again: "The spigots of capital are going to flood into this sector, like you've never seen. So for those of us that can invest in it now—you're getting ahead of what's going to be a huge wave of interest when policy occurs."

We saw many crypto bros unironically sporting the black El Salvador Bitcoin Bond T-shirts that had apparently been printed prior to Bukele's cancellation and distributed widely. Like the pre-printed shirts of the losing World Series team, they found their way to a willing host who was unconcerned with their accuracy. The Bitcoin bros didn't care—they hadn't been to El Salvador. It was free merch and it represented a cause that, at least in theory, they believed in.

For the people of El Salvador, the consequences of Bitcoin adoption were far more serious. At the conference, we connected with two exiled Salvadorans in Miami: Mario Gomez and Carmen Valeria Escobar. Mario, thirty-six, was a critic of Bukele's Bitcoin policy. He had been arrested on September 1, 2021, just days before the Bitcoin law was to take effect. While driving his mother to work, he came upon a police barricade that seemed to have been set up just for him. The police confirmed his identity and hauled him down to a local station, where they separated him from his mother and placed him in an interrogation room. When he asked why he was being detained, Mario was told it involved an investigation into financial fraud. He never saw any documentation that this was in fact the case and he was never charged with any crime. Nonetheless, the police took his phones and tried to take his laptop from his mother, who was waiting outside the station. Thankfully, Carmen, a young reporter and friend of Mario's who had been alerted to his arrest, interceded and prevented the police from confiscating it. Mario was eventually released, but a question remained: Why had he been arrested in the first place?

The day before, while watching a government presentation about the new Chivo Wallet system, Mario noticed something odd. There was a QR code on one of the slides in the deck, and when you scanned it, it took you to an address that had previously been used to scam people. In 2020, approximately 130 high-profile Twitter accounts had been compromised and used to promote a Bitcoin scam. The scammers only managed to make off with $121,000, but the case had briefly attracted global attention. To Mario, this was alarming. The government was using a scam wallet address in the promotional materials for the new Bitcoin monetary system they had developed in secrecy and were about to deploy. Maybe it was the work of a technical novice who googled "crypto wallet QR code" and used the first result that came up, or perhaps it was some scam by a contractor. Either way, it was a disaster, and Mario alerted his fellow Salvadorans via Twitter to the ridiculousness of the situation. The next day Mario was arrested.

Mario knew his stuff. A longtime technologist working on civic-minded projects, he had done stints with organizations like the United Nations World Food Programme. For him, the rush to implement the Bitcoin as legal tender wasn't an indication of a groundbreaking, innovative government policy, but rather smelled of old-fashioned corruption. While it was unclear exactly what Bukele and his cronies were up to, both Mario and Carmen speculated that it could be a way to facilitate money laundering associated with the drug trade while enriching a close circle of insiders. (Large amounts of South American cocaine flows north through El Salvador.)

Even if none of that were true, for Mario, Bitcoin was bad tech and bad economics. I asked him what he thought of Bitcoin advocates using El Salvador's adoption as an example of progress: "You cannot separate the people from the technology. What you are doing is . . . enabling a government to shut down anyone they don't like."

Mario was never charged with any crime, but he still feared for his safety. On the day the Bitcoin law went into effect, September 7, 2021, he fled the country, escaping first over land and then by plane to the United States, where he is now seeking asylum. He had to leave his sister, his mother, and his entire extended family behind. He told his sister that she should be prepared not to see him for a long time.

He said all this with a sense of civic principle, with grace under severe mental pressure, and with a remarkable amount of good humor. Mario had a joyful, almost childlike, high-pitched laugh. He was hard not to admire and harder not to like. On the conference floor we had watched as Salvadoran Bitcoin enthusiasts walked up to him and asked, with defiance, Why are you here? Some of the approaches were more than a bit threatening. He took it all in stride, sometimes engaging his antagonists in long, stem-winding conversations, punctuated by bursts of chest-shaking laughter. This, I thought, was the truth about Bitcoin and El Salvador: It had made Mario, a dignified, ethically engaged person worried about his people, into the world's first Bitcoin refugee.

Carmen was soon to follow. Her journalism had already angered the establishment enough that her mother was fired from a government job. She had recently secured a position with a foreign news agency, which potentially offered some protection, and began spending time in Mexico City. It might be past time to move permanently. The week we were together in Miami, one of Carmen's friends became the subject of a local social media campaign that tarred him as the brother of a gang member—a quick path to arrest under Bukele's militarized crackdown. Except Carmen's friend didn't have a brother. The truth didn't matter. The risk was too great. While we stood outside the press room in which Bitcoin moguls extolled El Salvador's burgeoning economic utopia, Carmen's friend called to tell her he was leaving for Mexico.

Bitcoin hadn't set Mario and Carmen free, and I doubted, no matter the surrounding conditions, that it could liberate any of the rest of us. Still, as much as I trusted their stories—and as much as I had been moved by their pathos in the face of all the profoundly stupid Bitcoin hucksterism surrounding us in Miami—I had to see it for myself.

It was time to go to El Salvador.

CHAPTER 7

THE WORLD'S COOLEST DICTATOR

"There is enough money for everyone when no one is stealing."

—Nayib Bukele's slogan during his successful campaign for mayor of Nuevo Cuscatlán

UNITED FLIGHT 1425 landed at El Salvador International Airport near midnight on Sunday, May 15, 2022. From the plane emerged two haggard, middle-aged fathers, underslept and overworked. After a cursory stop at immigration, Jacob and I left the sleek modern airport and met the warm embrace of the humid night and the welcoming smile of Napoleon, our airport driver. He was easy to spot. He held a placard with the alias I use when traveling, Don Drysdale, and wore a Batman T-shirt. Napoleon turned out to be a fan of *Gotham,* the Batman prequel TV show I starred in that centered on a young police lieutenant (and future commissioner) named Jim Gordon. I stumbled through some mangled Spanish thank yous: "Gracias por ver mi programa de televisión de *Batman*." After a few sentences of small talk, I settled into the backseat of Napoleon's Corolla. With the windows down and a brand-new country flashing by us, I was invigorated.

Half an hour later we arrived at the Sheraton Presidente San Salvador, the massive aging landmark hotel nestled in the city's foothills. Waiting for us was our fixer and translator, Nelson Rauda, a tremendous journalist. A thirty-year-old Salvadoran sporting a chinstrap beard, Nelson exhibited a nervous intensity that we would soon understand was his default setting. Sometimes he wore a mask as much for COVID protection as so he wouldn't be recognized as that young journalist-agitator who had argued with the president on TV. It was one AM on a Monday morning, but Nelson was there, ready to go. Did we want to eat something? Sure we did. We threw our bags in the rooms and Nelson drove us around what appeared to be one of the pricier neighborhoods in the city. Bright lights illuminated restaurants, car dealerships, and assorted branded franchises targeting the wealthiest of Salvadorans. The combination of the weather, the hills in the background, and the neon-flooded commerce reminded me of a more humid West Hollywood.

After several failed attempts at more interesting local options, we settled on the one place still open in the wee hours: Denny's. The actual location may have been Central America, but the spic and span all-American dining establishment with gleaming pickup trucks in the parking lot reminded this Texas boy of home. I ordered a burger sin queso, Jacob had a big platter of huevos divorciados. (His body would pay for it later.) The restaurant was strewn with signs depicting anthropomorphic entrees inviting us to pay in Bitcoin; we opted for dollars.

Over our meal, we queried Nelson on the state of play in his country, which was, to put it mildly, not good.

o o o

In 2019, a brash young politician named Nayib Bukele was elected president of El Salvador, shocking the political establishment. The small mountainous Central American country—population seven million and roughly the size of New Jersey—had previously been dominated by two political parties: ARENA on the right and FMLN on the left. Over time, they had become entrenched political forces defined by corruption as the nation's politics stagnated. Bukele rocketed to power by promising a different path. The son of a wealthy businessman of Palestinian descent, Nayib grew up surrounded by privilege, yet keenly aware of his outsider status as a Muslim in a deeply Christian nation.

In his school yearbook he jokingly dubbed himself the "class terrorist." Bukele proved unremarkable academically, although he took an interest in computer science. With a rebellious sense of humor and a dramatic flair, he found his true calling after he left school. After running several businesses, including nightclubs and a Yamaha dealership, Bukele was hired by the leftist FMLN party to manage their marketing campaigns.

It was here Bukele came into his own. Nayib intuitively understood the power of media, particularly social media, and displayed a knack for publicity, updating FMLN's antiquated PR offerings for the internet age and improving their fortunes at the polls. He eventually graduated to running for office himself, becoming the mayor of a city called Nuevo Cuscatlán, and later of San Salvador. At each stop, Bukele touted his stewardship of the government's good works, such as issuing scholarships and opening medical clinics. He was less focused on how to pay for them, leaving both Nuevo Cuscatlán and San Salvador saddled with debt after his departure.

In his campaign for president, Bukele formed his own party, Nuevas Ideas, and his bold style, as well as a wave of popular discontent with the old regime, swept him into office at the tender age of thirty-seven. Much as Donald Trump had done in America, Nayib Bukele bucked conventional political wisdom in El Salvador, marketing himself as both a man of the people and a successful businessman, despite inheriting much of his wealth.

Almost as soon as he was in office, the ambitious young president set about exercising power. On February 9, 2020, just eight months after assuming office, Bukele ordered armed soldiers into the halls of the Legislative Assembly in an attempt to intimidate lawmakers into passing his agenda. The president sought congressional approval for a $109 million loan to fortify the same security forces that were then occupying the building. The audacious stunt was successful. Bukele's Nuevas Ideas further consolidated power in the 2021 legislative elections. After winning a majority of seats, they formed an alliance with three other parties, thereby controlling some three-quarters of the body. The same day they took power, the Legislative Assembly voted to remove five justices of the Supreme Court as well as the attorney general.

Shortly thereafter, the newly reconstituted court creatively reinterpreted the Salvadoran constitution to allow the president to run for reelection, which had previously been illegal. The naked power grab was widely condemned by members of the opposition as well as the international community.

Bukele's most daring economic wager was yet to come. In June 2021, he announced that El Salvador would begin accepting Bitcoin as legal tender in September. It wasn't long to prepare. While the actual plan was closely held, the marketing pitch was simple and potentially compelling: If Bitcoin could be used as money—at least when it came to making cross border payments and encouraging tourism—it could be a game changer for the country.

El Salvador's economy depends on remittances. The money that the two to three million people of Salvadoran descent living in the United States send home to their families and loved ones accounts for one-quarter of El Salvador's GDP. The average Salvadoran makes about $400 a month, and 70 percent of the population lacks access to traditional banking, so most business is conducted in cash. (El Salvador "dollarized" in 2001, abandoning its local currency, the Colon, in favor of greenbacks.) Most Salvadorans rely on services such as Western Union or MoneyGram to accept remittances from relatives overseas, despite the sometimes high fees those services charge. On the face of it, Bukele's plan appeared promising: If he could convince Salvadorans to eschew traditional means and use a government program built on Bitcoin instead, it could be a win for his administration as well as the people. It would fill government coffers while lowering transaction costs for Salvadorans living at home and abroad, boosting economic growth.

The pitch when it came to tourism was equally simple. El Salvador is small and mountainous, making large-scale agricultural production difficult. The country's biggest export is cheap textiles, but that pales against remittances, which are, as mentioned above, a quarter of its annual GDP. With few natural resources, El Salvador's options are limited. It does have excellent surfing, offering some of the biggest swells in the Pacific Ocean. For so-called Bitcoin nomads, who own a lot of Bitcoin and don't want to be under the thumb of any government, Bukele offered up a vision of El Salvador as a crypto-Switzerland in the heart of Central America.

With the government's blessing, Salvadoran entrepreneurs, and their wealthy foreign allies, rebranded an area formerly known as El Zonte into "Bitcoin Beach." It would be a paradise for coiners, a place where they could spend their Bitcoin without tax obligations. Bukele's plan was bold—basically throwing up the middle finger to the rules governing international finance—but it held some potential. If Bitcoin and cryptocurrency were to work as actual money, rather than as a speculative investment, El Salvador seemed as good a place as any to try it out.

Could crypto work IRL? We had come to El Salvador to find out.

o o o

We woke at dawn and headed to Bitcoin Beach. We were joined by a film crew: Neil Brandvold, an American cameraman/DP who happened to live in the area; Victor Peña, a cameraman and still photographer; and Omnionn, a sound engineer who had produced some of this century's best Central American hip-hop albums. Nelson, Victor, and Omnionn were on loan from *El Faro* (The Lighthouse), a newspaper legendary in the region for its hard-nosed investigative reporting.

As we left the ritzy trappings of the Presidente Hotel, I was reminded of another similarity between San Salvador and Los Angeles: traffic. Aging cars and beaten down buses packed with commuters clogged the roads as Nelson fearlessly navigated his Nissan Rogue through the maze of morning rush hour. After a half hour, the traffic thinned out, as we cruised down country roads dotted with small stands selling fruit and pupusas (a puffy form of tortilla often filled with cheese or meat). Eventually we turned off the paved highway and onto a rocky dirt road leading down the hill to the beach.

Bitcoin Beach itself was extremely modest: a collection of small sandy hotels, shops, and restaurants overlooking the rocky black sand beach below. Known formerly as El Zonte, it's located in the town of Chiltiupán, population 13,000. On that overcast Monday morning, it was deserted. For several hours we searched for people to talk to about cryptocurrency. We messaged Mike Peterson, the San Diego–based surfer and concession stand owner who started the Bitcoin Beach project via what he claimed was an anonymous Bitcoin donation in 2019. In El Zonte, he had become a major entrepreneur, property owner, and community leader. He wasn't in town and tried to connect us with others who were perhaps suffering from journalist fatigue. (We were hardly the first reporters to roll through town that summer.)

To kill time, we grabbed breakfast at a local hotel. Jacob spotted a Bitcoin ATM and decided to purchase a little as an experiment, despite a worker warning him the machine sometimes ate your money while providing no Bitcoin. Paying a fee of about 10 percent, Jacob managed to buy thirty-two dollars' worth of Bitcoin and send it to a wallet on his burner phone. "No KYC/AML," Jacob said proudly, referring to Know Your Customer and Anti-Money Laundering processes, which are standard in mainstream finance and often ignored in crypto. His little pile of crypto, in other words, was basically anonymous, unconnected to his name.

As the marine layer burned off and gave way to the scorching sun, we met Dana Zawadzki, a sweet Canadian woman operating a juice stand a few blocks from the beach. We chatted about her somewhat convoluted journey to El Salvador and her work rescuing stray dogs in the area. Unlike many ideologically driven immigrants to the area, Zawadzki didn't care about crypto. If it helps drive business here, great, but so far the results were mixed. She accepted Bitcoin at the juice stand, and it usually worked, but for the most part people still paid cash. While Zawadzki was lovely, I hadn't traveled two thousand miles to talk about sterilizing stray dogs in the brutal heat of the ninety-degree day. As a Hail Mary, I asked her about Bukele and the mass arrests that had taken place inside the country since he had imposed martial law some six weeks prior.

"Oh," Zawadzki said. "Do you want to talk to Mario Garcia? He was arrested and I helped get him out."

o o o

Like seemingly everything when it comes to cryptocurrency, the launch of President Bukele's Bitcoin initiative did not go according to plan. On September 7, 2021, Bitcoin was officially introduced in El Salvador to much propagandistic fanfare and some discontent, including social protests. That day, the global crypto markets crashed as Bitcoin's price tumbled 15 percent in a few hours, with a number of exchanges unexpectedly shutting down. It may have been connected to El Salvador's own botched Bitcoin adoption, but it could easily have been typical volatility in a marketplace notorious for it.

In El Salvador, numerous reports of fraud and identity theft accompanied the rollout of the government's Chivo Wallet system, which promised each citizen thirty dollars' worth of Bitcoin. One local coiner told us that his friend used a photo of a dog to verify his identity. Even Nelson, our fixer, had his identity stolen—and his thirty dollars' worth of Bitcoin.

In the months that followed, even as technical improvements arrived, Salvadoran Bitcoin adoption remained minimal. Most people still preferred to use US dollars. Nor had Bitcoin proved useful for sending money between the two countries; less than 2 percent of remittances sent to El Salvador ended up using the Chivo Wallet system. At the end of the day, the Bitcoin rollout in El Salvador suffered from some of the same problems that plague cryptocurrency adoption more generally: It just didn't work very well, it was centralized rather than decentralized, and it was prone to fraud. The Bitcoin project itself was run by a tangled mess of government and private interests, some of them foreign. Average Salvadorans, already living near the margins with little room for error in their own financial lives, refused to gamble alongside their president.

Unfortunately for his people, the young leader refused to accept defeat, instead doubling down on his Bitcoin wager. Bukele changed his Twitter handle to "world's coolest dictator," and his profile picture sported laser eyes favored by Bitcoin maximalists, or maxis, who believed that Bitcoin was the one true cryptocurrency and the rest imposters, mere shitcoins. Bukele bragged that he bought Bitcoin, using the state treasury, on his phone while sitting on the toilet. Bukele never posted the wallet address he used, but if his claims of purchasing several thousand Bitcoin were real, he'd lost tens of millions of the people's money on those transactions alone. In addition, the Chivo Wallet system cost the government a reported $4.7 million of taxpayer funds. Perhaps most dangerous of all was Bukele's truculent defiance toward the international financial system, which had crippled his country's bond ratings. By early 2022, there was open speculation as to whether El Salvador would eventually default on its sovereign debt.

The farcical crypto rollout was hardly Bukele's only problem. Since his election, gang violence, a decades-long problem, had fallen sharply. The number of homicides fell precipitously, and the new president was quick to take credit, even going so far as to refer to himself as "The Batman" for his ability to root out crime. But just seven weeks before our arrival, a horrific spree of gang violence forced Bukele to cancel his appearance at the BTC Conference in Miami. Eighty-seven people were murdered over the course of a weekend in late March, an astonishing number for the small country. (The equivalent figure for the United States would be over 4,000 Americans killed in a weekend). More than sixty people were killed on March 26 alone, marking the single deadliest day since the civil war ended in 1992. In response, Bukele instituted martial law, vowing to round up the estimated 70,000 gang members inside the country.

Mario Garcia was one of those supposed gang members. He sure as hell didn't look the part to me: forty-six-years-old, pot-bellied, and not much more than five feet tall. To provide for his family, Garcia worked as a minutas, or shaved ice, seller in El Zonte. Garcia was used to pushing a cart through the sunshine, lugging around supplies, selling sweet ice treats to locals and tourists, including coiners, some of whom were buying up property in the area. He was almost a Bitcoin Beach mascot; Mario had appeared in YouTube interviews, been tweeted about by influencers, and featured in *Diario El Salvador*, a government-owned newspaper. *Bitcoin Magazine*, which has offered extensive, enthusiastic coverage of El Salvador's use of Bitcoin as legal tender, highlighted a sign on Garcia's cart that read, "aceptamos Bitcoin," calling the minutas seller and his wife "Bitcoin pioneers."

But on April 11 in El Zonte, the police, acting on a tip, pulled Garcia over. They stripped him down and checked his decades-old tattoos for gang symbols (a faded one on his left hand reads, in English, "FUCK YOU!"), and he was arrested and hauled off to jail. After two days in police custody, he was taken to Mariona, the country's largest prison. There he was beaten and shoved into a large cell packed with eighty other men. The inmates were routinely harassed, malnourished, and denied medical care. When one inmate violated protocol by daring to rest his arm outside the bars of the cell, prison guards threw tear gas into it, suffocating the men inside. Over the course of his imprisonment, Mario witnessed five men die. With no access to a lawyer or formal charges filed, Garcia was told he might be imprisoned there for years, even decades.

Under the state of emergency introduced by Bukele and his Nuevas Ideas party, civil liberties in El Salvador were suspended in the name of fighting rampant gang violence. People regularly disappeared in arbitrary arrests, and families heard nothing. Prisons once open to visitors and journalists became closed shops. Police were given triple-digit daily arrest quotas. In the first ten weeks, an estimated 36,000 people were arrested, and according to the human rights organization Cristosal, at least sixty-three people had died in detention as of July 20, 2022, when the Bukele regime extended the state of emergency for a fourth time. Bukele said that the error rate for innocent people arrested was no more than 1 percent.

Zawadzki knew Garcia, describing him and his family as "very near and dear to my heart." She worked with Garcia's wife, Dominga, to start an online campaign in which they called for the local Bitcoin faithful, some of whom were well-known online influencers with lines of communication to the Bukele administration, to oppose Garcia's detention and to donate money to his family. Eventually the campaign attracted attention on Bitcoin Twitter. Weeks later, Garcia was mysteriously freed. He was lucky to get out.

As I sat and talked to Garcia, he appeared dazed from his experience. He wore a sleeve on his right arm to cover his tattoos, lest he be arrested again, and stoically recounted his trauma, occasionally gesturing to his ribs and the various undiagnosed internal injuries he suffered during the weeks he was in prison. Despite his suffering, he said he was grateful. Grateful to Dana and his wife for helping him get out, grateful to God for watching over him, and grateful to his president for listening to his family's pleas.

After the interview, we trudged up the hill to Garcia's house. It was meant to be a grand home, but it had been stopped mid-construction and later abandoned by the bank. Garcia and his family squatted on the property, making good use of the modest half-built structure, which lacked running water or electricity or even any doors. Behind the house was the empty shell of a swimming pool, unfinished and overgrown with algae. The family got its water from a creek that ran through a nearby ravine. We found Garcia's wife laying on a hammock, a small child nestled in her arms. She had been ill and her face shined with sweat. He smiled warmly at her, and she at him, clearly still basking in the glow of their recent reunification. It was a simple moment, but it nearly broke my heart.

o o o

The next morning we drove more than a hundred miles to La Unión. A sleepy farming town of some 35,000 people, La Unión is tucked between Volcán de Conchagua and the bay separating it from Honduras. Locals farm corn and beans, and there are plentiful opportunities for fishing. La Unión is also the site of Bukele's most ambitious plan of all: Bitcoin City.

The government's disastrous rollout of the Chivo Wallet system left them with few good options, but Bukele, ever the gambler, refused to concede defeat. In November 2021, Bukele announced what he called Volcano Bonds. Half the money raised would be used to purchase Bitcoin, the other half would finance the construction of Bitcoin City, a tax-free paradise for coiners in eastern El Salvador. The showpiece city would be built in the shadows of Conchagua Volcano, and the Bitcoin would be mined by harnessing geothermal energy extracted from the mountain. Bukele promised to build another international airport to service the town, apparently so coiners wouldn't be burdened by the few hours' drive from the current one in San Salvador.

It didn't make much sense, economically, environmentally, or politically. El Salvador is the largest net *importer* of electricity in Central America, meaning it didn't produce enough electricity to meet its domestic needs. The reason it had not previously utilized geothermal energy from Conchagua was simple economics: To do so is prohibitively expensive. The terms of the bond were worse than just buying Bitcoin directly. There was no incentive to buy in—unless you were a Bukele ally looking to lend support. By the time we visited in May 2022, the issuance of the bond had been delayed, seemingly indefinitely. Despite the ill-conceived scheme, there were still consequences for the local population.

Wilfredo Claros, 42, lived with his wife, two children, and other family members on a small plot off an unpaved road in a verdant area called Condadillo, in the mountains around La Unión. Chickens, dogs, and one frequently annoyed turkey roamed the property. Over the course of a decade, Claros built his cinder block house by hand. He fed his family by farming, fishing, and plucking the mangos that grew in abundance in his yard. The community had access to fresh water from a well and cistern system, which an earlier generation of family members built under the shade of parota trees, a broad-canopied member of the pea family that yields a rich, caramel-colored wood. Claros credited its cool water with keeping his family healthy during the COVID-19 pandemic.

But each time Claros visited the well, he was reminded that his modest but idyllic life may soon come to an end. The parota trees were now marked with a stripe of orange paint: the government's marker designating the trees for removal. Like dozens of his friends, relatives, and neighbors, Claros's land was set to be cleared to build the new airport to serve Bitcoin City. They would be forcibly removed from their homes with compensation of only a few thousand dollars, far less than their land and homes were worth. It was unclear how many people would be affected. The Salvadoran government hadn't done a census in at least fifteen years.

Despite the tense environment, Wilfredo welcomed us to his home with open arms. I immediately noticed what I would come to understand as his signature expression: a broad, easy smile revealing several gold-capped upper teeth. As we fumbled to communicate, first through my poor Spanish and then by way of Nelson translating, he was patient and wry with his replies. Here was a famous Hollywood actor who wanted to film and interview him, to tell his story, yet no one in his own country could tell him when he would be kicked off his land or where he might go.

Wilfredo had the same attitude when it came to Bitcoin itself: How could he use it when he had no information on how it actually worked? He said his sister, who lived in the United States, had warned him against using Chivo Wallet or any of the other crypto platforms. You will lose all your money, she said. Wilfredo and I agreed it was smart to listen to the women in our lives.

Wilfredo was sharp. Although the airport was supposed to bring economic growth and jobs to La Unión and his community, for him it was a cruel joke. No doubt the government would use guys like him as labor to build the airport. And then what? With no formal education, he might be lucky to get a job mopping the floors, picking up the trash of the Bitcoin tourists. Wilfredo would rather fish, farm, eat mangos, and live in peace. He was proud that for forty-two years he had provided for himself, needing nothing from the government. Why did they need to take his land?

Wilfredo also worried for his seventy-year-old mother. She was traumatized by the threat of losing her home. I listened as he spoke clearly, simply, and convincingly. Sitting in peace under his mango tree, it was hard to understand why any of this needed to happen.

o o o

That night our small crew gathered in a nearly deserted tourist hotel outside La Unión. Nelson, Victor, and Omnionn were on edge. *El Faro* was set to publish a bombshell report documenting confidential negotiations between the gangs and government. Leaked audio recordings revealed Carlos Marroquín—a top official in Bukele's government—admitting to having forged a secret deal with MS-13, one of the country's powerful gangs, to tamp down violence after Bukele's election. In the recordings, Marroquín admitted he coordinated the clandestine release from prison of a top-level gang member and escorted him to Guatemala to show his "loyalty and trustworthiness" to the gang.

The historic peace between the gangs that the new president had boasted of so proudly? It was predicated on a lie.

In the leaked audio, the gangs expressed their displeasure to Marroquín about a breakdown in relations with the government. For his part, the minister said he had passed the message to "the Batman"—Nayib Bukele. As the story went live, Salvadoran social media exploded. Everyone was talking about it and Nelson, Victor, and Omnionn were ecstatic, but also worried. Those asking hard questions of the government had targets on their backs. Journalists' phones had been hacked using the Israeli spy software Pegasus. Government officials visited the workplace of Omnionn's wife and inquired about him, a clear act of intimidation. They all knew people who had been followed or arrested, their family members fired from their jobs, or threatened at home. Not knowing what might happen, Nelson had brought along his passport just in case he needed to flee across the border to Honduras.

o o o

The next morning, in the predawn black, Neil and I picked up Wilfredo and drove to where he kept his boat. A massive fork of lightning arced across the sky, an early storm that gave way to sun and calm waters. We piled into Wilfredo's modest power boat and set off to catch lunch. As we did, a brilliant orange-red sun rose above the volcano, Conchagua. It felt like something out of a Ray Bradbury novel—a massive fiery foreign planet looming above the feeble rock we call Earth.

We settled in a quiet spot and Wilfredo taught me how to throw out the massive twine net he used. He taught me to stomp on the bottom of the boat with large PVC poles to scare up the fish. We waited. The fisherman dispensed some advice. He spoke of the Bible, of chance, luck, and life. He talked about paying attention to what nature was saying. He shrugged. "Fishing is a little knowledge and a lot of luck," he said. "But you never say that you are good."

Wilfredo confessed he had lost a child years earlier. The boy wandered onto the road and was struck by a car, killing him instantly. Although he knew many people who had made the perilous journey north to the United States, including one of his other sons, Wilfredo himself had no interest. Many people leave, he said, and they say they will return to their families or send money back, but often they don't. They are gone forever. For Wilfredo, to leave his family was unimaginable. He just wanted to be left alone, to fish in peace.

CHAPTER 8

RATS IN A SACK

Dark Helmet: How many assholes do we have on this ship, anyway?

Entire Bridge Crew: Yo!

Dark Helmet: I knew it, I'm surrounded by assholes!

—*Spaceballs*

IRONICALLY, WHILE JACOB and I were in El Salvador finding out if crypto could work in the real world (no), the online marketplace for it cratered. And fittingly enough, all it took was three thirty-something bros gambling wildly for fissures to emerge.

If there was ever going to be a single domino—a Bear Sterns or Lehman Brothers moment—to knock over the rest of crypto, I always assumed it would be Tether. The company's dubious behavior had been well chronicled by journalists and regulators. It oozed suspicion, with its overseas headquarters, murky ownership structure, peculiar banking relationships, and refusal to provide a long-promised audit. Tether acted like the quasi-central bank of crypto, the maker of the poker chips used in every casino, the lender of last resort, and several other roles that probably shouldn't be commingled in a many-layered, offshore firm. But at least on the surface, Tether would play almost no role in the crypto nosedive of the spring of 2022.

In April, the crypto economy market cap stood at about $2 trillion. It was basically an imaginary number—there's no way all of that crypto could ever be cashed out for two trillion real US dollars—but it still signaled something about the state of the industry. Token prices had declined steeply in the first few months of the year, down from a peak overall market cap of more than $3 trillion the previous November. The slide continued throughout April. But venture investments were still coming in—major venture capital firms like a16z and Paradigm were on their way toward raising multibillion-dollar crypto investment funds to supplement the previous year's multibillion-dollar crypto investment funds. These firms, which profited by buying tokens at a friends-and-family discount that could later be sold at higher prices to retail investors, weren't yet feeling the effects of the crypto slide. They had enough capital in reserve to keep the machine going.

And then, in the first week of May, everything blew up.

Do Kwon was a shit-talking thirty-year-old South Korean crypto entrepreneur who, after graduating from Stanford in 2015, founded and sold a wireless networking startup before getting involved in crypto projects, sometimes pseudonymously. Eventually he launched a company called Terraform Labs, which managed a dollar-pegged stablecoin called TerraUSD (UST) and another token called Luna (LUNA). The two were bound together via an arbitrage system designed to keep Terra, a so-called algorithmic stablecoin, at one dollar. This was accomplished via a trading mechanism, allowing Terra holders to exchange one UST token for one LUNA token at any time. The LUNA token was then "burned," or destroyed, helping to drive up the value of the remaining LUNA by decreasing its supply.

It's all a bit complicated, so think of it this way: Luna is the counterweight to Terra, a way of balancing supply and demand for the supposed stablecoin. When Terra trades at a price that's higher than its 1:1 peg, that should mean that demand for the stablecoin is higher than supply, so the supply of Terra ought to be increased to match demand. The protocol incentivizes users to create (or "mint") new Terra and destroy (or "burn") Luna. With more Terra created, its price drops. With fewer Luna, its price goes up. Users continue this arbitrage process until Terra trades at its target peg price.

Or so went the plan. There was also a "staking pool" called Anchor, which was also created by Do Kwon and his company, Terraform Labs. (They always call them "labs," don't they?) Investors were encouraged to buy Terra coins, which they could then "lock," or deposit, onto Anchor in exchange for an improbably high yield of 20 percent. Terra became a popular stablecoin, with exchanges like Binance marketing it as a safe investment. FTX also listed it. Some South Koreans put their retirement savings into it.

In early 2022, Do began to attract attention for both his flippant comments and, more important, for his plan to buy up billions of dollars' worth of Bitcoin as a financial backstop to his crypto empire. Major investors and day traders flocked to him, supporting his projects financially, sharing his roguish media appearances, touting his tokens as the future of stablecoin economics, and generally hanging on his every word. He developed a cultish following of fans who proudly called themselves Lunatics. Mike Novogratz, a billionaire Goldman Sachs alumnus who ran a New York City–based digital asset firm called Galaxy Investment Partners, got a Luna tattoo inked on his shoulder. Do Kwon even named his daughter Luna. "My dearest creation named after my greatest invention," he tweeted.

Sure, there was the occasional bit of criticism. The economics of Terra, Luna, and Anchor were clearly Ponzi-like, involving the circular flow of money common to such schemes. Where was the 20 percent return on Anchor coming from? There were multiple red flags of a Ponzi scheme: an impossibly high rate of return marketed as low risk, a complex strategy to achieve said returns, and unregulated products sold in an unregulated marketplace. That the whole thing smelled like a Ponzi was no secret, but rather a fact discussed by some big industry names on Twitter, podcasts, and in other media.

Do Kwon had a variety of other projects, including something called The Mirror Protocol. The Mirror Protocol was essentially a replica (a "mirror") of licensed, regulated stock exchanges on which real companies trade real stocks. But on Mirror, people weren't trading real stocks in a regulated market. They were trading synthetic copies of real stocks on a market overseen by, well, Do Kwon. The SEC subpoenaed Do at a conference in New York, with Do publicly refusing to comply, responding to the government's principal securities regulator with a defiant lawsuit. Can you imagine the gall it takes to set up a fake copy of the New York Stock Exchange, one that, given its shaky underpinnings and nonexistent oversight, might attract who knows what kind of shady players? And then to refuse to even account for it?

There are a few possible signs of trouble with almost any stablecoin. One is if it depegs, that is, if its value goes below one dollar. The lower it goes—a few cents is considered significant—and the longer it stays there, the worse the situation may be. Another obvious sign of trouble is if users seem to be moving their funds out of a particular stablecoin and into other tokens, especially competing stablecoins. By the first week of May, Terra was exhibiting both.

On May 8, UST slumped to $0.985 as the markets showed signs of big holders fleeing Terra. On Twitter, Do Kwon joked about the risk, even as his company was taking extraordinary measures, loaning out billions in crypto to trading firms to allow them to prop up his tokens. "So, is this $UST depeg in the room with us right now? No?" he asked. "I prescribe 24 hours of pegging over the next 7 days."

The next day, the bottom fell out from the once-stable Terra. UST plummeted to thirty-five cents. In the midst of the collapse, Do tweeted a statement that would enter crypto infamy: "Deploying more capital - steady lads."

It didn't work; confidence in the scheme evaporated. Over the next week, UST remained massively off its peg while its associated token, LUNA, became nearly worthless. Positions were liquidated across crypto markets, as large UST and LUNA holders found their tokens plummeting in value. On May 12, the Terra blockchain was halted—essentially put on ice—as exchanges began to delist the organization's tokens, removing them from the proverbial trading floor. In every important sense, TerraLuna was dead. On May 16, the Luna Foundation Guard, the organization that helped backstop UST with billions of dollars' worth of Bitcoin, claimed that it had spent more than 79,000 Bitcoin to buy Terra in a fruitless attempt to pump up the price. The coming weeks would reveal huge losses—hundreds of millions for some of Do Kwon's investors and financial partners, which ranged from venture capitalists to important crypto hedge funds.

These big players weren't the only losers. Many ordinary retail investors, especially in South Korea, where Do Kwon was based before moving to Singapore, bought into his vision of easy riches. Tragic stories emerged of retirees who lost everything by staking their wealth in a system they were assured was low risk. A Korean family of three was found dead in their car at the bottom of a lake. The father left a note mentioning "Luna coin," "sleeping pills," and "ways to make an extreme choice." Destroyed financially due to TerraLuna's implosion, he had apparently killed himself, his wife, and their ten-year-old daughter.

An estimated $40 billion or more of value was wiped out, leading not only to a loss of personal wealth but a cascade of liquidations and loan defaults as a thicket of interlocking financial products, many of them flowing through unregulated DeFi protocols, began to unravel. As the first domino fell, we began to see that crypto was, quelle surprise, far less decentralized than advertised. It revolved around a handful of interconnected players, who all seemed to owe one another money, real and fake. They also owed investors and customers, who wanted their money back. But few had liquid assets on hand to pay up. It was time to keep watching for dominoes.

Many things about the Do Kwon saga angered me. But what I couldn't believe, even by the rock-bottom standards of crypto, was that weeks after Do's TerraLuna empire blew up, he tried to do it all again, barely pausing to catch his breath, or to take accountability. And he had much of the industry's support.

On May 28, Do Kwon launched what some called TerraLuna 2.0. There was no algorithmic stablecoin this time, but there was a new coin with the ticker LUNA, though, confusingly, it was called Terra. Its decimated predecessors were renamed Terra Classic (LUNC) and TerraClassicUSD (USTC) and remained widely tradeable. Almost a year later, one LUNC was worth about one thousandth of a cent, but the token's overall market cap was still in the top fifty of all crypto tokens. That signaled two things: Crypto was dominated by what were essentially penny stocks, and even in a disaster like TerraLuna, a lot of people hadn't given up hope. They were holding on.

The financial products known as TerraLuna 2.0 were from the same crypto huckster who had managed to wipe out $40 billion in investor value weeks earlier. Many major exchanges listed the new coin. Its value dropped 80 percent on the first day. The project, it was immediately clear, was a failure that would never do anything to make the last round's victims whole. Like practically all crypto, it had no utility beyond irrational speculation—a dead prospect at this point. And yet, many crypto fans cheered on Do Kwon or even believed that LUNC could make a comeback.

In the midst of all this, Terraform Labs' entire legal team quit at once. The company's Korean employees were forbidden by authorities from leaving the country, as South Korean law enforcement launched a number of investigations into different crypto exchanges and tokens, including, of course, TerraLuna. Do Kwon managed to abscond to Singapore and holed up in semi-seclusion there, citing death threats and needing to spend time with his family. Later he appeared to be in Serbia. His tweets became less frequent, but he expressed little real contrition or introspection regarding the damage he had wrought. His revamped coins, far diminished in price and any speculative possibility compared to their predecessors, continued to trade on most major exchanges. Do had the industry's support.

But there wasn't much time to focus on Do because other dominoes began to fall. Based in Singapore, Three Arrows Capital (3AC) had started as a small hedge fund run by former boarding school classmates Kyle Davies and Su Zhu, both thirty-five years old. As the crypto markets mushroomed in size during the 2020–21 bull run, so did 3AC's portfolio. The fund swelled to a purported $18 billion in net asset value before collapsing in a matter of weeks, having sunk an embarrassing amount of money into the TerraLuna "ecosystem." According to a source quoted in *New York* magazine, their stake in Luna, once valued at half a billion dollars, collapsed to just $604.

If 3AC had been cordoned off from the rest of the crypto market, the damage might have been contained. But the firm had borrowed enormous sums from multiple major players in the industry. Genesis Global Trading, a crypto prime brokerage and lending behemoth, was owed the most: $2.3 billion. Voyager Digital, another crypto lender, said 3AC owed it more than $650 million when it filed for bankruptcy in July. Blockchain.com, a crypto exchange, was due $270 million. The contagion had spread.

What did the 3AC guys do with the money they were loaned other than gamble with it? It was crypto, so of course they bought a yacht. (This one was worth $50 million and called *Much Wow*.) Their prudent investments also included a promising piece of NFT art called *CryptoDickbutt #1462*. 3AC was deeply overleveraged, bankruptcy filings revealed. Davies and Zhu, who once worked for Credit Suisse, had spent lavishly and bet poorly, embracing huge risks, refusing to hedge, loaning out the same tokens to multiple parties, and other practices that might provoke a call of "What the hell are you doing?!" if there were any adults in the room. The 3AC bros, who were once rabble-rousers on Twitter gloating about their empire, tweeted meekly that they'd like to work all this out and then went radio silent. Reportedly on their way to Dubai, they disappeared. Even their lawyers couldn't find them. Macabre rumors began to circulate about some grisly end, a result of having built 3AC on a pile of dirty capital. But as is often the case with crypto, no one could discern the actual truth.

TerraLuna and 3AC may have been an ocean away, but they brought the growing crypto collapse home. Genesis and Voyager were both based in New York, but they were not alone in their exposure to the collapse. Celsius, a leading crypto lender headquartered in New Jersey, paused customer withdrawals on June 12, citing "extreme market conditions." To anyone paying attention, the signs of trouble at Celsius had been long apparent. Our colleague Dirty Bubble Media had chronicled the company's strange movements of tokens, CEO Alex Mashinsky's apparent effort to pump the token price and cash out for tens of millions, and dubious investment and lending practices. I recalled my interview with Alex at SXSW just two months prior and his cavalier attitude toward risk and speculation in crypto. Only 10–15 percent of the money in crypto was real, he had said. And as Celsius was about to show, even getting that pittance of real money out can prove to be impossible for the average Joe, especially when the bank shuts its doors.

You didn't have to dive into Celsius's financials or interview its carnival-barker CEO to get a whiff of bullshit. Celsius's core offering—an 18 percent yield on staked coins—was ridiculous, far higher than any traditional bank interest rate, and could be achieved only through Ponzinomics. What's more was that the company's terms of service, which apparently few people read, essentially gave Celsius custody and control over one's deposits. Once you handed your crypto over to Celsius, it was no longer yours. If Celsius fell into bankruptcy, there was a good chance you'd never get your tokens back.

For a month, Celsius twisted in the wind, as reporting emerged that, like 3AC, it was deeply overleveraged and made risky bets with its customers' tokens. Possible rescue packages were floated—offers from crypto companies and traditional banks to salvage what was left of a firm that, as recently as a few months earlier, managed more than $20 billion in crypto assets. Mashinsky, who once held boisterous weekly confabs with customers on Twitter Spaces, and who exhibited the chronic arrogance endemic to crypto CEOs, also went dark. In the financial press, stories appeared claiming that Celsius—a professed nonbank that allowed people to "unbank" themselves with unregulated, uninsured bank-like services—was seeking the help of Citigroup. The irony was delicious.

In the meantime, other crypto companies began to wobble. A crypto exchange called CoinFlex went bankrupt over a claimed $84 million debt owed by a single customer named Roger Ver, who liked to call himself Bitcoin Jesus. An early crypto investor who was once imprisoned for selling illegal firecrackers online, Ver renounced his US citizenship in favor of the tax-free island nation of Saint Kitts and Nevis. "You don't need even to file a tax return at the end of the year," he told an interviewer. "That just feels like paradise." Ver later obtained citizenship in Antigua and Barbuda, where he invested in a bank and was named Barbuda's nonresident envoy to Japan.

After devouring tech talent the previous year, big exchanges like Crypto. com (usurpers of the naming rights to Staples Center) and the Winklevoss twins' Gemini conducted multiple rounds of layoffs, sometimes without any public announcement, in just a few months. Coinbase rescinded job offers it had already handed out, leading to some bad press. Crypto lenders that, following Celsius's model, offered improbably high yields and gamified rewards, abruptly paused withdrawals. It appeared likely that few of them would ever open again. Bankruptcies proliferated, as did emergency capital infusions and loan packages from FTX and Sam Bankman-Fried, who had ended up in the business of picking survivors for the oncoming crypto winter. One of them was BlockFi, another crypto lender that offered huge, and unsustainable, interest rates on customer deposits. SBF gave BlockFi an emergency loan of $250 million on June 21—only to buy the company a month later in an odd deal that valued BlockFi as low as $15 million. A year earlier, BlockFi had attempted to raise funds at a company valuation of $5 billion. As it would turn out, both numbers were too high.

How much real money was left? How much had gone into this bubble?

The curtain was being slowly peeled back through a steady diet of leaks, bankruptcy filings, and the first wave of lawsuits. Important revelations were emerging, some of which confirmed earlier criticisms from skeptics. First, these companies were willing to embrace enormous risk, employing massive amounts of leverage, taking on huge loans, and sometimes loaning out the same crypto more than once. Companies handed over millions or even billions of dollars in crypto to commercial partners they barely knew, sometimes without even a written agreement. And throughout, there were lies—about solvency, about risk management, about not mixing customer funds with a company's prop trading desk. I was beginning to understand just how far some fraudsters would go, and how few incentives they had to tell the truth. Never apologize, never explain—that might as well have been the mantra of crypto kingpins standing over the ashes of their creations. And some would follow that perverse logic all the way to prison.

On July 18, court documents from Singapore leaked in the media, revealing cooperation from 3AC's legal team with creditors who were unlikely to be made whole. As for the once high-flying owners of 3AC, they had gone completely underground, the rumors around their, well, permanent disappearance only intensifying. Five days earlier, on July 13, Celsius ran out of options and filed for bankruptcy. Alex Mashinsky, who had seemed on top of the world when I had spoken to him earlier at SXSW, was revealed as a deceitful showman who led his company right into bankruptcy through a number of stupefying actions, not least of which was the housing bubble–style faith that crypto prices would always go up. When it filed for Chapter 11, Celsius reported $5.5 billion in liabilities and $4.3 billion in mostly illiquid assets. Technically, it had been insolvent—meaning it owed more than it had—since 2019. But Mashinsky and his cronies kept the plates spinning, until eventually they couldn't.

With Celsius's failure, the real victims were everyday retail investors who had trusted Mashinsky's overwrought promises about revolutionizing finance. Celsius had claimed to have 1.7 million customers, but even though the real number turned out to be closer to 300,000, the company's failure inflicted enormous financial pain, often borne by those least able to afford it. In statements to the bankruptcy court, hundreds of Celsius customers related stories about promises broken, lost fortunes, despair at not being able to pay bills, guilt at letting down family members, and being on the brink of homelessness. These people had trusted Celsius. Maybe they had a glint of greed in their eyes and chose to overlook warning signs, but in their defense, Mashinsky and Co. were presenting themselves as an alternative to those evil greedy banks that paid customers little interest and kept the profits for themselves. With Celsius's collapse, the depth of that lie was now laid bare. Celsius customers were victims of a fraudulent company run by con men, and now they would have to suffer without recompense.

I hadn't forgotten about Tether. It was implicated in all this as an investor in Celsius and other companies, and as a key business partner of many more. The entire crypto economy depended on Tether's stablecoin—it was by far the most traded token each day. But its murky operations, uncertain financial backing, and bloviating executives—to say nothing of those executives, like CEO Jean-Louis van der Velde, who were almost never heard from—didn't seem like the makings of an organization that could weather a major industry downturn. At some point, I believed, the bill would come due for Tether, and it would be one it couldn't afford to pay.

But while Tether was processing billions of dollars in redemptions for major customers, the company remained quietly tenacious. Through some clever paper-shuffling and a quirk in bankruptcy law, Tether managed to claw back $840 million in collateral from a loan it made to now-bankrupt Celsius right before Celsius went bust. The move was unusual, but it seemed perfectly legal. "We're in an area where the law is quite uncertain and quite at odds with the market's general expectations," one lawyer told the *Financial Times*. Ah yes, the market's general expectations. Its vibes, if you will.

While the peculiarities of bankruptcy law as applied to crypto needed some refining, the industry's major players were already turning on one another. Tether's $840 million move proved that. In my own conversations with industry executives, I began to hear more badmouthing of peers who, in public, were held out as friends or respected colleagues. On Twitter, the sense was no longer WAGMI and more cutthroat, with open sniping among formerly peaceful crypto titans and strong disagreements about the future of the industry. It turned out that the "community" of participants in a zero-sum, strictly competitive game actually all hated each other. Everyone was punching wildly, with SBF criticizing Binance and CZ suing a magazine publisher for a cover line that read "Changpeng Zhao's Ponzi Scheme." That was along with accusations of market manipulation, fears of government intervention, and more rumors than even a gossip-hound like me could handle. And all the while, scams, rug-pulls, hacks, and Potemkin crypto projects proliferated, adding billions more to the toll that comes with being part of the web3 community. As our skeptic colleague Frances Coppola observed, the crypto bros began fighting "like rats in a sack." The circle jerk had become a circular firing squad.

Perhaps the most disturbing part of the crypto crash of the spring of 2022, which wiped out more than $2 trillion in notional value and wrecked the nest eggs of everyday traders all over the world, was the utter lack of humility shown by the industry's leading figures. Materially, most of them were fine: Their predictions might have been ludicrous, and perhaps they lost oodles of money—but it was usually someone else's money, and they had made enough insider profits along the way to simply hop over to the next project, should the current one fail. Many had also bought in early to Bitcoin, which still held some value, even if it was 60 percent or more below its peak. The system was designed to insulate the people operating it from any consequences for the huge risks they took. Sure they might express some sympathy for retail traders who lost everything, but it usually seemed like an empty gesture. After a hack struck thousands of wallets on the Solana network, Sandeep Nailwal, the cofounder of Polygon, a competing blockchain, tweeted, "My heart goes out to #Solana community members who lost their life savings in the ongoing attack. Stay strong, these are the growing pains the entire blockchain industry has to go through. These moments, if handled correctly, lead to a lot of strength for any ecosystem. 🤙"

It was an emotionally tone-deaf thing to say—sorry about losing your life savings, but these are necessary growing pains!—and it was all too typical. In fact, it was far more sympathetic than some of the comments I heard, which included hyper-libertarian bluster that anyone who fell for a scam or lost money, especially on a crypto besides Bitcoin, probably deserved it. DYOR. Not your keys, not your coins. Keep your tokens off an exchange and on a secure hardware wallet. (Hell, maybe bury it in concrete in your basement, like John Wick.) The hard-nosed rationalizations, and the complicated procedures around securing one's crypto against calamity, were endless.

As spring and summer 2022 rolled along, many crypto industry members excused the accumulating losses, citing a few bad actors, the aforementioned growing pains, or a sense that these were just bumps in the road. In March 2022, when Axie Infinity—an exploitative, pyramid-scheme-style game that, after players buy in, pays them crypto tokens to keep playing— was hacked for more than $600 million in crypto, industry figures, and Axie itself, shrugged it off, touting vague notions of community and resilience and emerging stronger. Less than a week later, Axie received an emergency infusion of hundreds of millions of dollars from a16z and Binance, two of the industry's most powerful players. The story was different for people who couldn't withdraw their funds for weeks, who lost everything, or who were mired in an exploitative economic relationship that strung them along for meager crypto rewards. For these people, their losses couldn't be shrugged off. They weren't a prelude to future riches. They are the whole event: These gamblers lost.

As trillions of dollars of wealth evaporated—if it was ever really there to begin with—we started to hear the occasional smidge of public criticism, a slowly dawning realization that perhaps the scammers and Ponzi artists should not have been allowed to run wild. A few crypto CEOs resigned, mostly citing other priorities or new opportunities. Yet there seemed to be no honest reckoning. If crypto's true believers wanted to promote positive use cases for their products, then perhaps they would have already dealt with the industry's many unscrupulous operators, rather than allowing them to proliferate. It wasn't like the scammers weren't known, although many operated under pseudonyms and recycled identities. The crypto world is in fact quite small, and most industry players know one another. Instead of calling them out, the crypto "community" had done almost nothing. In many cases it had been far worse: The fraudsters like Do Kwon were held up as innovators, pillars of the industry designed to grant self-sovereignty and liberate the masses from the shackles of TradFi. Constantly preaching ideas of community, democratic empowerment, and individual liberty, crypto's leaders and influencers had instead created an anarchic set of markets that invariably funneled money from information-poor retail investors to well-connected insiders and whales. The outright scammers—the NFT con men and rug-pulling DAOs—were there to take advantage of an already fragile situation, cleaning up what the exchange CEOs and VCs and insiders hadn't added to their own coffers. The truth is that most of the scammers and con men were tolerated—or even encouraged—by the wider crypto industry because there was no economic incentive to do otherwise.

o o o

If all this is giving you flashbacks to the subprime crisis, your instincts are correct. While I had been shouting to the Twitter rafters trying to warn people of the impending financial disaster I sensed looming, seasoned academics were articulating a more nuanced version of the same. Hilary Allen, professor of law at American University, wrote a paper in February 2022, just three months before the crash, referring to cryptocurrency and its assorted DeFi products as effectively a new form of shadow banking.

Broadly speaking, shadow banking refers to a company offering banking services while avoiding banking regulations. For example, during the subprime crisis, money market funds (MMFs) offered customers higher rates of return than they could get in licensed banks. To do so, however, they needed to take on more risk. MMFs began investing in a form of corporate debt called *commercial paper*. When investment bank Lehman Brothers fell in September 2008, there was a run on what's called the Reserve Primary Fund, a large $60 billion MMF. The fund held only 1.2 percent of its portfolio in Lehman commercial paper, but given the uncertainty in the markets at the time, even this relatively modest allocation caused investors to panic. As the equivalent of a bank run ensued, the government was forced to step in to make sure money market funds didn't go belly up. While MMFs didn't cause the subprime crisis, the shadow banking services they provided exacerbated an already fraught situation.

Collateralized debt obligations (CDOs), sale-and-repurchase agreements (repos), and asset-backed commercial paper (ABCP) were also part of the pre-2008 shadow banking system—and the attendant crisis. For our purposes, how these intricately structured financial instruments worked is not important. The crucial takeaway is merely that they are intensely complicated, and complexity itself is a risk to financial stability. Slightly adjusting for the layman what Professor Allen describes so well in her paper, there are three broad similarities between the systemic weaknesses revealed in the subprime crisis and the current construction of the crypto markets: leverage, rigidity, and complexity. They make the system very fragile, so that if a bank run occurs, it can trigger a crash.

Leverage + Rigidity + Complexity + Bank Run = Crash

Leverage is pretty simple: You borrow money to buy something. The more you borrow in relation to your actual money (equity), the more the upside, but there's also the downside. If what you are investing in (or gambling on) goes up in value, you can make a lot of money. If it goes down, you can lose a lot, and eventually the people you borrowed from will ask for their money back. If you don't have it handy, you may have to sell stuff, which pushes prices down on what you are selling. If other people also borrowed money to buy similar assets, now that their price is dropping, they too might have to sell. Fairly easily these things can get out of hand.

For this reason, leverage is restricted in regulated banks. However, bank leverage has a way of building up over time, sneaking into our regulated system through side doors and back channels in capitalism's insatiable hunger for profit. We know this happened during subprime, but as Professor Allen points out, the leverage in crypto, especially DeFi, is far higher. "The amount of leverage in the system can also be increased by simply multiplying the number of assets available to borrow against," she writes. "That is a significant concern with DeFi, where financial assets in the form of tokens can be created out of thin air by anyone with computer programming knowledge, then used as collateral for loans that can then be used to acquire yet more assets."

The people behind crypto coins can create endless amounts of fake money. Crucially, the exchanges themselves can also do so, in the case of coins like FTT (FTX) and BNB (Binance). If folks can use that fake money to borrow real money, that's a problem, as the leverage is potentially unlimited. Recall wash trading, discussed in chapter 3, whereby a coin's price can be manipulated by buying and selling coins back and forth among accounts controlled by a single party. Via wash trading and other means, the prices of the fake money can be bid up far beyond the actual money (or liquidity) backing them. With a rise in price, the inflated fake money can then draw in even more real money. Of course at some point it all comes crashing down when people want their real money back. And because in crypto there is no actual underlying asset beneath all that leverage—at least with subprime if you squint hard enough there were houses involved—there was also no floor to how low the price of crypto could drop. It could, in fact, go to zero. An asset whose value derives solely from greater fools is only priced as high as the last idiot willing to buy it.

Rigidity comes into play when leverage is being unwound. When parties use leverage, it's all fun and games when the numbers are going up, but if they go down people have to sell stuff. The more stuff that has to be sold and the more entities involved, the bigger the potential problem. Crashes happen in regulated markets, but at least there is some flexibility built into the system—whether it be negotiations between the parties, court cases, or even government bailout—that can mitigate the damage. At the end of the day, licensed banks in the United States are backstopped by a trusted third party, the US government. Cryptos are famously trustless, so no such third party exists. Not only that, but rigidity lies at the very foundation of crypto itself in the form of so-called smart contracts. Remember the first rule of thumb in crypto: Everything is the opposite of what it claims to be. It will shock you to discover smart contracts are, for many purposes, pretty dumb.

Smart contracts are basically small computer programs designed to execute their functions immediately, without the interference of a financial intermediary, a regulator, a court, or the parties themselves. The irreversibility of the blockchain—it's an immutable ledger that can only be added to, never subtracted from—and the smart contracts built around it means DeFi is far more rigid than TradFi. Most actions, once performed, cannot be undone. When an interconnected system falls apart, this is not a good thing.

Complexity leads to fragility. The more complicated the financial mousetrap you build, the more likely it is to fail. This doesn't necessarily mean we shouldn't build complex things, including financial instruments. They may serve a productive purpose, such as mitigating risk among multiple parties. But it does mean we need to account for their positive and negative attributes alike, as well as potential unintended consequences.

By now you recognize the complexity embedded in crypto. Much of crypto may be technobabble salesmanship, but the cryptography involved is real. Blockchain, consensus algorithms, smart contracts, and cryptographic signatures are all real human creations whose value we can debate. As individual components, they may all have positive attributes, but combining them together in a more or less unregulated marketplace has become self-evidently problematic. Unless, of course, you were just trying to use that complexity as a smokescreen to commit fraud.

With leverage, rigidity, and complexity galore, all crypto needed to set itself on fire was a match—a bank run. As you'll recall, a bank run can occur in a regulated marketplace, but the existence of a trusted third party back-stopping said banks is a mitigating factor. Since the FDIC was created in the 1930s, not a penny of FDIC-insured money in licensed US banks has been lost. But again, the lack of a trusted third party *is the entire idea of crypto*, so when the proverbial shit hits the proverbial fan there is no off switch to make the fan stop spinning. As my toddler might say, poopie go everywhere. The causes of the 2022 crypto bank run—or bank runs, if we're being more accurate—are still highly contested, but they may not matter. The system was so fragile, and based on such faulty economics, that mass liquidations and bank runs and all manner of contagion were practically expected. When the leaders of some crypto projects were unmasked as con men, the crypto economy tumbled faster toward its inevitable collapse.

Macroeconomically, the writing was always on the wall. When the easy money went away, crypto was bound to crash. Remember my initial thesis: When a bubble pops, the most speculative things fall fastest. Since crypto was entirely speculative, the investment equivalent of gambling, it was bound to go poof when the Fed started raising interest rates. That said, even I was surprised by the speed at which events played out. Over the course of 2021, inflation began to rise in the United States in response to easy money policies, supply chain disruptions, and changes to the labor market, among other factors. In 2020 it was a modest 1.2 percent, in 2021 it had grown to 4.7 percent, and in 2022 it would balloon to 8.2 percent by year's end. On March 17, 2022, seeking to counteract inflation, the Fed raised interest rates by a quarter point (or 25 basis points if you want to sound fancy). On May 5, they raised half a point and the carnage began. On May 8, crypto had a nominal market cap of $1.8 trillion. By June 18, it was $800 billion. A trillion dollars evaporated in less than six weeks. The joke was the lie that it had ever been there in the first place.

The crypto industry was wobbling like a drunk after last call. It was nearing its moment of subprime catastrophe. Of all the ironies crypto presented, this was surely near the top. Cryptocurrency, which was supposedly created as a solution to the myriad failures of our regulated financial system laid bare during the subprime crisis, had effectively reproduced and even amplified the same dynamics, leading to a similar implosion. Thankfully for the broader public, it had all happened on a smaller scale and the real banks were not involved (despite the crypto industry's efforts to the contrary). But once again, it was regular people who were left holding the bag.

o o o

The more we talked to victims, traders, lawmakers, Senate staffers, regulators, technologists, and finance scholars, the more I was stunned at the industry's recklessness and government's utter inability (or refusal?) to deal with it. Much of it was right there in the rapidly accumulating court record.

The adults weren't in charge. They weren't even in the building. I was sensitive to the fact that regulators might have been facing unknown political pressures, but it seemed that the Democratic Party was falling down on the job, too. Ostensibly the party of consumer protection and looking out for the little guy, many leading Democratic politicians were taking huge donations from the crypto industry—most notably, from Sam Bankman-Fried—and spending far too much time with industry lobbyists. (We saw the photos on Twitter before you deleted them, guys.) The revolving door between crypto and elected officials was ever present, attracting members of both parties to advocate on its behalf. Former lawmakers Senator Blanche Lincoln (D-AR), Senator Mark Pryor (D-AR), and Representative Sean Duffy (R-WI) joined the swelling ranks of crypto lobbyists in 2021.

We began to hear from politicians at the local level who talked about conflicts of interest among their colleagues, e.g., those who pitched pro-crypto bills while their spouses did crypto-connected work. The *New York Times* published a wide-ranging story showing that legislatures across the country were passing industry-written bills essentially as is—the same kind of regulatory capture that has plagued US politics for decades. In Florida, the state

House unanimously passed a crypto bill crafted with help from the industry. After a grand total of 75 seconds of deliberation, the Florida Senate rubber stamped it, sending the bill on to Governor Ron DeSantis for his signature. He obliged a month later.

It was not surprising, but it was disappointing and should have been antithetical to the kind of decentralized and democratized power structure that crypto claimed to stand for. But crypto, in practice, was nearly always the opposite of what it claimed to be, so of course it ended up becoming a tool for political influence. And because crypto was foremost a way to get rich, crypto investors celebrated the billionaires, like SBF, who were showering politicians with donations in order to legitimize crypto and shape its regulatory future.

As summer went on, it seemed like all roads went through Sam Bankman-Fried. Crypto's boyish king—who happened to be Tether's biggest customer—was making major interventions to determine who might weather the downturn. Notably, he considered buying Celsius, which filed for bankruptcy in July, before walking away from a potential bid days later. (Despite this, he continued to dangle the possibility that fall.) Such a move seemed prudent: Ties between SBF's business empire and Celsius ran deep. Dirty Bubble Media found that Celsius had allegedly used FTX to buy forty million of its own CEL tokens, then later used the exchange to liquidate millions of dollars of customers' assets. Celsius's bankruptcy proceedings also revealed Alameda Research as one of its biggest creditors, owing Sam's firm $12.8 million. Another firm that Bankman-Fried had ties to, the Pharos USD Fund, was owed $81.1 million. The previous fall, Bitfinex'ed told us the crypto industry was vanishingly small, controlled by only a handful of players. At the time it seemed far-fetched, but the more bankruptcy filings forced the opaque sector into the light, the more he was proven right.

Bankman-Fried was in the media constantly, appearing at conferences, doing CNBC hits, tweeting threads about lessons learned from the ongoing crisis, and generally trying to present himself as a steady hand at the tiller. Meanwhile, FTX was expanding, gobbling up shares of companies like Robinhood and moving into stock trading and derivatives markets. Perhaps most important, FTX was considered the leading force pushing for the underfunded Commodity Futures Trading Commission to assume greater regulatory authority over crypto, rather than the better-heeled, enforcement-ready Securities and Exchange Commission. There were other political battles at play—over derivatives regulation, over stablecoins and banking—and SBF seemed to have his hand in all of them. Not that he always won every hand he played: He poured $12 million into a congressional candidate's failed run in Oregon, only to have that candidate lose in the primary, receiving just 18.4 percent of the vote. He also gave a huge line of credit to Voyager Digital, which promptly filed for bankruptcy. It didn't matter: FTX ended up winning an auction for all of Voyager's assets a few months later for a reported $51 million. A few stumbles aside, for the moment, SBF was still perceived as the crypto wunderkind, and he had the public influence and the dollars to back it up.

He was being hailed as the "J. P. Morgan of crypto," originally by none other than Anthony Scaramucci, aka the Mooch. (Sam's venture capital arm FTX Ventures bought a 30 percent stake in Scaramucci's investment firm SkyBridge Capital in September.) Media outlets such as *Fortune* and Bloomberg soon picked up on the comparison, a reference to the prudent, visionary financier both revolutionizing an industry and shepherding it through its hardest time. In 1907, when bank runs roiled the US finance industry, Morgan, the top dog of his era, convened a group of powerful financiers and convinced them to lend emergency funds to quell the panic.

Crypto critics and good governance advocates worried about Bankman-Fried's growing political influence. One note of reassurance seemed to be that SBF, like some of his peers, said and did what he wanted, without much PR coaching. He seemed more honest about his intentions than the typical CEO whose public utterances were always laundered down to something bland and innocuous. In a way, his semi-plainspokenness (always served with a dollop of technobabble) seemed disarming, but it occasionally bit him in the ass.

In an April interview on the *Odd Lots* podcast, Bloomberg's Matt Levine questioned SBF about the seemingly circular flows of fake money in crypto. In response, SBF described DeFi staking pools as magic boxes out of which money was created. Bloomberg's hosts said that sounded, at best, like a Ponzi scheme. Sam agreed.

Sam started DMing Jacob on Twitter, trying to convince him—for reasons we could not quite figure out—that Tether wasn't a scam.

"Always happy to chat about stuff :)," SBF wrote to Jacob in June, offering "a bunch of cached info." "Could be helpful for pointing you to places that will in the end vindicate what you say/help you avoid things that won't age as well."

"Help you avoid things that won't age as well." It wasn't the first time a powerful person had tried to shape our reporting, but few were higher on the food chain than SBF. As in all relationships like this, the important thing was to not succumb to that influence, however it might be exerted. As a newly minted journalist, I had begun to realize that competing agendas were all around me, that sometimes we had to mingle with some unsavory people in order to find the truth while still keeping our ethics intact. (Also, it helped to hash it out periodically with Jacob over a beer.)

At the same time, I realized something: If these crypto bros were really as cocky as they appeared to be, maybe stirring some shit up on Crypto Twitter would yield results. To use a poker analogy, why not splash the pot a bit, piss some people off? On May 14, I fired off a tweet egging them on: "Anyone in the crypto industry wants to come at me, feel free. Fwiw, I have spent 20 years in showbiz, I can take a punch. Just a couple words of advice: don't miss."

It was puerile, but it was crypto, so of course it worked like a charm. I got all sorts of hate from dudes with laser eyes in their profiles. I did not anticipate SBF himself would respond.

"BUT WHAT IF IT GOES UP IN PRICE LATER??? DID YOU THINK ABOUT THAT?!?!!!?!? (but seriously—I totally agree that crypto needs more oversight and some cleaning up! I also think it presents huge opportunities for payments, underbanked, equitable access, and market structure.)"

I had, in fact, considered the possibility of "number go up." It was central to my understanding of what crypto was all about: gambling. I had been following Sam on Twitter, and he started following me back. I DMed him. It was the start of a periodic conversation that would continue for months.

As for Tether, our white whale, SBF should have had a great deal of firsthand experience with them. "It's not perfect—not close—but way less bad than the public thinks," SBF wrote Jacob on June 20, 2022, referring to Tether. "I think it's very likely to actually be more or less backed, historical lack of transparency notwithstanding (and would certainly bet as much!)." How true: SBF had bet billions of dollars on Tether, helping make it the industry's leading stablecoin as his own trading empire blossomed. If anyone knew what was going on there, Sam did.

It was time to speak to SBF. Jacob formally requested an interview. We both assumed it would never happen. Sam was no fool; he knew we were writing a book about crypto and fraud. It was in our Twitter bios! No way he would agree to be interviewed by a guy who wasn't buying what the bros were selling. What was the upside for him?

Sam agreed, almost immediately, and with no preconditions.

Fuck it, I said to Jacob. What do we have to lose? Ask if he'll do it on camera.

Sam agreed.

I was dumbfounded, but exhilarated. Whatever Sam's motivations, I was gonna get my shot with him. And I had a lot of questions for crypto's supposed J. P. Morgan.

CHAPTER 9

THE EMPEROR IS
BUTT-ASS NAKED

"In a closed society where everybody's guilty, the only crime is getting caught. In a world of thieves, the only final sin is stupidity." —Hunter S. Thompson

I DON'T SPEND MUCH time around billionaires. I've met a few in passing at fancy showbiz events over the years, but I never talked to any of them for more than a minute. Billionaires are always very busy and must be spared the burden of talking to non-billionaires whenever possible. I certainly never interviewed one on camera before. Most of my journalism experience had been on the other side of things, the subject of entertainment industry puffery.

Afraid of fucking up what might be my only chance at a sit-down with the public face of crypto, I needed a cram session on all things Sam Bankman-Fried. If the industry was the functional equivalent of an unregulated, unlicensed casino, as I strongly suspected it to be, it was highly improbable that the guy running one of the biggest casinos was completely on the up and up. But suspicions are not facts, and I was on the hunt for clues to fraud.

Thankfully, there was no shortage of information to be gleaned due to the fawning press coverage Sam had received. He had graced the cover of *Forbes* and would soon do the same at *Fortune*, with the latter subtly wondering if he was "THE NEXT WARREN BUFFETT?" The *Wall Street Journal* said he was gonna spend a billion to bail out crypto, Bloomberg and others breathlessly reported on his (undefined) plans to give away his enormous fortune. Sam floated the idea of spending a billion on the 2024 election cycle, "north of $100 million." He was everywhere: on TV, in print, and seemingly online 24-7. I dug in.

Sam Bankman-Fried was the child of Stanford law professors—an intellectual pedigree that later added to his nerd-king mystique. Growing up, he and his younger brother, Gabe, were engrossed with the card game Magic: The Gathering, as well as video games like *League of Legends* and *StarCraft*. Sam, who has ADD, was infamous for playing multiple games at once. He said he quickly grew bored with a single opponent; he needed more of a challenge. Ironically, Sam's public ranking in *League of Legends* was rather middling, an indication that the future CEO might have overestimated his own prowess.

Sam excelled when it came to quantitative reasoning, and graduated from the Massachusetts Institute of Technology in 2014 with a major in physics and a minor in math. While at MIT, Sam had a life-changing encounter with Will MacAskill, a proponent of a philosophical craze sweeping through Silicon Valley called *effective altruism* (EA). Conceptually, EA is straightforward: If you want to do the most good for the most people, you should strive to make the most money possible in order to give it all away. Philosophically, EA is predicated on utilitarianism, the doctrine that actions are right if they provide the most usefulness (utility) and benefit to the majority. In the abstract, utilitarianism sounds appealing: Who wouldn't want to do the most good for the most people? In practice, however, it runs into some immediate problems. How do you know what action will accomplish the most good for the most people? How are you supposed to constantly calculate what is the most-good thing at every moment, as the future is unknowable? Utilitarianism, whose roots stretch as far back as Jeremy Bentham in the eighteenth and early nineteenth centuries, has always struggled to answer these basic questions satisfactorily.

That said, if utilitarianism were to ever be practicable in real life, Sam's mathematical mind was as good a fit as any. He was born into it, steeped in his parents' own belief in utilitarianism. Effective altruism immediately resonated with him. Sam later claimed he had found his mission in life: Make a bunch of money and then give it away. Or as MacAskill put it: "Earn to give."

In order to advance Sam's EA aspirations, MacAskill offered him a piece of advice: Apply for an internship at Jane Street Capital. The prestigious Wall Street trading firm is known for hiring the most brilliant grads from elite universities. Sam got the internship, excelled in it, and was offered a full-time position following graduation.

At Jane Street, Sam could apply his considerable quant skills to figuring out ways to arbitrage minor differences in price to produce massive profits. He was tasked with providing market-making services trading global exchange-traded funds (ETFs). The specifics of that field are not important for us here, just the obvious: At Jane Street, Sam Bankman-Fried was still playing games. These games involved real money, and Sam was very good at making money. But playing the same game over and over again made Sam bored. He wanted to do something else, so he took time off and decided to look around. What he found was a new opportunity to make money via arbitrage, only this one involved crypto.

In the mid 2010s, the crypto market was much smaller and even more dysfunctional than its current manifestation (yes, this is possible). At the time, there was what was called the *kimchi premium*: The price of Bitcoin in South Korea was higher than in the United States and other Asian markets, sometimes by a difference of as much as 50 percent. There were various reasons for this, including capital controls and anti–money laundering laws set up by the South Korean government that limited the ability of its citizens to turn their local currency, the won, into US dollars. Sam quickly realized there was a lot of money to be made exploiting the difference—buy Bitcoin in the United States, sell it in South Korea, pocket the difference. He started his own trading firm, Alameda Research, to take advantage of it. Sam recruited a few close friends from MIT, including roommate Gary Wang, whom he had known since meeting him in high school math camp, and Jane Street colleagues like Caroline Ellison, with whom he had become close. They began operating out of a small space in Berkeley, not far from where Sam grew up. Eventually the kimchi premium dried up, but there were still massive inefficiencies to be exploited in the nascent crypto market.

In 2019, Sam moved Alameda Research to Hong Kong in search of a more favorable regulatory environment. Hong Kong benefited from being close to mainland China, where cryptocurrency had exploded in popularity, due in no small part to the desire of wealthy Chinese to avoid state capital controls. In Hong Kong, everyone seemed to be getting into crypto. Sam decided to gamble bigger. Why not start an exchange? In 2019, FTX was born. Six months after its launch, Changpeng Zhao, the CEO of Binance, reportedly purchased 20 percent of FTX for $100 million.

In late 2020 and early 2021, as the market for cryptocurrencies exploded, FTX emerged as an industry leader. But it needed more money to keep growing, so it tapped Sequoia Capital, a Silicon Valley venture capital firm, for more funds. Reportedly, Sequoia was blown away by Sam's grand vision of FTX during a Zoom call with him, only to discover afterward that he had been playing the video game *League of Legends* while on the call. While normies like us might think that to be a bright red flag, that is not the mindset of VC firms in Silicon Valley seeking enormous returns. This guy was that brilliant *and* playing a video game at the same time? Quick, give him as much money as you can! The Series B round of funding raised $1 billion. It was soon followed by a "meme round," so called because it raised another $420.69 million from sixty-nine investors (get it?), including the Ontario Teachers' Pension Plan.

Flush with cash, Sam moved FTX and Alameda to the Bahamas. Nassau provided a nice setup, free of the public health restrictions imposed in Hong Kong in response to the COVID-19 pandemic, and much closer to the United States, including the crypto hub of Miami. It was also closer to Washington, D.C., where the face of the crypto industry had been spending a lot of time lately. Sam and his inner circle lived in a superluxe development called Albany, which calls the likes of musician Cardi B and NBA star Steph Curry residents. But Sam kept his personal trappings modest, sporting an FTX T-shirt and shorts at all times, driving a Corolla and napping on a bean bag chair at work while sleeping as little as four hours a night. Despite living in one the swankiest developments in the Caribbean—Sam and a bunch of his buddies occupied a penthouse worth $39 million—the wunderkind of crypto professed no material needs. He was going to give it all away, you see.

○ ○ ○

The more I looked at SBF, the more red flags I saw.

The first was potential conflicts of interest. Sam owned an exchange and a trading firm that operated on that exchange. Imagine if J.P. Morgan owned an unregulated version of the Nasdaq. What was stopping him from manipulating the value of assets on his exchange via Alameda and pocketing the proceeds?

The second was his company's deep ties to Tether. In November 2021, Protos, a crypto media company renowned for its skepticism, revealed that Alameda Research was one of the largest (perhaps even the largest) customers of Tether. The notoriously shady stablecoin company had printed $36.7 billion for Alameda. We're supposed to believe Alameda gave over $36 billion to buy thirty-six billion Tether? Where would Alameda have gotten $36 billion from? According to public reporting, they had raised a few billion from VC firms and others, but nothing like what Protos found. If Alameda didn't give Tether the full amount up front, how did the arrangement work?

The ties between Tether and FTX/Alameda went even deeper. Daniel Friedberg was the former general counsel of FTX, and now its chief regulatory officer. He once worked alongside Stuart Hoegner, the general counsel of Tether, at Excapsa. Recall that Excapsa was the holding company of Ultimate Bet, the online poker site that had a secret "god mode" where insiders could see other players' cards. So FTX/Alameda's top lawyer worked with Tether's top lawyer at the parent company of the card cheating website. Huh.

Another bright red flag was how small the circle of trust appeared to be at FTX. Remember that when running a con, controlling access to information is crucial. The inner circle of the FTX/Alameda team lived in the same penthouse together and had personal ties to Sam. Nishad Singh, Director of Engineering at FTX, was a high school friend of Sam's brother. Gary Wang, FTX's cofounder, had known Bankman-Fried since math camp in high school.

Caroline Ellison, the CEO of Alameda Research, worked with him at Jane Street. Caroline and Sam occasionally dated. All nine of the roommates were thirty years old or less.

Another troubling aspect of Sam's operations was the size of his political donations. Sam was Biden's second-largest donor in 2020. He'd given $40 million to the Dems. His partner at FTX, Ryan Salame, gave $23 million to the Republicans. They were playing both sides, cozying up to Democratic and Republican politicians alike. Sam posed for a picture with CFTC Commissioner Caroline Pham and was a regular at CFTC offices. For an effective altruist, Sam sure liked to spend money and time forming relationships with people in power. And while he talked a big game of giving money to pandemic preparedness and animal welfare, it was awfully difficult to find hard numbers as to what he had actually spent on nonpolitical causes versus political donations.

There were many more red flags when it came to FTX/Alameda, but the final one worth mentioning is their location: the Bahamas. In just five short years, Sam had moved his operations from the United States to Hong Kong and then to a Caribbean island nation not exactly known for its stringent financial regulations. In 2020, the Bahamas passed the Digital Assets and Registered Exchanges Act (DARE), which set off a gold rush of crypto companies seeking a more favorable business environment. Like Binance, or Crypto.com or many other crypto exchanges, FTX had been playing the game of moving to where the rules of the game were most lax. Why was this important to their business model? If they were world-class and on the up and up, why not practice their craft stateside? It was impossible to answer that question at the time, but a simple observation offered a clue. One of the most difficult parts of running a crypto exchange is finding a banking partner. An industry that often ran afoul of know-your-customer and anti–money laundering laws meant most banks simply wouldn't touch crypto for fear of being fined or shut down. But banks in the Caribbean were often more willing to engage. And whether coincidentally or not, Tether's bank happened to be nearby. Deltec Bank, the one run by the cocreator of the *Inspector Gadget* cartoon series Jean Chalopin, was based in Nassau. Chalopin boasted of assisting the Bahamian government in drafting the DARE Act.

o o o

The night before the interview I could barely sleep. Somehow I managed to pass out for a few hours, woke at dawn, helped get the kids to school, and headed into Manhattan. Arriving at 1 Hotel Central Park, a luxury, earthy hotel where Sam was staying (think very expensive hand-carved wood furniture and mossy wall coverings that probably required regular watering), I was ready to set up a conference room to my neurotically precise specifications. But Sam was already there, doing an interview with *Fortune* that would lead to the "NEXT WARREN BUFFETT?" cover a month later, in the very room I had rented to use in an hour and a half. Through the glass, I saw him. The famously shabby CEO of FTX appeared exactly as advertised: dressed in a company T-shirt, shorts, and battered New Balances, and sporting a mop of messy black hair. Sam was turned toward the reporter in question, so he couldn't see me. I watched him, studying the body language of a man who was supposedly among the hundred wealthiest people in the world. He appeared nervous, but then again he always did, and I would be too if I was going to be on the cover of *Fortune*. In fact, I was exceedingly nervous at that very moment. After a minute or so of this nonsense, I realized it was getting a bit stalker-ish. I went back to studying my list of questions.

A young woman in her twenties approached, kind and petite. Natalie described herself to me as Sam's assistant, PR rep, and bodyguard. "Oh my God this is so exciting!" she said. "I'm a huge fan of *The O.C.*!" Maybe this was going to be easier than I thought. Sam's interview concluded, and he briefly passed me on the way out to his next one (remember, billionaires keep tight schedules). "I'm very curious about your project," he muttered, and was whisked away.

My team arrived: Jacob plus two top-notch cameramen—Neil Brandvold, up from El Salvador, and our mutual friend Ben Solomon, who was kind enough to help us out for the day. Ben has a Pulitzer and an Emmy Award (he would never tell you that, so I will), so he was a bit overqualified to shoot two dorks in a room pontificating about magic money. Still, I was glad he was there, as we quickly realized the room I had rented was too small to fit much more than the five of us in addition to the two cameras. But that also gave me an idea.

An hour later, Sam reappeared with Natalie in tow. Again, he looked nervous: head mostly down, trouble making eye contact, a general twitchy energy. It was impossible to miss, but I largely wrote it off to a combo of his social awkwardness and ADD. We exchanged pleasantries, and Natalie looked around the cramped room for a seat. "I'm so sorry, Natalie, the room is tighter than I thought with the cameras and whatnot. Would you mind terribly waiting outside?"

"No problem!" she cheerily replied.

I'm not a publicist, but I'm well aware that one of the cardinal rules of the profession is to never leave your client alone in a room with a reporter, especially one who might end up in an adversarial relationship with your client. But I can't really blame Natalie. Everything about Sam's situation was weird. If this guy was a billionaire, where was his security and his entourage of advisors? Who was protecting him from saying something stupid, even if in error? He had agreed to be interviewed on camera, with no preconditions, by a guy writing a book about crypto and fraud. And he was willing to be alone in the room with me. Sam's decision appeared to be a combination of extreme confidence and extraordinary stupidity, but I wasn't complaining. We began.

o o o

My general strategy as an interviewer is to smile a lot (physical cues are important), encourage an honest give-and-take whenever possible, and take no shit when it comes to prevarication or outright lying. As sincerely as I could muster, I introduced Sam as the "J. P. Morgan of crypto," running down a list of FTX's celeb endorsements, from Tom Brady and Gisele to Steph Curry and Larry David (sigh). I asked him how he explained crypto's 70 percent drop in market cap over the past nine months, as companies like Terraform Labs, 3AC, Celsius, Voyager, and BlockFi had either gone belly up or were threatening to do so. It did not seem like the decentralized, democratized future of money we had been promised in the ad campaigns, I said. Rather, it felt more like subprime 2.0.

Sam responded by relying on a favorite talking point of industry boosters at the time. Sure, crypto was down, but so was the broader market. And the riskier assets were ones that had fallen the most. We got into a long discussion of Fed policy, how rising interest rates increase the price of money (easy money, buh-bye), again leading to a selloff in risk assets like crypto. Sam tried to argue that the difference between the 0 percent interest rates due to the pandemic and the current 1.5–1.75 percent was not that significant. It was a strange moment, but I was forced to point out to the math savant that the percentage increase between 0 and 1.5–1.75 is actually infinite.

Sam quickly conceded that point. "It is an infinite increase," he said. "But if you had any business that made any kind of sense at all—"

"Well, that brings me to crypto," I interjected.

Sam chuckled uncomfortably and continued making his argument. Crypto's fall thus far was macroeconomic, he said, due to the Fed's plan to raise rates. A general shift in sentiment, he called it. A vibe shift? I offered. He again laughed uncomfortably, and kept going. I let him, but then needed to get us onto the real subject of the interview, and of the book: fraud.

I pointed out that Sam himself had publicly stated that most cryptos were in fact securities. He tried to duck it, saying he hadn't done a "thorough review of tokens 10,000 to 20,000." This was a common talking point from crypto evangelists; they all knew (or should have known) the bottom 10,000 coins were the functional equivalent of penny stocks, with ownership of the coins heavily concentrated in the hands of a few whales who could manipulate the market for them. Nonetheless, Sam conceded that "the majority are maybe securities by count."

Uh huh. Well, I said, if they are securities, then they are awfully weird securities. There is no product, good, or service that they represent a share of. They provide no utility. We agreed this was an important issue, so I pressed him to name just *one token* that did so.

"Can you name one? What's one crypto project moving forward that offers utility that can't be provided in other ways?"

"So, uh, let me actually go backwards on that and let me actually first talk about what ways crypto could actually ultimately provide utility and then I'll talk about projects."

"Okay."

"So three areas. First of all, payments. I do think that there is real potential there to make payments a lot cleaner. We go to a store and we lose a percent or two, every time we purchase things to paper over dysfunctional underlying payment rails that we have domestically. Internationally, it's way worse. Remittances are really, really expensive."

This pissed me off. I had seen firsthand how this common industry talking point was largely untrue.

"Well, I just want to stop you really quick because we went to El Salvador, which has Bitcoin as legal tender. And El Salvador's economy is heavily reliant on remittances. A quarter of the economy is remittances. And it's not being used. It's less than 2 percent. So how is it going to be used for payments? It's not working."

"I agree it's not working today. I think it could get there in the next five years. I think there are two reasons for that. The first is network effects. You need the sender and receiver to agree, you need somehow to get over that network barrier if you want to have bilateral payments with it."

"You need to have some trust."

"You need to have some trust and you need to have enough widespread adoption that you could actually have a bilateral payments method."

This was a core philosophical disagreement between us. I was trying to point out that you can't just create trust out of thin air, you need that trusted third party—such as a central bank—to serve as a bridge. Sam claimed that "network effects" and "widespread adoption" would magically provide that bridge; once enough people started using crypto, more people would be drawn into crypto, and a self-reinforcing cycle could begin. (Which is totally different from an MLM or Ponzi . . . for reasons.) To my mind, Sam and other crypto evangelists fundamentally misunderstood the nature of money.

He continued, "The second thing though, which is just a crucial part of this—let's pretend that you want to have a billion people using a blockchain for payments. If you have a billion people you're probably gonna have at least 100,000 transactions every second, maybe a million transactions a second. Unless you have a blockchain that can handle that, it's not going to be a scalable payments system."

Sam pointed out that Bitcoin can only process 5–7 transactions per second. By his own admission, Bitcoin was "four orders of magnitude" away from accomplishing this. It was never going to happen. Finally we agreed on something! But then Sam pivoted. He argued that other blockchains were faster.

"What does have potential is first of all the fastest blockchains today, they're continuing to improve on their latency, they get one to two more orders of magnitude of throughput and they actually could be a sustainable global payments network. Solana is probably the fastest today."

Solana? This was a pretty self-serving take. Alameda was a major investor in Solana tokens, to the point where it was jokingly called one of Sam's coins. (FTX/Alameda was later revealed to own more than fifty million Solana tokens, or $1 billion worth of the cryptocurrency.) Sam had even offered to buy people's SOL on Twitter to convince others of its value. Here he was again, pumping his bags!

But there was another issue when it came to Solana. It periodically stopped working. The Solana blockchain suffered numerous outages since its launch in 2020, with fourteen in 2022 alone. It also had an unfortunate tendency to be hacked, including a hack that would occur just weeks after our interview that cost users at least $5 million.

"Is Solana safe? Do you worry about it crashing?" I asked.

"So the basic answer is it depends on what you mean by safe . . ."

"I mean it's not going to crash. I don't know what other people mean! That's what I mean."

"Are you talking about the token or the network?"

"Both?"

Sam went into a long explanation that boiled down to sure, Solana and other blockchains had problems now, but through the process of experimentation and refining they would improve over time. It was a standard crypto argument (again, we're still early), and as always with crypto CEOs, a pretty easy one to make when it was other people's money at stake.

I decided to circle back to the point Sam was trying to make: that crypto's primary use case might be as a payment method. The data did not support that. The vast majority of people buying crypto were not using it for payments. According to a Pew poll, the top three reasons people bought crypto were (1) as a new form of investment, (2) a good way to make money, and (3) because it was easy. Didn't that fly in the face of the payments argument? Americans weren't buying crypto to send to relatives in other countries to avoid transfer fees, they were buying it to make money.

I asked Sam what percentage of crypto was being used for payments. He agreed the "majority of people today are not using it as a payment method" but instead as a "financial asset." He guessed "$4 billion" of crypto was being used as payments. Crypto's market cap was roughly $1 trillion on July 20, 2022. Four billion would represent 0.4 percent of that number. Seemed pretty insignificant to me, but then again, could you even trust that Sam's number—or the market cap number—was real? That gave me an idea.

"I had a conversation with Alex Mashinsky of Celsius . . ."

"Yep." Sam giggled awkwardly. Mashinsky's reputation preceded him.

". . . yeah, in the spring. I asked him how much real money is in crypto and he said 10 to 15 percent."

"And by real money, I'm guessing you're saying dollar, or euro, or yuan inflows into the ecosystem?"

"I didn't need to explain to him what real money is. If I was going to explain it to you, yes."

Mashinsky said 10 to 15 percent was real and the rest was speculation. Sam nodded, but argued that the real money in crypto was not wildly different from where it was in March.

"I think the number of dollars in crypto have not changed massively between then and now."

"Perhaps they've lessened?"

"They certainly have not increased. I don't think they've decreased massively though, which lines up with your thought that a lot of this was leverage leaving the system."

"Well, part of the problem, the reason they haven't left is that people can't get their money out. I mean they can't get their money out of Voyager, they can't get their money out of Celsius, all of these exchanges are just shutting down . . ."

"There are places with trapped money. Celsius is by far the biggest of these. Most of the other places are quite small."

Sam started attempting to quantify "total balance sheet whole size" and argue the amount of money that was frozen wasn't that significant. But I wasn't interested in arguing that point; I wanted to talk about the victims.

"Leaving the numbers aside, trying to talk about the people, how many people does that represent?"

"A million people would be my guess roughly." He said it so matter-of-factly it took me by surprise.

"I mean a million people that can't get their money out. Imagine this is a regulated bank, that would be a BIG problem."

"Oh yeah, that would be a big problem."

Sam expressed cautious optimism that eventually customers in Celsius and Voyager would get some of their money back. I was skeptical but I wasn't there to argue bankruptcy law. Eventually, Sam got back to the original question. He estimated that there were $100 billion of stablecoins left and that they were "roughly backed" 1:1. (No, I don't know what "roughly backed" means either.) He estimated there were "another one hundred billion of non-stablecoinized dollars that have entered the ecosystem." That would add up to around $200 billion of real money left in crypto. I pointed out to Sam that the number was roughly in line with what Mashinsky said to me in March.

"Yeah," Sam said. "His estimate doesn't sound crazy to me."

"See, that's interesting to me because I think when regular people . . . put $1,000 into crypto they assume they have $1,000. But if it's only backed 10 percent, for every dollar, don't they only have ten cents? If everything went badly, can they get their money back?"

"You could say the same of stocks," Sam said.

I pointed out I can go in and out of stocks in seconds via an app on my phone.

"The same is true of crypto."

"Except when the exchange shuts down."

Sam agreed, but then argued that a lack of 1:1 backing was not unique to crypto. He meant the total dollars of market cap in other asset classes aren't completely liquid either. While that's true, the difference to my mind was that liquidity in the crypto biz was far worse, and these exchanges were set up overseas in part to avoid complying with regulations that would provide investors with some protection. Instead, people rarely get any of their money back when an exchange shuts down. Sam again agreed this was a "big problem."

We moved on to stablecoins. SEC Chair Gary Gensler called stablecoins the "poker chips at the casino," I said. Tether was the biggest stablecoin in terms of trading volume by a country mile.

"Your company Alameda is one of Tether's biggest clients."

"Alameda does create and redeem Tether. We're one of the larger ones doing so."

"Okay, so there was an article from Protos, the crypto publication, from last year that said that Alameda and Cumberland, another trading firm, received $60 billion of USDT (Tether) over the time period they analyzed, which is equal to 55 percent of all outbound volume ever."

"Yep."

"Does that sound right to you?"

"Sounds ballpark correct."

"So that's a lot. That's $60 billion between Alameda and Cumberland. I've done a lot of research on Tether. They are a . . . pretty interesting company."

I rattled off a few facts about Tether: the twelve employees, the executive who was a plastic surgeon who settled with Microsoft over claims of counterfeiting.

"Their general counsel is the former chief compliance officer for Excapsa, which was the parent company of Ultimate Bet. Ultimate Bet . . . was famous for having a secret 'god mode' where they—"

Sam started laughing again nervously. "Oh boy!" he said.

"That's Stuart Hoegner. They've never been audited. They have been fined by the New York Attorney General. I just have to ask Sam, your company has billions of dollars of these Tethers. Do all these facts that I'm reeling off, are they of concern to you?"

"A few things. And this gets to what Alameda's core business is, and worth noting I don't run Alameda anymore . . ."

"But you own it, right?"

"Yeah. And I, uh, know in general what it does with stablecoins. And basically what happens is, to walk through an example which represents the bulk of what goes on here, is somewhere in the crypto ecosystem there is demand for Tether. . . . A company like Alameda or [the trading firm] Cumberland will wire dollars to Tether to create tokens and then go and offer those tokens on the venue [the exchange]. . . . It's not like Alameda, or I'm guessing Cumberland, would not have $60 billion and want to own $60 billion of Tether . . ."

"So you are using it, but you are not holding it."

"That's right. And I'm not saying zero Tethers, because of liquidity purposes. . . . It's a small fraction of the total transaction volume."

"Got it. So, by the way, your former general counsel, Daniel Friedberg, used to work for [the parent company of] Ultimate Bet as well. He's now your chief regulatory officer."

I paused. Sam appeared at a loss for words.

"I just thought that was sort of interesting."

Sam's nervous movements intensified. He tucked one leg under his body and turned his body ninety degrees in his seat, away from me and the cameras. He seemed to grab something from his pocket, and when he turned back he was nodding and twitching so much he needed to take a sip of water.

"So if you aren't holding the Tethers, maybe you're not so concerned about whether Tether could collapse. I mean, do you worry Tether could fall apart?"

"So I wouldn't say not at all concerned. . . . It is important to have a nontrivial amount to be an active market-maker in crypto."

Sam launched into a long-winded explanation of how market makers like Alameda and Cumberland work in crypto. He moved on to stablecoins, and how he thought two of them, USDC and Paxos, were safe. Eventually he turned to what he described as "the other end of the spectrum" risk-wise: Terra, the algorithmic stablecoin that blew up a few months prior.

Sam continued, "In retrospect, I've obviously thought a lot more about this than I did prior to it. In retrospect, I think the answer was that every year there was like a 25 percent chance that [Terra] was going to crash to less than 50 percent. . . . Crashing to zero was a real possibility."

"And you mentioned on Twitter, you said, 'The system was transparently going to falter.'"

"Yes."

"But FTX listed Terra."

"So, again, part of this was it wasn't until after this happened that I did as deep of a dive—"

"But you said it was transparently going to falter—"

"Transparently, what I meant by transparently there was that there was publicly available information that implied that."

"So transparently to someone else, but not to you?"

"Transparently—"

"Not to you at the time—"

"Transparently, to the world, to anyone who chose to do—"

"To 'do their own research.' "

"Right."

"But that didn't include you at the time?"

We went back to Tether, and Sam rambled on attempting to assess the risk that Tether might not be backed "quantitatively." It sounded like gibberish, some kind of post hoc rationalization, but there was little point in debating it. Instead, I asked a simple question: Why should we trust Tether, or Terra, or any of this stuff? It's one thing for FTX to list Terra, but it's another thing entirely for a regular person to buy in. Remember, the people who believed in Luna (the coin whose price floated but could always be converted into Terra) were notoriously hardcore, calling themselves Lunatics and worshiping the ground its founder, Do Kwon, walked on. Some of them bet everything on TerraLuna, and they lost everything.

Sam conceded that change was necessary, ". . . is the system set up so that the regular person can get enough information and comfort to give what they have been giving? And I think . . . the answer is no. . . . There needs to be more oversight, more transparency."

"But where does that come from? The industry is notoriously free of much regulation and has been promoting this notion of 'self-regulation.' "

"Right."

"I have to tell you, Sam, I'm the father of three small children. Self-regulation? That's not a thing. That's chaos. I just don't believe that self-regulation really ever works. What it becomes is this increasingly levered situation where you see the results right now, where things fall apart and everyone sues each other."

Sam agreed that crypto needed "federal oversight." He then made an interesting observation, which I've bolded below:

"Today, we are regulated in a lot of countries as an exchange. Our core exchange is not regulated as an exchange in the United States. . . . In the US, our core spot order book falls into a little bit of a no-man's-land where there is anti–money laundering oversight today through FinCEN and others, but from a customer protection point of view, from a systemic risk point of view, **from a fraud point of view**, from a market integrity point of view, the core exchanges in the US do not have preemptive federal oversight—"

"Right."

". . . and I think that should change."

Something was off in the room. My two cameramen were giving each other knowing looks and mouthing something. Jacob, sitting in the back of the room, joined in the silent communique. They all looked up, gazed around, inspecting, searching, gently tapping headphone cups, improvising hand gestures. I tried to focus on asking Sam about regulatory battles between the CFTC and the SEC, but I also wanted to know what the hell was going on. Some sound issue, maybe.

Later it became clear: The peculiar mechanical noise wasn't a faulty AC unit or an electrical line in the walls—it was a fidget spinner. Sam had pulled one out and started, well, fidgeting with it mid-interview, just as he had done in appearances before congressional committees.

Sam then claimed he was "less prescriptive" about whether the CFTC or SEC or some combination of the two should be in charge. I decided not to mention the picture he posed for with one of the CFTC commissioners, Caroline Pham. Instead, I used it as an opportunity to segue into a conversation on lobbying and political influence. I pointed out that Sam was the second-largest donor to Biden in 2020, that he was one of the largest donors to Democratic political action committees, and that he was amassing political influence.

"I think our political system is pretty broken," I observed.

"I agree."

"I think capitalism is eating our democracy in many respects, and I have to say the crypto industry and the recent push—I think something like $30 million has been spent over the last six months or year toward regulation or influencing regulators and politicians. I think this is a very dangerous thing we are playing with here."

"So most of the political donations I have made are not related to crypto, and this is a complicated, nuanced thing . . ."

"In what sense?"

"Um, so there's FTX the company—"

"Right . . ."

". . . and there's Sam the person."

"Right . . ."

"And, you know, most of what I'm doing for crypto regulation is not contributions, it's going and talking to people in DC and having meetings, trying to explain as much as I can about how the industry works, trying to point out the parts I think most need oversight. When you look at the contributions that I've made, most of those have to do with pandemic preparedness. Totally unrelated to my day job. I fell into finance to donate what I made and, um . . ."

"How much money have you donated to things like that versus how much you have donated to politicians?"

"Umm, I've donated, um . . . I wanna say . . . ballpark, fifty to one hundred million?"

"Wow." I wrote that number down in my notes. Sam watched me, twitching even more than usual.

"Sorry, there's some pending donations so . . ."

"Fifty to one hundred million for pandemic preparedness?"

"And then a bunch more to global poverty, animal welfare, and other causes . . ."

"How much have you donated to politicians?"

"So, um, um, I . . . don't remember the latest . . . I can get back to you on that."

"Do you have a round number?"

"Ballpark . . ."—Sam's head was down now, and he was not looking me in the eye—"in the tens of millions is where the contributions have been so far."

The entire exchange was extremely awkward. Sam paused a lot, shifted in his seat uncomfortably, and looked around the room trying to avoid eye contact. I'm no genius, but in poker these would be obvious tells that something was amiss. The fact that he really didn't want to give hard numbers on political donations also seemed dumb because much of that information is public. According to Open Secrets, a nonprofit that tracks data on campaign finance and lobbying, in the two years leading up to the 2022 midterms, Sam Bankman-Fried had given $39.8 million to Democrats, making him their second-largest individual donor. So even if you took his pandemic preparedness numbers at face value—perhaps a dubious proposition—on the low end ($50 million) they would be similar in size to his recent political donations. And yet Sam seemed to be trying to evade the question in the most obvious way possible. It was strange, and at the time I couldn't figure out what it meant.

Sam wanted to change the subject back to pandemic preparedness. While he bemoaned the lack of a timely response to COVID, I pointed out yet another irony: The easy money that had flooded into the economy because of that lack of preparation had, in my analysis, laid the foundation for the wild speculative gambling that is crypto. Unsurprisingly, Sam disagreed. He was never going to agree that crypto was only gambling, but we did have a moment where we found common ground. He pointed out that even if you were a Keynesian and believed in letting the money supply increase in times of crisis, you should then pull back when times were good so as to have tools at your disposal for the next time they went south. Instead, "It was a toggle between easy money and easier money," Sam said. Lo and behold, we had found something on which we broadly agreed.

Just then, Natalie returned bearing an embarrassed expression. She reminded Sam of his next appointment, that we needed to wrap it up. We had been talking for about an hour at that point, and so I asked for time for just one more question. I needed to get to the heart of the matter. Who knew if I would get to interview the emperor of crypto ever again? I decided to focus on utilitarianism, and whether Sam's vast holdings were just a massive exercise in hypocrisy.

When I look at the crypto industry, I don't view it as utilitarian, I said. First it's hard to find utility that isn't illegal activity or speculation. Worse, to me the industry seems built from getting retail customers, aka regular people, into the crypto casinos to gamble. Some of them win, but most of them lose; it's what keeps the lights on in the casino. And the people that profit are the owners of the casinos, i.e., the owners of the exchanges, as well as the people that own the trading firms. The implication was clear: Sam was both of those things.

I spoke about how crypto has targeted lower income people, those least likely to be able to afford to lose money gambling. I mentioned the number of people taking out payday loans to gamble on crypto.

"It doesn't feel like it's creating a lot of good for people. It feels like a net negative. I'm just, I'd like to be honest with you about that, and get your reaction to that."

"Yeah, and I think I disagree. I understand where you are coming from. Here's what I'd say, but obviously you are certainly entitled to your own opinion on it, is first of all, like, there are multiple ways to frame everything. You can frame it in terms of people who have lost money, you can frame it in terms of people who have made money on it—"

"I'm saying more people have lost money now and will lose money."

Most people who had ever purchased crypto entered the market in 2020 and 2021, and most of those people had lost money. Sam argued that the people who invested before then had made money, which didn't refute my point. Sure, a minority of people who got in early did well. He tried to pivot away from a discussion of price and toward an "ultimate use case." I was fine with that. One of my biggest problems with crypto was that it didn't actually do anything productive. To that end, I repeated my ask from earlier: Give me one use case for crypto. Sam went back to the argument about use cases today versus in the future. When pressed again on something crypto could do in the present, he reiterated the point that one day it could be used for remittances. We were getting nowhere, so I decided to simplify.

"Your belief system seems to have been driven by the fact that you have made so much money. You were a trader before, and you were making money [at] Jane Street, and now you're in crypto. Isn't it still driven by the same thing? I mean, you are making a lot of money."

"So the thing that caused to start FTX, the thing that cause me . . . to, um . . . So I spent a year trading crypto, late 2017 to late 2018, and over the course of that year . . . when I first got involved in crypto I had no idea what it was. And so when I first got involved it was just numbers on a screen. This is just an asset class on a screen. And I wasn't building any products, I wasn't doing anything consumer-facing. And I didn't have any beliefs about the industry in any direction. Over the course of that year I learned a lot about blockchain but I also learned a lot about our current financial ecosystem. And what became clear to me over that year was that already there was a lot of messiness on the crypto side. There were a lot of things that needed to be cleaned up. One of the impetuses behind FTX was addressing some of the problems behind the current crypto venues. But the other was realizing how difficult it was to operate within the current financial ecosystem, and the ways in which crypto was way, way cleaner, as a technology . . . the single hardest thing about trading crypto was sending a wire transfer."

In a roundabout way, Sam had gotten to the heart of the matter. While getting a wire transfer can be a major pain in the ass, and I agreed we could improve our payments system and our broader financial system, one of the reasons a wire transfer is cumbersome is that it runs through our banking system, which has safeguards in place: anti–money laundering laws, know-your-customer laws, the ability to protect against fraud. These regulations exist for a reason. We can and should argue over how to improve our system and amend those regulations when necessary, but claiming crypto was better simply because it was "cleaner" and moved faster was either disingenuous or deeply ignorant. Sure, it moved fast, but at enormous cost. Crypto opened the door to facilitating all sorts of criminal activity, and "trusting the code" often meant having to live with hacks, scams, and fraud as a cost of doing business. Plus, the irreversibility of the blockchain meant you couldn't correct an honest mistake. You lose money? DYOR, man.

I decided to move on. I asked him how he felt about all the people who had lost money in TerraLuna, which FTX had listed, or who were unable to get their money out of places like Celsius. I was searching for some semblance of heartfelt contrition on his part, some gesture of sympathy toward the naive crypto-buying masses, but mostly I came up empty. Sam reiterated a generic need for federal oversight. I expressed a hope that, at a minimum, we skeptics could find common ground with industry players like him and work toward eliminating the myriad scams and pervasive fraud in crypto. Sam nodded, his head hanging low.

And with that, the interview was over.

Except that it wasn't. As Sam stood up and got unmiked, he turned to Natalie. "I'm an idiot and left my hotel key in my hotel room, can you...?" Natalie disappeared, and Sam and I posed for an awkward photo.

We said our perfunctory thank-yous. But Sam kept talking.

"And always if you guys have any thoughts or questions about the ecosystem. Feel free. And Tether, there's a lot more I could say off-the-record."

(Off-the-record is by mutual agreement; we never agreed to it.)

"Frankly, they're emotional guys. And I don't want to piss them off. Weird fucking dudes. Like really fucking weird. They're honestly not scammers, but they are difficult people. And I think the *FT* article on Giancarlo is an amazing article..."

In July of 2021, the *Financial Times* published an article on Giancarlo Devasini, the CFO of Tether and the exchange Bitfinex ("Tether: the former plastic surgeon behind the crypto reserve currency"). The story included many juicy details: Devasini's brief career as a plastic surgeon before he quit the profession ("All my work seemed like a scam, the exploitation of a whim"), his settlement with Microsoft, and his selling of used electronics (one buyer complained that he paid $2,000 for memory chips and instead received "a large block of wood").

"And the most unbelievable thing is that he chose to tell that story to *FT*. That tells you a lot about, whatever. He's a passionate guy. I would not run a company the way he does. They fucked a lot of things up. They're not trying to scam people. They're trying to be honest. They also have become really, really frustrated with and burnt out by the regulatory ecosystem and sort of given up on it. Which is not healthy. On the audits point, okay they have not done nearly all the things they should be doing to get an audit. [But] they have tried to get audits. And they have gotten auditors to go through their books and confirm them, but then those auditors were vetoed, were not allowed by their firms to publish the audits for PR reasons."

This smelled like bullshit. Brock Pierce and others had made similar excuses as to why Tether had never been audited, but none of them made sense to me. If the audit showed a solvent company in good standing, what was the problem? No legit company should fear an auditor, nor should an auditor worry about endorsing fraud—if it has its own house in order. The only reason I could think of that an auditor would initially engage with Tether, but then refuse to release their findings, would be a concern about the reputational hit the accounting firm could take if those books turned out to be cooked. See Arthur Andersen and Enron.

Sam was willing to place some blame on Tether. "You only end up in this situation as Tether if you're really difficult to work with and if you're not doing everything you could be doing to get audits," he said. "And in practice they're like, if they start to get a sense that you don't respect them, they will get turned off real fast and they will just become dicks to work with. It is very messy and it's not how a business should be run at all."

So that was, allegedly, the deal with Tether. They were "messy as shit but not dishonest or scamming," he said. The company executives were just "paranoid and burnt out," a headache to work with. "It bears some resemblance to Binance as a company," Sam said. There was brief awkward laughter as we seemed to have similar suspicions regarding Binance, the industry giant that Jacob and I had been tracking. It was a bit odd for Sam to throw shade at them; Changpeng Zhao, the CEO of Binance, was one of FTX's first investors.

Jacob asked if USDD, a new stablecoin, could be an eventual replacement for Tether. Recently Alameda had announced a financial partnership with Justin Sun, the entrepreneur behind USDD. Sam responded as if he had never heard of USDD.

"USD what?"

"USDD."

"Which is DD?"

"The new Justin Sun algorithmic stablecoin."

"No, no. I don't know where on the scale from DAI (another algorithmic stablecoin) to LUNA it is, but I think it might be on the bad end of that spectrum."

It seemed odd that Sam either didn't know what USDD was or had to be reminded of its existence. Alameda was named the first member of the TRON DAO Reserve, an organization designed to support USDD. Alameda was also the first company granted the right to "mint" USDD on its own.

Justin Sun was a well-known figure, one of a dozen or so crypto moguls who exerted a profound influence on the industry. In the colorful world of crypto, he stood out not only for the size of his crypto empire—a varied group of blockchain companies, exchanges, DeFi protocols, and stablecoins that likely made him a billionaire, at least on paper—but also for his peripatetic travels and strange affiliations. In his relatively short career, Sun had already moved away from China, the US, and Malta. In December 2021, Sun declared that not only had he taken citizenship in Grenada—yes, the tiny island nation that Reagan invaded—but also that he was now a diplomat, Grenada's ambassador to the World Trade Organization. He changed his Twitter display name to H.E. Justin Sun, and he began referring to himself, seemingly unironically, as His Excellency. He said that he was stepping away from most duties at TRON, his main blockchain company, but he continued to promote the company and, as always, himself.

Sun struck more deals and started more ventures, from tokens to exchanges. He agreed to help create an official token for the island nation of Dominica, and he was appointed to the board of Huobi, a major exchange, which then embraced Sun's crypto products and gave him millions of dollars' worth of Huobi's native token in return. At the same time, one of Huobi's cofounders sold his share of the company, potentially worth billions of dollars, and many suspected the buyer was Sun, though he denied it. Sun seemed to control at least three crypto exchanges.

In this roundabout of favor trading, dealmaking, and citizenship shuffling, Sun may have been seeking both profit and political protection.

Sam said he hadn't done a deep dive into USDD, but he was "pretty skeptical of it." Still, Sam's own trading firm was a key player on the project.

We asked about TRON, Justin Sun's blockchain and the main one for which Tether seemed to be minting its tokens. Sun and Tether clearly shared close business ties—$30-plus billion worth of Tether were on the TRON blockchain—and Sam was in a position to know something about them. TRON wasn't a great blockchain, Sam said, but "the scam is not the blockchain. The scam is *the token* [emphasis mine]. It's basically worthless." While TRON had been useful for its low transaction fees, he thought it would eventually die out. "I don't think it's an important role in the ecosystem," he said.

And with that, we finally parted company. Crypto's would-be J. P. Morgan ambled off through the moss-covered hallways of the ritzy Manhattan hotel toward his next appointment, leaving me behind, perplexed. I had many, many questions, but essentially they all boiled down to one: What the fuck was that all about?

○ ○ ○

In our journey through the wilds of crypto, Jacob and I had encountered numerous bizarre characters, but none quite like Sam Bankman-Fried. I knew from previous communiques that he would try to shape my perception of him and his businesses, and it was equally clear from his deliberately crafted public persona that he had cast himself as the responsible steward of a fledgling industry that was, to his regret, rife with fraud. Sam played the role of the awkward California kid/math genius decently well, and his credentials bolstered his résumé. From his childhood in the Bay Area, Sam had been surrounded by left-leaning intellectuals and the much-lauded visionaries of Silicon Valley. He was fluent in both languages, promoting progressive values and bemoaning social ills while worshiping at the altar of technology, with "innovation" as a magic societal cure-all. But the previous decade of Sam's life had also been instructive. From his time at MIT and then at Jane Street, he had learned how to speak the language of complex financial engineering—the lingua franca of Wall Street. His ability to execute quantitative, bloodless arbitrage in a dysfunctional crypto market was one of his prime selling points to prospective investors.

When I spoke to him, one thing was obvious: Sam wanted me to like him. He was desperate to find common ground. Whenever possible he tried to agree with me broadly, then quickly pivot to lengthy vague discourses on another subject: inequities in our financial system, political paralysis, or pandemic preparedness. Sam always had a conversational out and someone else to blame. Sure, crypto needed cleaning up, but so did our regulated financial system. Yes, crypto wasn't being used for payments now, but one day it could be, right? If Sam could shift focus from the here and now, then we could agree to disagree as to crypto's future, and he could argue the present sordid state of the industry was immaterial in the long term.

I found his justifications completely unconvincing, but that was not what fascinated me. I wanted to know why Sam wanted me to like him. According to the Bloomberg Billionaires Index, he was one of the hundred wealthiest people in the world. He was a titan of industry, a beloved philanthropist. Why did he care what a guy writing a book about crypto and fraud thought? I was fixated on understanding his motivation.

o o o

While throughout our escapades in crypto Jacob and I had been bombarded with weirdos, scammers, and others with undefined agendas, we had also been fortunate to develop some meaningful relationships with people who earned our trust. One of them was a former FBI agent named Jim Harris.

Jim grew up a computer geek. He was well into a thriving career at IBM when 9/11 prompted him to make an abrupt shift. He joined the FBI, and his background led him to investigating cybercrimes. Working out of the Sacramento field office, his initial focus was on crimes targeting children online, including child sexual abuse material. Over time, he ranged across the full spectrum of issues that fall under the broad umbrella of cybercrime. Jim served more than a decade, ascending the FBI ladder and becoming a liaison with DHS and the intel community. In 2013, he rejoined the private sector. Along with a few colleagues, he had approached Jacob and me early on in our journey, offering to provide some expert advice from people who had been on the law enforcement side when it came to crypto. In trying to decipher what the hell had just happened during my interview with SBF, I decided to talk to Jim. What he said fascinated me.

Most people consider themselves good people, Jim said, no matter what bad things they may have done. The overwhelming majority of the population is not evil. They care what others think of them, but even more importantly, it's crucial to their own self-image that they justify their own behavior. Jim explained Sam's desire to get us to like him as "not unusual in white collar cases." Jim had seen the worst of the worst during his time at the FBI, but when interrogating someone suspected of a crime, no matter how brutal, he tended to employ the same simple tactics. Just listen, he said. Tell the suspect you know he is a good person, but you need help understanding what happened because the facts aren't adding up. If given the opportunity to explain their behavior, most suspects will take it. They need to see themselves as good people; they desperately want to be understood. They will justify their behavior, as Sam did constantly.

I've played a cop on several TV shows, but apparently I knew nothing when it came to actual interrogation tactics. What Jim said, and the simple way in which he said it, changed my perception of what my job entailed, at least when it came to SBF. Unlike on TV, the most effective strategy was to listen honestly. Jim advised me to keep the lines of communication open with Sam. Who knows what he might say next? I took his recommendation to heart.

o o o

The interview with Sam left me feeling unsettled. On the surface, Bankman-Fried seemed to have all the angles covered—a major exchange, his own personal crypto trading firm, a deep portfolio of investments, political influence, the benefits of living and doing business in an overseas jurisdiction, and a public reputation as a madcap mogul on the make. On crypto Twitter, he tended to be treated with a tongue-in-cheek, dark reverence—jokes about Sam liquidating traders, ironic Darth Vader comparisons. Seemingly every strange market movement or diabolically savvy trade was attributed to him, usually just on the strength of rumor. Sometimes these tilted into anti-Semitism—as a Jewish billionaire leading a centralized crypto empire, he was a ripe target for crypto's conspiratorial fringe. But if there was one thing that everyone could agree on, it was that Sam Bankman-Fried had it all figured out. Even among the most die-hard crypto skeptics, it was broadly assumed that Sam was making money hand over fist, and whatever shenanigans he might be up to, he would most likely get away with it. No way the regulators and politicians he befriended would touch the golden boy from California.

These assumptions seemed reasonable, but several things didn't add up. First, if Sam was a crypto God, why were his answers to basic questions so unsatisfying? He seemed woefully unprepared to handle even the mildest cross examination. Invariably, we would go around and around again on some issue, and while I would cite facts and figures, the purported quantitative genius would respond with incorrect numbers, vague homilies, or pseudoscientific guesswork. For example, "every year there was a 25 percent chance that [Terra] was going to crash to less than 50 percent." Where did that number come from? Interviewing Sam was like punching against air. If this was the king of crypto, was it a kingdom made of sand?

Second, if Sam was a billionaire mogul overseeing a vast conglomerate, why did his job seem to be primarily about garnering as much publicity as possible? He was constantly on the move, hopping from interview to interview, jetting off to Capitol Hill, appearing on TV as often as possible. FTX/Alameda were notoriously small shops, so who was actually doing the work? If Sam Bankman-Fried really was the bean-bag-napping workaholic CEO he claimed to be, how did he have time to spend an hour and seventeen minutes with an actor writing a book about how his entire industry was a scam?

I went back to the fraud triangle: need, opportunity, and rationalization. The opportunities for him to commit fraud were undeniable, as he owned both an exchange and a market-making firm trading on that exchange, both operating in a jurisdiction (the Bahamas) not exactly known for its strict regulatory environment. While perhaps rationalization wasn't quite the right word—I had no hard evidence Sam had committed crimes and thus couldn't accuse him of anything in particular—he was extremely evasive. He always had an excuse handy, or at least a way of deflecting blame elsewhere. But that still left the first part: the need. Why in the world would Sam Bankman-Fried need to commit fraud? He was a genius, a guaranteed moneymaker, a sure thing. No way he would have to do anything illegal. He could make money in the time-honored (if unseemly) tradition of Wall Street and its capitalist antecedents, using his supposedly brilliant mind to arbitrage small discrepancies in price.

But then a more disturbing thought flashed through my head. Sam Bankman-Fried loved playing games; he was addicted to them. He played them not just compulsively, but simultaneously, and not always well. Sam was literally playing a video game while seeking a billion dollars from a Silicon Valley venture capital firm. While the game he was playing with me was clear, it begged the question: What other games was Sam Bankman-Fried playing?

CHAPTER 10

WHO'S IN CHARGE HERE?

"Most people don't know what they're doing,
and a lot of them are really good at it." —George Carlin

T O INDUSTRY BOOSTERS, the spring crash of the crypto markets in 2022 was billed as just another trough before the next bull run. Part of a familiar cycle. But to skeptics, and to people unlucky enough to have invested more than they could afford to, the implosion represented something more severe. Crypto was on life support. A market worth $3 trillion in November of 2021 had been reduced to less than $1 trillion—and even that number seemed aspirational at best. As some bankrupt crypto companies stopped allowing customer withdrawals, it was hard to know how much real money was left to back the fake stuff. When I spoke to him in March, Alex Mashinsky of Celsius had estimated that number at less than 15 percent—and that guy was allegedly running a Ponzi scheme that soon went bankrupt. He might have been exaggerating; it was probably even less.

While Sam Bankman-Fried was busy buying up companies (and their crypto assets) for pennies on the dollar, many industry executives cut bait. Michael Saylor, CEO of MicroStrategy, and the guy who encouraged people to mortgage their houses to buy Bitcoin, resigned his position in August. (Fun fact: Saylor is the answer to a Trivial Pursuit question: "Who holds the record for most money lost in a day?" He lost $6 billion in one day during the dot-com boom.) Jesse Powell, the anti-woke CEO of crypto exchange Kraken, resigned in September, as did Alex Mashinsky himself that month. By October, more than two dozen "high-ranking" crypto executives had quit in 2022, according to Bloomberg. They often did so publicly, writing long Twitter threads, explaining they wanted new challenges beyond crypto, or emphasizing how they wanted to spend more time with their recently redis-covered beloved families.

The massive crypto advertising campaigns went poof, and with them the celebrities who endorsed crypto out of their deep love for and understanding of blockchain technology. There was the shocking disappearance of NFT avatars from Twitter and other social media. It was no longer so cool to be a bored ape if your JPEG was now worth a few hundred thousand real dollars less than when you had FOMO'd into it. Analysts argued over whether the NFT market had collapsed by 97 percent or 99 percent. In its public filings, Tesla revealed that it had lost hundreds of millions of dollars on its crypto investments. Elon Musk, the supposed genius billionaire who had gone on *Saturday Night Live* the year before and promoted Dogecoin, a cryptocurrency he admitted was "a hustle," had apparently been hustled himself. (Musk was simultaneously in the midst of receiving the most expensive lesson in contract law in history with his ill-conceived bid for Twitter.) Everyone was suing everyone. Musk was the main defendant in a $258 billion pump-and-dump lawsuit filed by an aggrieved Dogecoin investor, contending that his *SNL* appearance amounted to market manipulation. The supposed crypto "community" splintered into thousands of beefing factions. Major crypto players no longer hid their hatred of one another, airing their grievances publicly on Twitter. It was, in the grand tradition of recently pierced financial bubbles, an unruly mess.

What was clear was just how widely the crypto virus had infected the general public. Most Americans who bought into crypto did so in 2020 and 2021, when the market was at its peak, having been lured by promises of mind-boggling profits in the crooked casinos. That same majority, on average, lost money as the price of virtually all of these cryptocurrencies had crashed, most by 70 percent or more from their all-time highs. In court filings from bankrupt companies like Celsius, investors who had lost their life savings submitted devastating testimonials. They came from all walks of life: young and old, rich and poor, some sophisticated investors, others novices. There were a significant number of retirees. One elderly widow wrote that while she understood crypto's volatility, she was not aware she was investing in a Ponzi scheme. "The devastation to my life situation is irreparable, its despair, hopelessness, its failure, a slow death, that eats at you every minute of the day." Unlike Musk and his Silicon Valley VC buddies, many regular folks could not afford to gamble in the crypto casino. They did it anyway, and they lost.

The problem with an industry predicated on "number go up" philosophy is that numbers do not go up forever. While die-hard crypto advocates continued to try to sell the story that crypto could one day rise from the ashes (or that token prices didn't even matter in the long run), as the losses piled up, their appeals rang hollow. Now that the contagion from the crash was spreading, it became increasingly difficult for those in power to ignore the issues of fraud and consumer protection. Perhaps, belatedly, they might even summon the courage to do something about it.

Earlier that spring, government authorities increased scrutiny of the industry, albeit mostly from a safe, fence-sitting distance. In March 2022, President Biden issued a broad executive order marketed as a whole-of-government approach to "ensuring responsible development of digital assets." The first objective listed was to "protect consumers, investors, and businesses." There was a lot to "ensure" and "protect" when it came to crypto. The Federal Trade Commission estimated, "Since the start of 2021, more than 46,000 people have reported losing over $1 billion in crypto to scams—that's about one out of every four dollars reported lost, more than *any* other payment method (emphasis in original)." Even that number vastly understated the losses incurred. The statistics cited by the FTC represented only the more obvious and reported scams. They did not include potentially tens of millions of other victims who had been playing cards at a casino with a cut deck. The trend line was ominous. The agency reported that losses due to crypto fraud were sixty times what they had been in 2018.

How in the world was this massive speculative bubble in an industry rife with fraud—and built upon an incredibly shaky economic foundation—allowed to metastasize to such a degree? Cheating people out of their money is supposed to be illegal, right? What the hell happened to the rule of law around here? Oh right.

In the midst of all this, crypto lobbying expenditures were at an all-time high, and politicians from both parties were touting pro-industry legislation. Leading the charge was Sam Bankman-Fried, the baby-faced effective altruist who had charmed institutional investors (from his offshore Bahamas compound) and was supposed to make crypto safe for Americans. As he told me, he took frequent trips to Washington, the evidence of which could be seen in donation records, televised congressional hearings, and chummy photos with regulators.

It seemed like we were at a tipping point. The industry's inherent faults were being laid bare, but politicians from both parties didn't seem to care. The revolving door kept spinning—there was still a lot of money to spend on poaching government officials for high-paying jobs—and so did the sense that all political power rested with CEOs like SBF. There was a lot of pressure to do something—to provide "regulatory clarity," in the industry's preferred phrasing, which really meant to pass a bill or two and let the industry-friendly CFTC lead the regulatory program. And soon they might get it.

Jacob and I ventured to Washington, D.C., that summer to try to find some answers. Was anyone in power concerned? And could something be done to stop companies like FTX before they planted their hooks deeper in the mainstream financial system?

o o o

As the crypto bubble inflated massively during the pandemic, the industry realized that it faced a potentially existential threat: meaningful regulation. Because crypto was basically running every sort of scam that was at least theoretically outlawed in regulated markets, any new law or policy that might treat crypto even with the soft touch shown to Wall Street banks sent shivers down crypto's collective, oh-so-delicate spine. The stateless, peer-to-peer currency that would avoid all intermediaries and democratize and decentralize the future of money now needed to kiss Washington's ass in the present and throw some of the real stuff around. It was either that, or watch their industry go bye-bye.

On the other hand, an opportunity presented itself. If the nascent industry could instead get D.C. to enact some "light touch" legislation, carving out special rules for crypto under the guise of "innovation," that would encourage institutional players like banks and pension funds to put their money into it. Crypto companies formed lobbying groups and political action committees, and executives donated lavishly to political candidates, with little apparent criteria for their donations except "could be friendly to crypto." According to Bloomberg, "donations from people working in digital assets reached $26.3 million" in 2021 and the first quarter of 2022, more than donations from execs in big pharma, big tech, or even the defense industry. While many of crypto's true believers were conservative, it was an equal opportunity industry when it came to influence-peddling. Sam Bankman-Fried largesse toward the Democrats was quickly becoming legendary, but lest you think this was a partisan issue, his colleague at FTX, Ryan Salame, as mentioned earlier, donated $23 million to the Republicans. FTX also gave $1 million to a PAC linked to GOP leader Mitch McConnell right before the election. Crypto was playing both sides.

In April 2022, just days before the crypto collapse kicked off, FTX hosted a crypto conference near their headquarters in the Bahamas, where SBF shared the stage with such luminaries as Bill Clinton and Tony Blair. The location was fitting for a couple of reasons: First, to avoid regulation most big players in crypto had moved offshore in search of more favorable legal environments, and second, just steps away from the Baha Mar resort where the event was held stood the Caribbean's largest casino. Ironically, even Michael Lewis, author of *Liar's Poker* and *The Big Short*, was in thrall with the boy wonder, according to reporter Zeke Faux of Bloomberg. Interviewing him onstage at the event, he marveled: "You're breaking land speed records. And I don't think people are really noticing what's happened, just how dramatic the revolution has become," before openly wondering how long it might be before crypto swallowed Wall Street itself. As someone who is a big fan of his work, I grimaced. It seemed even Michael Lewis was buying the bullshit.

For all of his high-level networking and profligate giving, SBF did not always receive much in return for his largesse. But publicly, Sam remained undaunted. While he wouldn't tell me when I interviewed him how much he had spent on political causes, in another interview, he floated the possibility that he might spend up to $1 billion in the 2024 cycle. As always with crypto, it was difficult to take that astronomical number seriously.

While the long-term vision was muddled, what was clear was that a lot of dough was being spent by folks hoping to shape crypto legislation. By the time Jacob and I visited D.C. that summer, it was impossible to ignore the results of what so much crypto lobbying had bought. The industry may not have won over the cynical hearts of some national politicians, but they had certainly gotten their attention. Numerous pols of both parties suddenly were paying tribute to blockchain technology and talking abstractly about economic empowerment. Leading the charge on the Senate Banking Committee (which oversees the SEC) were ranking member Pat Toomey, a Republican from Pennsylvania, and Cynthia Lummis, a Republican from Wyoming. Coincidentally, they were the only senators who owned Bitcoin. (Lummis even added Bitcoin laser eyes to her Twitter profile picture in February 2021.) On the Senate Agriculture Committee, which oversees the CFTC, one of the industry's biggest boosters was Kirsten Gillibrand, a Democrat from New York.

Toomey spun his ownership of Bitcoin and the potential conflict of interest as a source of important "expertise" when deciding on regulatory policy. He argued that Washington needed to offer "respect for consumers" to make their own investment choices, despite the fact that the very lack of disclosures inherent in cryptos not being classified as securities kept investors in the dark as to how they might be getting swindled. Both he and Lummis were also deeply worried about losing the competition over financial innovation, now spreading to noted innovation hubs such as Kazakhstan and Romania.

The politicians weren't the only problem. A swiftly revolving door between high-level government positions and far more lucrative jobs in private industry meant that the oversight process seemed hopelessly compromised. As in other sectors, cozy relationships between regulators and those they regulated had become the norm. According to the Tech Transparency Project (TTP), there were "nearly 240 examples of officials with key positions in the White House, Congress, federal regulatory agencies, and national political campaigns moving to and from the industry." Crypto's roster of boosters now included two former chairs of the SEC (Jay Clayton and Arthur Levitt), two former chairs of the CFTC (Christopher Giancarlo and Jim Newsome), and one former chair of the Senate Finance Committee (Max Baucus). A representative example was Brian Brooks, who was chief legal officer of exchange Coinbase before he became Acting Comptroller of the Currency, only to leave that governmental position to become the head of Binance's US division. He lasted all of three months at that job, before resigning due to "differences over strategic direction."

Despite these headwinds, many of the people in Washington that Jacob and I met with were sympathetic to the cause of protecting consumers and rooting out fraud. Crypto just smelled bad, and it reminded them of the predatory lending schemes leading up to the subprime crisis. The last time it was the banks and mortgage lenders saddling folks with unsustainable debt; now it was the easy allure of an unregulated get-rich-quick scheme.

But no matter how much crypto skepticism these officials expressed, in almost every room a sense of resignation prevailed. Sure, crypto posed some huge problems, but crypto leaders had bought influence, which was evident in bipartisan support for some industry policies. Democrats, traditionally the party of consumer protection, were divided. Who would want to be seen as popping a bubble?

Amid this political passivity, the scuttlebutt was that the crypto lobby could well get legislation passed in the new Congress. One bill going around at the time was known as Sam's Bill, or the SBF Bill—which tells you all you need to know about his influence at the time. Its official name was the Digital Commodities Consumer Protection Act (DCCPA). It was bipartisan, and it had powerful friends. It was backed by Senate Agriculture Committee Chairwoman Debbie Stabenow (D-MI) and ranking member John Boozman (R-AR). It would give oversight of the crypto spot market—where financial instruments like securities and commodities are traded for immediate delivery—to the CFTC rather than the more powerful and better funded SEC. Crypto broker-dealers would be required to register with the CFTC and submit to oversight from it.

Even if the DCCPA didn't pass during this Congress, these and other proposed bills indicated a desire on Capitol Hill to create a more favorable regulatory environment for crypto's leading players. Eventually, via sheer force of lobbying muscle, it seemed, the industry would get some version of what it wanted: further legalization of the crypto casino and deeper access to the US banking system—and all the potential retail cash that came with it.

This bleak future sent chills down the spines of experts in fraud and financial malfeasance. Mark Hays is senior policy analyst for fintech at Americans for Financial Reform, a nonpartisan, nonprofit coalition of more than 200 groups that aims to address systemic issues within our financial system. Hays made a career out of studying money laundering and other financial crimes. What he saw in crypto gave him flashbacks to the wildly risky financial products that underwrote the 2008 financial crisis. And much like the subprime crisis, those least able to afford a financial setback had been targeted. According to a study from 2021, 44 percent of crypto traders were people of color. Many had been excluded from the mainstream financial system and saw crypto as a way of creating generational wealth. Expensive marketing campaigns starring world-famous athletes and celebrities sold them on this story.

One of the most glaring examples of this was Bitcoin Academy, a project "personally funded" by Jack Dorsey, cofounder and former CEO of Twitter, and hip-hop artist and mogul Jay-Z. The project attempted to educate residents of the Marcy Houses, the housing development in Brooklyn where Shawn Carter (aka Jay-Z) grew up, on the wonders of Bitcoin. Apparently these wonders included expensive lessons in crypto's volatility. Bitcoin Academy was announced on June 9, 2022, when Bitcoin's price was a shade over $30,000 a coin. The next day it cratered. By June 18, it was less than $20,000. If you bought what Jack and Jay were selling, you would have lost a third of your money in a matter of days. Unfortunately, like the majority of crypto investors, most people of color entered the market near its peak in the bull run of 2020/2021 and were now among the ones left holding the bag.

Despite this, Mark Hays held out hope it wasn't too late to do something, if only to prevent further losses by the general public. "Right now we have an opportunity to create guardrails and a firewall around an asset class that at best is risky and unproven and at worst could be much more problematic," he said. Hays tried to remain optimistic, but he was chastened by his experience navigating a political scene dominated by corporate interests that learned few substantive lessons from the 2008 crisis. Regulation was not innately good, and given the amount of industry money flowing into D.C., bad legislation could make an already bad situation worse. "If you do it wrong, instead of creating safeguards and protections for consumers and investors and anyone exposed to this, you're actually legitimizing the assets and bringing the risk closer, not further away," said Hays. At that point, crypto's volatility and risk could infect the mainstream financial system.

Hays was right, but he was a voice in the wilderness. Jacob and I talked to whomever would listen and shared some of our research, which seemed to indicate a shit-ton of industry malfeasance, from insider trading at major exchanges to pump-and-dump boiler rooms run via Telegram. On Capitol Hill, good people listened and nodded, offering murmurs of genuine public concern. Many of these issues were known to them, in some form, even if they hadn't been publicly acknowledged, much less acted upon.

There was hope that a brave legislator or two would push back on the industry's misleading rhetoric—aka its lies—or promise to introduce legislation focused on protecting consumers, not venture capitalists. Instead, there was an inevitable acknowledgment of the political complexities at play. Every meeting basically ended the same way: Let's stay in touch. They had to move slowly, sensitive to political realities. It was an election year, remember? As

Jacob said, it was as if the spirit of SBF and the crypto lobby had preceded us in every room. Well, its spirit and its money.

o o o

The United States of America is unique in the way it separates its regulation of securities from its regulation of commodities. It's basically a historical fluke. You'll recall that securities are defined extremely broadly under American law, often under what's called the Howey Test. It has four conditions: (1) an investment of money, (2) in a common enterprise, (3) with the expectation of profit, (4) to be derived from the efforts of others. The expansive definition is purposeful: Human beings are incredibly creative in coming up with new and exciting ways to turn some amount of money into a larger amount of money. Investors, and the general public more broadly, need to be protected in these endeavors. Securities laws are predicated primarily on disclosure. Put simply: When you invest money, you need to know who you are giving your money to and what they are doing with that money. Crypto had almost none of that. In addition, given that there was no product or service provided by crypto companies, they strongly resembled a particular type of illegal security: the Ponzi scheme. That's right, in the eyes of the law, Ponzi schemes are a form of securities fraud and therefore regulated by the SEC. The agency lists seven "red flags" for Ponzis on its website. Crypto checks off five, arguably six, of the seven (see Appendix).

Commodities, on the other hand, were originally things tied to physical goods: wheat, corn, soybeans, beef, pork, oil, gas, aluminum, etc. Things that you grew, animals you killed to eat, minerals you dug from the ground—you know, stuff. Initially, you could gather capital to invest or trade commodities among people in your community, but for both securities and commodities to scale they needed proper marketplaces where numerous buyers and sellers could transact freely.

In the late eighteenth century in America, securities markets developed where the majority of the money was: the major cities of the east. The first stock market actually started in Philadelphia in 1790, but only two years later the New York Stock Exchange (NYSE) followed.

Commodities markets, on the other hand, were centered in Chicago. As western expansion resulted in explosive economic growth, transporting the fruits of labor that came from farms, ranches, and mines from the rest of the country back to the population centers of the East Coast became imperative. Likewise, the industrial products manufactured in the east needed to travel west. Both of these required railroads for transport and telegraph services for communication, and it all ran through Chicago, the great emerging Midwestern metropolis. The Chicago Board of Trade was created in 1848, and it became the locus of commodities trading, both in America and, eventually, the world.

A funny thing happened at this point: innovation. Commodities trading originally meant trading the physical goods themselves, but over centuries it grew to include what are called *futures contracts*—the obligation to buy or sell specific commodities at a future date at a set price. There are endless iterations of this basic concept, but all you really need to know is that futures contracts were created to hedge against risk. They are a crucial tool for a modern economy to function effectively. Any futures contract tied to a commodity is by extension regulated as a commodity under the Commodity Exchange Act (1936), which defines commodities quite broadly to include not just the physical stuff like grain, beef, etc., but also "all services, rights, and interests (except motion picture box office receipts, or any index, measure, value or data related to such receipts) in which contracts for future delivery are presently or in the future dealt in."

This is why things like currencies and interest rates are regulated as commodities. Basically anything that involves a derivatives contract on an underlying asset can be deemed to be a commodity, unless it's already been classified as a security. The broad definition of commodities created a gray area between the legal definitions of commodities and securities that could be exploited.

Both the SEC and the Commodity Exchange Authority (CEA), the predecessor to the CFTC, were born out of the depths of the Great Depression. By the mid 1930s, lawmakers realized financial products of all kinds needed federal regulation to avoid the free-for-all of earlier periods. The CEA became the CFTC in 1974, and the inclusion of futures contracts in its remit allowed the agency to assert authority over an array of increasingly complex financial products.

Which brings us to Bitcoin. In 2014, CFTC Chairperson Timothy Massad staked his agency's claim to crypto derivatives. "Derivative contracts based on a virtual currency represent one area within our responsibility," he said. Another CFTC commissioner, Mark Wetjen, helped lead the initiative to make a company called TeraExchange the first regulated Bitcoin derivatives exchange. And thus, Bitcoin followed in the financial lineage of beef futures. For many coiners, it was taken as good news, a way of legitimizing the first cryptocurrency by enshrining it under the existing regulatory regime.

One year later, the CFTC announced that TeraExchange had engaged in illegal wash trading surrounding that very first Bitcoin derivatives transaction. TeraExchange settled with the CFTC, with the crypto exchange agreeing to stop violating the law and to acknowledge the CFTC's authority. There was no fine or criminal prosecution. CFTC Commissioner Wetjen, in the grand revolving door tradition, later entered the crypto industry. In 2021, FTX US hired Wetjen to be its head of policy and regulatory strategy—the mirror to his former governmental position. To recap, the first derivatives exchange in crypto to be classified as such under American law was later found to have engaged in illegal activity, got off the hook, and then later another exchange hired the regulator who oversaw that decision to help guide their maneuverings on Capitol Hill. You can't make this stuff up.

Bitcoin is a commodity, then, mostly because CFTC officials exercised a regulatory power grab. They got there first. Former chair Massad and others considered derivatives contracts commodities, which was justifiable under a strict reading of the Commodity Exchange Act. Because such contracts existed for Bitcoin, the cryptocurrency itself was one. Bitcoin's a pretty weird commodity, in that it obviously isn't tied to any specific physical good, as commodities were traditionally defined. To be fair, its "decentralized" nature in terms of the code means it's more difficult to say who the exact issuer is. (Think of a regular security, like a stock. It has a clear issuer: the company itself.) But the reality is that Bitcoin's ownership is actually extraordinarily centralized, concentrated in a tiny group of whales and mining pools. In fact, just two mining pools account for 51 percent of its global hash rate, meaning just two large groups control the majority of new Bitcoin created. Additionally, just because we don't know who came up with Bitcoin originally doesn't mean no one did. Whoever Satoshi Nakamoto is, it's a real person or real people. Once again, code does not fall from the sky. One day we may well find out who started this whole nonsense. If so, break out the popcorn, law nerds.

Regardless, by the summer of 2022, two things were clear on the otherwise murky regulatory front: (1) The law considers Bitcoin a commodity—cat's out of the bag on that sadly—and (2) there was a massive battle between the CFTC and the SEC for jurisdiction over the 20,000 or so cryptocurrencies out there.

The crypto industry desperately wanted the CFTC to be in charge. Sam Bankman-Fried and other crypto heavy hitters praised the agency's light touch approach to Bitcoin as a model and met with its leaders. Commissioner Caroline Pham tweeted photos of herself meeting with SBF as well as Brad Garlinghouse, CEO of the crypto exchange Ripple—who was engaged in litigation against the SEC. One meeting included one of Pham's former colleagues who had gone over to the crypto industry and now was publicly lobbying her. As was the case across government, the revolving door was moving faster than ever, and few public officials seemed to feel any shame in passing through it.

The CFTC chief at the time was Rostin Behnam, with whom Sam Bankman-Fried met over ten times. Behnam and the CFTC were supporters of Sam's Bill, which would put crypto exchanges under the agency's domain. Behnam was a former aide to Senator Debbie Stabenow, who was overseeing that bill. Behnam publicly touted that if his agency got more money and authority, it'd be good for crypto: "Bitcoin might double in price if there's a CFTC-regulated market," he said at a conference in September 2022.

The CFTC has approximately one-quarter the budget of the SEC. It's a smaller, less powerful agency. If there was to be a regulatory regime governing crypto, the collective industry consensus went, better that it be under a pliable agency whose leaders liked posting smiling pics with CEOs. (That's not to overlook the efforts of SEC Commissioner Hester Peirce, whose enthusiasm for the industry is legendary. In late May 2022, after the spring collapse was already underway, she complained: "We're not allowing innovation to develop and experimentation to happen in a healthy way, and there are long-term consequences of that failure.") The concern from a consumer protection standpoint was that the competition between SEC and CFTC could create a race to the bottom, in which both agencies were incentivized to stake out as much regulatory authority as possible, but then tread lightly when it comes to actual enforcement.

There was a parallel turf war going on inside the halls of Congress. The SEC is overseen by the Financial Services Committee in the House and the Banking Committee in the Senate. The CFTC is overseen by the Agriculture Committee in both chambers. While this distinction may be immaterial to you and me, for the members of Congress vying to serve on these committees, it's a pretty big deal. Securing a coveted slot on one of them means CEOs and companies seeking influence are incentivized to develop a relationship with you. Maybe they'll make some donations to support your campaign or promise to do more business in your state. As Otto von Bismarck said: "If you like laws and sausages, you should never watch either one being made." Personally, I think that's unfair to the sausage industry.

Economists look at incentives, and the competition between the SEC and CFTC likely created perverse ones. Regulatory arbitrage—taking advantage of gaps in regulation in different jurisdictions—had proved essential to the spread of the crypto virus. That's why so many crypto exchanges were based in overseas island nations known for having practically as many shell corporations as people.

Even if the divide between the SEC and CFTC were papered over, there was still a gap in their collective remit: Neither was principally a criminal enforcement agency. They can fine people and bar them from trading in the future, but typically they refer potential criminal cases to the Department

of Justice for prosecution. When it came to crypto entities in foreign jurisdictions, even the Department of Justice was at a disadvantage. It's difficult
to go after companies set up overseas with the express intent of avoiding
American laws and regulations. At least some help was on the way. In
October 2021, the National Cryptocurrency Enforcement Team was created
within the Department to tackle "the criminal misuse of cryptocurrencies
and digital assets." In February 2022, it appointed its first Director, Eun
Young Choi.

The very fact that shady overseas exchanges had gained access to the most
valuable market of them all—the average American's wallet—spoke volumes
about how deep the failures of the system ran. With crypto advertising running in tandem with online sports gambling during the biggest media event
of the year, the Super Bowl, one was reminded yet again of the parallels
between online poker and crypto. With online poker, it was the Feds who
had been forced to shut the whole thing down. Which begged the question:
Were we in for round two?

o o o

One sunny morning, Jacob and I went to visit a source of ours in a leafy
Maryland town not far from D.C. John Reed Stark, the now-retired chief of
the SEC Office of Internet Enforcement, welcomed us with the ebullience
of a contented suburban dad. Stark left government in 2009 to become a
private-sector consultant, working on issues ranging from ransomware to
regulation. He is also helping to train the next generation of regulators; John
is a senior lecturer of law at Duke University. An affable, fifty-something
guy who seems ready to have a chat about whatever you'd like, Stark was the
kind of person you'd want as a neighbor. Relentlessly friendly and commu-
nity-minded, he came bearing a strong moral code.

Stark was a libertarian with a zeal for consumer protection, two beliefs
that, I joked with him, might be in conflict. He laughed and shrugged it off.
Since leaving government, he too had fallen down the crypto rabbit hole, and
in his mind, the government was utterly derelict in its law enforcement and
regulatory responsibilities. Stark had emerged as a vocal and unapologetic

opponent of crypto, considering the tokens to be unlicensed securities little different from the kind of penny stock fraud cases he tackled in the 1990s. Blazing a scorched-earth path across various media—Twitter, cable news, even the normally placid terrain of LinkedIn—Stark called out former colleagues without hesitation. To Stark, someone like Hester Peirce, a famously pro-industry SEC commissioner, was both brilliant and a huge disappointment. No one was spared. John's lifelong best friend—someone who he thought was the smartest, toughest kid he knew growing up on Long Island—was Anthony Scaramucci. That's right: the Mooch, who had lasted ten days as President Donald Trump's communications chief. Scaramucci was also a major crypto investor, running the firm SkyBridge Capital, which had deep ties to Sam Bankman-Fried. It drove John nuts.

"There really is no legitimate side to crypto," said Stark. To him, crypto had simply repackaged the traditional get-rich-quick scheme in a shiny, fraudulent wrapper.

Stark's public emergence as a crypto critic rankled some people. They said he was just a salty ex-regulator or that his rejection of all crypto was unreasonable. Any time someone's bags were threatened, there was potential for strong backlash, and John's voice had begun to carry across crypto media. He started receiving violent threats. "It's like nothing I've ever experienced in my life," said Stark. He owned a gun and maintained a home surveillance system. For reasons he couldn't quite pinpoint, during the height of the COVID pandemic, he bought a massive, eight-foot-tall safe and had it installed in his garage.

We met John and his family at his house, from where he took us to a local sports club that catered to the neighborhood. The club was nicely appointed—it had a large pool and clay tennis courts—but unassuming. It was the kind of place where families could hang out all day; the kids could go to sports camp while their parents played doubles. A little slice of Americana, in a classic American suburb. The facility was open only to area residents and maintained low dues—points of pride for Stark, who overflowed with neighborliness and social concern. He was like Ned Flanders with a law degree and a better backhand.

In the interests of fairness—and Stark's mind often seemed concerned with what was fair or just—Jacob and I decided to face off against our host in the sport of kings, two versus one. Given that John was a well-practiced semi-retiree and we were two haggard dads of relative middle age who hadn't played tennis in decades, it seemed evenly matched—or as even as could be. As John schooled us with a smooth forehand, we struggled to hit the ball between the lines. Somehow, in the midst of the occasional volley and Jacob diving nobly but futilely to return a laser-like serve, we managed to talk a little crypto.

As usual, Stark was fired up. He was tired of official D.C.'s relative inaction and thought it would only lead to more consumer harm down the road. To him, these issues were black and white—or could be, if only regulators and lawmakers had the proper information and the political will to do the right thing.

"To me, the solution first and foremost is the criminal prosecutions," said Stark. "I really think so. So much of this stuff—it doesn't have to be securities fraud. It's just fraud." People liked to describe crypto as the Wild West, but to John it was something worse. "It's like *The Walking Dead*," he said, citing the TV show about a zombie apocalypse where the living can be more brutal and inhumane than the titular flesh-eating monsters. "Everybody just does what they want."

Stark liked free and fair markets. Crypto was neither. And that it was being presented as a system for financial inclusion, a way to help the unbanked, seemed especially troubling. "If anything, it's worse," Stark said. "You're trading one system that exploited people for one that's a lot worse. And that's disturbing."

Stark reframed crypto in a way that I thought some of the best critics did. He cut through the rhetoric and technological mystification and called crypto what it was: a predatory financial product in the manner of payday or subprime loans.

"For me it's all so obvious," said Stark. "When you ask anybody, 'Give me one legitimate use for crypto. Give me one thing you can use crypto for?' I just don't see it, and nobody can ever tell me anything."

What I found most refreshing about Stark was his concern for people who got caught up in crypto. "You can blame the victim if you want. But the reality is, it's really not the victim's fault. They're being taken in by really sophisticated hustlers."

It was something Stark had learned while at the SEC. "You meet victims of all kinds," he said. He had seen other people buy into fraudulent investment schemes and various unlicensed securities that, at their core, were not much different than crypto. People were always trying to get rich quick, and there was always someone around willing to promise fantastic wealth while picking their pocket. "You start to realize, anyone can be vulnerable."

It was a sentiment that we both wished policymakers in D.C. would understand. Some did. The Labor Department issued guidance in March 2022 encouraging people to "exercise extreme care" before investing their retirement savings in crypto. But just three months later, in June, Senators Cynthia Lummis and Kirsten Gillibrand went on cable news to push back. Senator Lummis: "I think the Labor Department is wrong. I think [401(k) investments in crypto are] a wonderful idea. It should be part of a diversified asset allocation." Senator Gillibrand agreed.

"It made me want to throw a brick through my TV," John said. "They're enabling it."

For many lawmakers raking in large political donations from the crypto industry, it simply wasn't in their political or financial interest to look out for the "little guy." It was up to critics like Stark—who had no skin in the game, who didn't make money off of his crypto criticism—to put forward that argument. And for now, he was one of the more effective voices doing it, at some personal and reputational risk.

As for me, I desperately needed a tennis lesson.

o o o

After returning from D.C., I got called for the excruciatingly boring exercise in civic responsibility that eventually claims every American: jury duty. It was my first time serving on one, and I have to admit that although there was the requisite tedium, I thoroughly enjoyed getting to know a group of people I would never have met otherwise. I also learned a lot from the case—a lawsuit over a decade-old slip and fall case that seemed more about acting out tangled emotional grievances between the two parties, who were former roommates, than actually reaching a just legal settlement. Observing the elaborately convoluted case—who knew there was so much to learn about roof leaks!—I saw firsthand that the application of the law is messy. Elected lawmakers create the law, professionals argue about it, judges interpret it, and public servants assist in the process of implementing it, but often, ultimately, a randomly selected group of citizens decides it. Like all human endeavors, it is as flawed, and prone to unexpected twists of fate, as we are. It might also be the best we can do.

On one of the last days of my jury service, I fell into a conversation with the officer of the court, Officer Gelan. He revealed he was formerly an auditor for a large bank, but he left his job during the 2008 recession and made a career switch to law enforcement. But the subprime crisis wasn't done with him. It followed Gelan to his new job. For years, he explained, the courts were full with lawsuits between banks and customers—the combined wreckage of a generational housing crisis slowly moving its way through the legal system.

Why did I get the feeling a similar wave of litigation was brewing as some $2 trillion of crypto wealth had vanished overnight? Then an even more chilling thought ran through me: Because crypto had been purposefully set up to avoid regulation, would everyday victims have any shot at justice? Or would the "decentralization" of fraud leave millions of regular folks with less real money in their pockets and even more distrust of a system that had already repeatedly failed them?

o o o

The week after my jury duty ended, former president of the United States Donald J. Trump was charged with fraud. His family business, as well as three of his children, were accused by the New York Attorney General of lying about the value of various assets they owned to the tune of billions of dollars. Having cast Trump as the symbolic figurehead of the golden age of fraud, it was remarkable to see him—even if only potentially—held responsible for his actions.

Two weeks later, Kim Kardashian, the subject of our first article in October 2021, was fined $1.26 million by the SEC for her participation in shilling the shitcoin EthereumMax. Kardashian also agreed "not to promote any crypto asset securities for three years." It had taken a year, but at least there was some accountability. Getting arguably the most famous person in the world to acknowledge the impropriety of her role in a sleazy pump-and-dump scheme was certainly a PR coup for the agency, albeit with a fine attached that the uber-rich Kardashian could easily afford to pay. Still, it was important. In combating a false economic narrative, it is crucial to put forth an alternate true one, to reveal the hucksters and con men for who they really are. But Kardashian and her fellow celebs were, at least for the most part, not those fraudsters. They were just a tool, a megaphone used to spread the lies of crypto more effectively.

To my mind, the much larger question still loomed for those actually perpetuating the fraud. Would anyone in crypto ever actually see the inside of a jail cell?

CHAPTER 11

UNBANKRUPT YOURSELF

"It is easier to rob by setting up a bank than by holding up a bank clerk." —Bertolt Brecht

"There are no rules in this business." —Alex Mashinsky

G ROWING UP IN Michigan, James Block developed an interest in fraud at an improbable early age. When he was in third grade, he dressed up for Halloween as Kenneth Lay, the CEO of Enron who became synonymous with illegal financial engineering around the turn of the millennium. "I was a weird kid," James admitted, laughing, when we spoke to him in early 2022. The interest didn't wane. Years later, when he and his future wife were dating, they developed a drinking game for *American Greed*, a CNBC show about corporate malfeasance.

As a child, James would spend the day with his grandfather, an accountant, crashing public hearings to hector local politicians about failing to live up to their campaign promises. His granddad, James made clear, was more avuncular than angry—passionately civic-minded. He was not impressed by authority—politicians were there to serve them—and he expected public servants to be exactly that. James took away some lessons from his principled progenitor that would serve him well years later as a self-taught blockchain sleuth. He wasn't impressed by a CEO title or power or money—those were just more opportunities for corruption. Companies that promised outsized benefits to their "community" should be able to withstand a little well-intentioned scrutiny.

In the fall of 2021, as he started to immerse himself more in crypto, James saw a tremendous amount of hype and salesmanship that rarely matched reality. He didn't have a full understanding (yet) of how crypto markets could be manipulated, he said, "but the one thing I could recognize was a company claiming that they could generate above-market returns with these deposit type products as something that was incredibly suspicious and has a very long and very bad history."

As a leading crypto lender offering yields as high as 18 percent—far greater than that offered by any regulated bank—Celsius stood out. So did its CEO, the eccentric Ukrainian-Israeli tech entrepreneur Alex Mashinsky. Mashinsky's résumé was gilded with a long list of supposed innovations and business accomplishments. For example, he professed to have invented voice over IP (VOIP), the ability to conduct phone calls and multimedia sessions over the internet (think of the companies Skype and Zoom as successful examples in the field). But there was little evidence backing Mashinsky's bold assertions. Now, he claimed, he was using his experience and business acumen to help bring wealth to the crypto masses. "He was different because he was this guy who was like, 'I was this big CEO and I did all these great things.'" Later, James would find that Mashinsky had either exaggerated or invented a great deal of his professional history.

With crypto lenders offering unsustainable interest rates and hucksters like Mashinsky at the helm, James sensed fraud in the system. He just had to unravel it. Fortunately, some major pieces of evidence were sitting there in a complicated array of blockchain transactions. He had little idea how to interpret them, so he taught himself. It wasn't necessarily that hard. It took a bit of reading, the requisite YouTube tutorials, and time spent on blockchain-tracking sites like Etherscan. Put it all together, sprinkle with some data visualization (James had a knack for that, too), and you can start seeing how a modern-day crypto Ponzi is assembled.

"All I wanted to do was figure out how the stupid thing worked," said James. "I never thought it would go farther than that."

It helped that a lot of crypto fraudsters weren't subtle. They left clues. People made mistakes. Some people were dumb. And some people, especially in crypto, didn't care about secrecy. They wanted credit.

Alex Mashinsky was a combination of all the above. Neither an innovator nor a genius, he had a certain showmanship and I'm-just-winging-it confidence. In an industry of colorful figures, Mashinsky the carnival barker wasn't necessarily that different from the crackpot VCs, fugitive stablecoin dealers, or serial scammers who promised that this new project was legit (just trust me, bro). In short, he wasn't atypical, which meant that he didn't strike me as someone to trust with my life savings. Still, an astounding number of people did just that; at the time of its bankruptcy filing, Celsius claimed 300,000 active customers, to whom it owed $4.7 billion. These customers had been tempted by the high yields and regular payouts of Celsius's rewards program, which offered high-interest rates in return for customers handing over their crypto. Some customers might have known that the promised yields were based on juiced numbers, but in crypto, the word *Ponzi* had been practically rehabilitated. Ponzinomics were suddenly everywhere. The dollar was now considered a Ponzi—only a bad one. DeFi protocols and many crypto tokens were Ponzis—but they were usually good, because a smart trader would get out when they could (as for those unlucky enough not to, well, best not speak of them).

Mashinsky spoke in brash sweeping statements about "unbanking yourself" and the glory of his nonbank's bank-like offerings. He sometimes wore a T-shirt featuring the words "Banks are not your friends" underneath the Celsius logo. Like many crypto CEOs, he talked about overthrowing the existing financial order and empowering people in the face of insidious TradFi institutions that had failed them. It was recycled industry shtick, but it worked well enough when the payouts were so good. Some may even have seen kind of an ironic or folk quality in Mashinsky, a Ukrainian-Israeli who spoke mostly in exclamation marks, liked to mix it up with customers at conferences, and made a lot of bad jokes. He was goofy but he was also making it rain.

"TradFi has been socializing losses by using too big to fail to force bailouts and have the little guy pay for it via Taxes," Mashinsky tweeted in December 2021, weeks after the crypto market peaked. "CeFi @CelsiusNetwork is socializing #Crypto profits to the little guy by charging institutions fees to borrow Crypto while helping millions Unbank."

Mashinsky encouraged his customers to HODL—*hold on for dear life*—through the bad times, saving their crypto for the long term and buying every dip. Some customers found their accounts put automatically in what Celsius called HODL mode, preventing them from cashing out. In a practical sense, this was a Ponzi artist trying to prevent his victims from withdrawing their money, which would make the entire scheme collapse. During a period of market volatility in September 2021, Mashinsky tweeted, "Don't let these flash crash ✳ low volume swings sway you. Others may need cash and so sell their coins at a discount, you are going after financial freedom so #HODL on. ETH is a great buy at these levels."

Besides outsized rewards and financial freedom, Mashinsky promised his customers "community," that empty, horribly overused word that seems to be deployed even more often after a company tells its customers that they can't return their money. Oops. We apologize to our community.

In Mashinsky's telling, everything was being done for Celsius's community of "unbanked," financially empowered customers. For Celsius the corporation, its "community" was paramount. It was mentioned in nearly all of their tweets, press releases, ads, and rambling speeches by executives in Twitter Spaces events. Even the company's press release announcing its bankruptcy filing contained a few nods to its community—clearly an attempt by the company at cooling the mark. They were assuring jilted customers that this wasn't a normal company; it was a community, and they were looking out for you even in hard times.

For a couple years, the Celsius community was enjoying fat returns thanks to the definitely-not-a-bank's proprietary trading methods. It was based on a lie, that of profitability, but the public either didn't know or didn't want to ask what made the scheme possible.

"Nobody cared," said James. "It's funny how that works."

When I stumbled upon Mashinsky at SXSW in early 2022, Celsius seemed to be in decent shape. Sure, some regulators were nipping at its heels, but that came with the territory. Meanwhile, Celsius claimed to have more than $20 billion worth of assets under management, offering a place where customers could "stake" their crypto tokens for high yields and other rewards. According to the strange tokenomics of the decentralized finance protocols underpinning these staking schemes, a virtuous cycle would ensue—more fake internet money for everyone! James called it the Celsius flywheel, a mechanism by which fake digital assets could be pumped up, insiders could cash out, and the whole whirligig would just keep spinning ad infinitum—until it couldn't anymore.

There were numerous warning signs. Free money was rarely ever free. But few people felt incentivized to look under the hood.

James started to investigate. Early on, he didn't like what he saw—lots of borrowing, circular movements of crypto, high and seemingly unsustainable yield rates. "At a minimum, Celsius Network is a highly leveraged debt machine that is exposed to multiple counterparty risks," James wrote under the pseudonym Dirty Bubble Media in his newly founded Substack. "Importantly, the individual account holders in this situation—both depositors and borrowers—are unsecured creditors of Celsius Network. This means they occupy the unenviable position of being last in line to recoup losses in the event the debt machine malfunctions."

That point would become sadly pertinent months later.

Dirty Bubble Media began to attract attention. What started as a fly-by-night crypto publication began to emerge as a serious industry watchdog. Investors, traders, and crypto company executives started to pay attention. When James published a post suggesting that Celsius might be insolvent, it got more than one million views.

James has a calm, almost steely affect that reminds me of what he described as his grandfather's confident defiance toward Michigan politicos. It paid off in one of his few actual exchanges with Alex Mashinsky. In November 2021, as the Celsius CEO held court during one of his weekly Twitter Spaces meetings, during which he usually touted his company's unfettered growth and its success at enriching its community, James decided to ask a question—not something canned from a Celsius cultist, but a real question.

Celsius's CFO Yaron Shalem had been recently arrested in Israel as part of an alleged fraud scheme connected to Moshe Hogeg, who was also arrested for alleged sex crimes, according to the *Times of Israel*. (Through lawyers, Hogeg "vehemently" denied the allegations and said he was "cooperating fully with his investigators," and Shalem said he "acted in accordance with the law and strongly and utterly rejects any attempt to associate him with any act of fraud.") As soon as Shalem was arrested, he was basically erased from Celsius's history. The company said nothing about his arrest until it was confronted by critics online. Celsius eventually issued a vague statement without naming Shalem, hired a new CFO, and moved on, dodging questions about him during public events. During one of Mashinsky's regular Twitter Spaces sessions, James, under the guise of Dirty Bubble Media, decided to press the Celsius CEO about the relationship between Shalem, Hogeg, and Celsius.

James later recounted the exchange on his Substack publication:

> *DBM: Ok, so you're denying any knowledge or anything about this case, or where your CFO is right now?*
> *Mashinsky: I, I . . . the guy you're talking about, there's nothing to do with Celsius, ok, so . . .*
> *DBM: Yaron Shalem has nothing to do with Celsius Network?*
> *Mashinsky: The guy you talked about, this Hogeg guy, has nothing to do with Celsius.*

Far from the first or last time, Mashinsky was lying. As DBM would go on to prove, Hogeg had been an early advisor to Celsius, and the two had a tangled business history going back years. That's how it was in crypto: Fraudsters tended to move from project to project, sometimes concealing their participation, advising each other, investing at a discount, and hyping the latest coin offering. "This Hogeg guy" was actually an important part of Mashinsky's professional rise.

Building on his childhood interest in fraud, James was curious about deception, puzzles, and the human mind. He found himself attracted to medicine and psychiatry. He received a dual MD/PhD and then moved on to a psychiatry residency at a Michigan hospital. He liked talking with people about their problems and exploring the ways in which people fooled one another and themselves. Physically unassuming, with short brown hair and soft eyes, his relaxed attitude served as a mask for a clever, searching mind.

Crypto was in many ways a confidence game, based on promises of riches that for 99 percent of participants would never come true. It was, writ large, a fraud, not unlike the kinds of schemes that James had been fixated on since he was a child. The psychology of it—and why people who have been burned keep sidling up to the table, time after time—fascinated James. You could see so much of it playing out in public, on Twitter, Discord, YouTube, and other social apps, and in the livestreamed conferences and cable news appearances in which viewers were reminded that the promised crypto utopia, or simply the next big asset pump, was always just around the corner.

You could also see it on the blockchain. Because crypto transactions are publicly recorded on a shared ledger, it's possible to track movements of most tokens. You might not know who owns a particular wallet, but you can see the crypto tokens leaving that wallet—and perhaps they end up in a wallet that's familiar to you or to another online sleuth. Along the way, the crypto might pass between various exchanges, staking pools, DeFi protocols, and other crypto services. These waypoints can reveal something about a person's intentions, what kind of transactions are taking place, and where the money is headed. It's fun nerdy detective work, if you can understand it.

An industry trope has it that the blockchain is public, which means it's transparent, which helps suss out bad actors and secure transactions. But in practice, it's not so simple. These monetary networks are not as transparent as one might be led to believe. Some tokens are more private than others; there are ways to mask transactions or swap out "dirty crypto" for "clean crypto" via what's known as a *mixer*. (Mixers became a target of the Treasury Department's Office of Foreign Assets Control, which sanctioned Tornado Cash for facilitating money laundering.) There are also what are known as *over-the-counter*, or OTC, trades, which might be as simple as me giving my private key to another person, who then gives me cash or some other asset. The crypto hasn't "moved," but the other party now has my private key, which gives them control over the crypto. Maybe I had to take a haircut—my $10 million worth of Bitcoin might be worth only $4 million in USD at an OTC desk. But I've been able to convert crypto into something else without leaving much of a trail, if any. OTC transactions take place all the time in mainstream finance, and they're not inherently suspect, but you can see why they might be a favored tool of financial outlaws.

What you see on the blockchain is only part of the story, but it is an important part. And plenty of crypto fraudsters have been lazy enough with their operations security that they are regularly tracked and unmasked (or doxed) by online sleuths, who are also known as *on-chain investigators*. Some of them work for respected security firms and have access to powerful analytic programs and deep stores of data. Others are anonymous and self-taught and rely on free online services like Etherscan, a blockchain explorer tool, but they can be just as consequential in exposing skullduggery, especially when the relevant authorities and the financial and tech press aren't doing their jobs. James fell into this latter category. A self-taught on-chain sleuth, he used publicly available data and open-source tools to do what others had failed to do before him: Follow the money.

And he did. Sensing blood in the water with Celsius, Dr. Block's investigations intensified.

He started mapping Mashinsky's crypto wallets and those of his wife, Krissy Mashinsky. James discovered a range of sketchy behavior, much of it centering on hyping the CEL token so that the Mashinskys could cash out as the price rose. Between just March and August 2021, James estimated, the Mashinskys cashed out for at least $40 million—and perhaps much more. But Mashinsky had been careless, rarely obscuring his tracks. James was able to discover Mashinsky-controlled wallets that had profited from several ICO scams run by former Mashinsky business associates. In one instance, James used Mashinsky's Twitter profile picture to track down another of his many wallets. The profile picture was an NFT—a stylized image of Mashinsky in the form of a Roman bust. The picture was linked to the wallet that owned it. It was startlingly simple, just clicking on a profile photo to find one of Mashinsky's wallets, but no one had bothered to look. The NFT wallet, it turned out, had sold more than six million CEL tokens, for which Mashinsky received about $12 million worth of USDC stablecoins.

It was clear that, besides being a Ponzi scheme run by some truly unimpressive operators, Celsius was a money machine for the Mashinskys. Whatever crypto rewards Mashinsky may have been returning to his customers, he was also profiting himself.

Mashinsky and the Celsius team didn't handle James's findings with much equanimity. Neither did Mashinsky's wife, Krissy, a sort-of influencer whose clothing company handled all of Celsius's merch orders. A relentless defender of her husband and Celsius, Krissy liked to do battle on Twitter with activist Celsius investors.

Dirty Bubble Media was vilified by die-hard Celsius fans—and by other members of crypto-dom who were suspicious of a pseudonymous account offering some potential bad news. At the time, before many industry players turned on one another, there was a collective omertà against bad-mouthing competitors. Every "project" had its merits and success was shared—a rising tide lifts all Ponzis, perhaps. Talking about systemic issues or manipulated asset prices might ruin everyone's good time. DBM was different: He was saying that key industry players were committing fraud, with potential implications for everyone investing in crypto. In the eyes of industry and desperate gamblers, DBM had committed a mortal sin: He hadn't reported the truth or asked hard questions; he was spreading what crypto bros liked to dismiss as FUD—*fear, uncertainty, and doubt.*

Celsius executives began seeing James and other online critics as adversaries endangering their business. Months after his company filed for bankruptcy, Mashinsky was still playing victim, blaming everyone from Sam Bankman-Fried to crypto media that "publish[ed] false and misleading stories about Celsius and almost never covered any positive news." The cognitive dissonance was bewildering: What was there positive to say about a Ponzi scheme?

James tried to keep himself anonymous online. Dirty Bubble Media provided a shield, a barrier between his day-to-day life and that of his investigator-journalist persona. In his writing, he sometimes used the more inclusive *we*, referring to DBM as a publication. It didn't hurt to be cautious. People could be hysterical and over-the-top on Twitter, and he could be seen as threatening some people's investments.

His putative anonymity didn't mean that people, some unknown adversary perhaps, couldn't mess with him and make his life difficult. The first indication something was wrong came when James received an email confirming that his Twitter password had been changed. That set off an internal alarm: He hadn't changed his password, but someone had, bypassing James's two-factor authentication in the process. His Twitter account was hacked. And he happened to have some important (private) communications there with sources.

Having kneecapped his Twitter presence, someone came for his Substack account, where he published articles about Celsius, the murky economics of celebrity NFTs, and other crypto malfeasance. Substack suspended his blog, apparently based on some copyright takedown notices that he wasn't alerted to until they had already been processed. As he tried to figure out a way to get his first Twitter account back, he started another. That, too, got hacked. He wondered if his devices were compromised.

In his online sleuthing, James had made more than one enemy. He published articles about celebrity NFTs (and the sketchy financing behind them), people pouring absurd amounts of crypto into digital assets (which always raised the specter of money laundering), and of course, the delightful characters at Celsius. Any of them could be behind this.

There were some clues. After he finally heard back from Substack, James learned that the DMCA takedown notices came from an Indian company named Mevrex. It appeared to be some sort of low-rent content-and-PR shop. We reached out to them but never heard back. Soon, James discovered that Chain.com, a murky startup with a lot of crypto but seemingly only one employee, may have been behind it. James and Jacob had been looking into Chain, and James wrote a piece about the CEO's extravagant purchases of multimillion-dollar NFTs. It turned out that after James published his Dirty Bubble Media article about Chain, someone had created similar, competing articles that, while containing much of the same content, painted Chain in a more positive light. Whoever was behind this had also done something clever with this copycat-ish content. Through Mevrex, their apparent cut-out, they submitted DMCA takedown notices claiming that James violated their copyright. As James and Jacob painstakingly explained to Substack's PR, it was quite the opposite. Jacob confronted Chain's CEO via Telegram. He denied ever having heard of Mevrex or hiring them. Eventually, after a fair amount of badgering and pleading with communications people at the respective companies, James's Twitter and Substack accounts were restored.

As the crypto market started to slide in the spring of 2022, Celsius ran out of runway. The company paused withdrawals on June 13. A month later it filed for bankruptcy. The company's collapse wasn't just a disaster for Celsius and its investors. Hundreds of thousands of everyday people, retail traders, had been led to believe that their money was safe. Some might have been desperate or greedy or willfully ignored signs of trouble, but all were victims. Testimonials poured in, with heartbreaking stories of people who couldn't retrieve their funds to pay essential bills, cover medical care, or afford their kid's tuition. Beyond the sense of having been robbed, some of these aggrieved customers blamed themselves or fell into depression. Scams always appear more obvious in retrospect.

Journalists failed the public on this one. Anyone could have dug a bit into Mashinsky's background and realized that he had made a career out of inflating his accomplishments. James found that and more—that Mashinsky was connected, through business and financial relationships, with alleged Israeli money launderers and crypto scammers.

"I'm just a random guy, screwing around in my spare time," said James, speaking about crypto media being asleep at the wheel. "You could have found all of this and more in like five minutes."

That's partly what motivated James. "I got kind of frustrated when people weren't paying attention," he said. "This is a major red flag that, like, anyone who's investing should be seriously concerned about, and nobody cares, right?"

Practically every claim about Mashinsky's glittering résumé was inflated, it turned out. He was not nearly the technological trailblazer he had presented himself as. And some of his past companies relied on associations with dubious, even criminal characters, especially in Israel, a center for fintech innovation—and money laundering and fraud. Subsequent reporting by the *Times of Israel* filled in essential details, helping to form a dark picture of the professional criminal network with ties to Celsius.

In many ways, Celsius was a simple Ponzi. It promised payouts that it couldn't sustain via the gains from its own investments and financial jiujitsu, so it used money from new depositors to pay out previous ones. Textbook case. Along the way, the company's executives lied about their solvency and investment practices, cashed out for themselves—including when Celsius was facing bankruptcy—encouraged customers to keep pouring in money to a failing scheme, and made any number of strikingly reckless decisions. They also treated their critics— some of them simply well-meaning customers who wanted to know how their assets were being handled—with utter derision. Even at the time, the contempt and anger toward people asking good-faith questions of the company, based on solid evidence, had an air of projection. Every time Mashinsky accused his evil critics of spreading FUD, I assumed that DBM was probably on the right track. The proof was often in the block-chain data, waiting to be interpreted.

Beyond its embrace of Ponzinomics, Celsius was built on a rickety foundation of fabulist projections and false promises. That extended to how Celsius conducted its trading. In the eyes of the public, Celsius took advantage of price movements across exchanges while also leveraging various decentralized trading protocols to turn a bunch of fake digital money into more fake digital money. Their strategy was supposed to be hedged against risk, based on solid trading practices, and reliant on the expertise of longtime traders and asset managers. Celsius turned out to be none of that. In late 2021 and in 2022, in the company's waning days of solvency, Mashinsky himself was directing company trades—often to disastrous effect, leading to millions of dollars in losses. In one case, he refused an offer to cash out his company's position in Grayscale Bitcoin Trust (GBTC), a Bitcoin-based financial product. According to reporting from the *Financial Times*, when Mashinsky eventually approved the deal six months later, Celsius lost more than $100 million on its investment.

Celsius's deceptions helped facilitate broader fraud in the crypto markets. In late 2020, Celsius came to a verbal agreement with a small crypto trading firm named KeyFi. Run by a man named Jason Stone, KeyFi ostensibly made big returns by finding overlooked opportunities in decentralized finance. Celsius gave KeyFi and Stone as much as $2 billion worth of crypto and digital assets like NFTs—initially with no written agreement and no lawyerly intermediaries. Celsius expected him to trade on their behalf, generating the kind of large, market-beating returns that Celsius's customers had been promised.

By collaborating, Celsius was able to tap a supposedly cutting-edge trading outfit while KeyFi could reap fees from a major client. According to a lawsuit filed by KeyFi, Celsius pumped the price of the CEL token, which helped keep the whole scheme solvent. But there was more at stake in the arrangement. Stone also maintained an online crypto trading persona known as 0xb1, named after the main wallet holding "his" crypto. Because of his massive holdings, 0xb1 developed a reputation as a major crypto whale, with a valuable NFT collection and savvy market instincts. On Twitter, where he has more than 100,000 followers, he established himself as a well-known crypto shitposter—memes, trash talk, industry predictions, you get the idea—knee-deep in crypto riches.

As the crypto markets soared in the fall of 2021, 0xb1 leveraged his growing portfolio—which is to say, Celsius's portfolio, which he secretly helped manage—and his online fame into a contract with Creative Artists Agency.

CAA is arguably the most powerful talent agency in Hollywood and an investor in OpenSea and other crypto companies. According to a statement from the agency, 0xb1 was going to advise CAA clients on web3 opportunities and would work with the firm on monetizing his own NFT collection. On the surface, it sounded a little silly, but it actually spoke to powerful financial interests—Hollywood talent agencies, digital asset exchanges, top crypto traders, influencers, and celebrities—combining to help steer the markets in their favor. In the nexus of all this self-dealing was 0xb1, the guy whose fortune was based on a fiction. The actual crypto underwriting his supposedly market-leading NFT collection came from Celsius, which was riven with deceptive practices and outright fraud.

The relationship between KeyFi and Celsius eventually fell apart, as one might expect in an industry built on unscrupulous practices and verbal agreements. KeyFi sued Celsius, claiming the company committed fraud—the lawsuit called the whole thing a Ponzi scheme—and failed to pay him for $838 million in profits he allegedly generated. Celsius decided to countersue, arguing that Stone had pocketed millions of dollars' worth of crypto, used Celsius funds to buy his own NFTs, and made private investments with Celsius assets. It's possible both sides were right. Neither side exhibited much moral authority.

In the largely accountability-free world of crypto, it seemed no one really cared—besides perhaps the hundreds of thousands of customers who had been robbed—about Celsius's deceptions. While Mashinsky had developed a reputation as a huckster, Celsius was still deeply enmeshed in relationships with key companies like Tether. As the company stumbled into bankruptcy, Sam Bankman-Fried was reportedly considering picking over its corpse, gobbling up its depreciated assets. It wasn't just the crypto vultures pursuing their self-interest. The victim pool was large, and not everyone agreed about how or if they could get their money back—or even what had happened. Competing factions appeared. Lawyers flocked in, some seemingly more on the side of angels than others. There were arguments and accusations and quixotic recovery plans—much of it debated in public on Twitter and Telegram and in bankruptcy court. Whatever community Celsius might have nurtured had been torn asunder.

According to people involved in one Telegram group, which contained nearly a thousand victimized customers, about a quarter of the group members exhibited some form of denial. If they didn't think that Mashinsky had been unfairly maligned, then they still thought that the company might turn around or that there was more than a distant chance of getting their money back. They hadn't given up on the dream of accumulating huge sums by just parking digital currencies in an account, and they certainly hadn't given up on Celsius. Asked if some of this might have been sock puppets from Celsius insiders or loyalists—that kind of digital skullduggery isn't unknown in crypto—the Celsius customers said no. These people seemed to really believe that this bankrupt company, built on Ponzinomics by unscrupulous operators already up to their eyes in litigation, could all be turned around. The capacity for rationalization was astonishing and sad in equal measure. It seemed like one last dagger in the ribs from a scammer: Not only did he steal their money, he made such a psychic impression on them that they still thought there was a chance of getting their crypto back. Some refused to admit that they had been robbed. That they had been fooled.

While he became less voluble on Twitter, Mashinsky still issued occasional tweets or popped up in a Twitter Space, sometimes as a listener, just one icon among many others in the audience. The possibility of criminal action still loomed.

His wife, Krissy Mashinsky, became a Twitter warrior, challenging any critics to battle with febrile, emoji-laden tweets. Sometimes it was hard to know what she was talking about. (After I asked a question about her business interests, she bizarrely tried to set me up on a date with a spurned Celsius customer.) Krissy was unrepentant. Never apologize, never explain. Stick to the story. Ignore any inconsistencies and just move on to the next thing. Somehow, Celsius had done no wrong. It was a victim of unseen forces— shadowy hedge funds, pseudonymous online investigators, Sam Bankman-Fried himself—or was, weirdly, just misunderstood. While extolling Celsius's innocence, Krissy Mashinsky simultaneously marketed a line of T-shirts, produced by her apparel company, with the bizarre mantra "Unbankrupt Yourself." Was this all a joke to her? She continued to fight her Twitter battles and rally the last loyalists going down with the ship.

Just because Celsius was bankrupt didn't mean that the grift was over. Anything can be monetized, including a campaign to convince fraud victims that they haven't really been defrauded. And there's always another scheme to try, a Hail Mary that just might fix everything—if only the authorities and those damn greedy creditors would get out of the way. For Celsius, it was a plan with the codename Kelvin. Its details don't matter; it lasted a matter of days, never making it off the drawing board. But it was a typical example of crypto hubris—like Do Kwon launching Terra 2.0 just weeks after the collapse of his $50 billion Ponzi scheme devastated so many retail traders. It was ridiculous to think that anyone could rescue Celsius, so of course Mashinsky thought he was the one to do it.

Despite promising to go down fighting, Mashinsky finally resigned as Celsius's CEO on September 27, 2022. "I will continue to maintain my focus on working to help the community unite behind a plan that will provide the best outcome for all creditors," he said in an announcement. Mashinsky continued his denials, claiming he acted in the community's best interests. His former customers felt otherwise, with many of them expressing, in ever-more colorful terms, their wish to see him incarcerated for his crimes.

As for James Block, who eventually revealed his name after journalists began peppering him with requests for tips and commentary, he was offered a job by a hedge fund shorting crypto. He decided to stick to medicine. He became a key source for crypto observers, and was a hero to some Celsius victims. He had revealed to them both the scale of the fraud and the utter banality of its operation. It was a bitter medicine that they needed to take. With his investigative reporting, Dirty Bubble Media "saved countless people who did get their funds out" before the company paused withdrawals, said a Celsius borrower involved in litigation against the company. "Imagine if the scam had gotten bigger, how much worse it would have been."

Playing out across Twitter and crypto media, Celsius devolved into farce, filled with accusations and counter-accusations and improbable rescue plans led by dubious characters. I became acquainted with the term *launchpad scammer*—someone who uses a disaster like the Celsius bankruptcy to elevate their own profile and use their new influencer status within the community to peddle their own scams. There was no shortage of launchpad scammers picking through the Celsius wreckage.

As always, there was one overriding question: Where did the money go? Celsius's executives managed to cash out at multiple points, moving funds that might never be recovered (much less turned back into more useful dollars). At one point, at least forty state regulators were investigating Celsius, along with the federal authorities. But like blockchain transactions, much of the damage was irreversible.

Even the victims were at war with one another. During the summer and fall of 2022, as some investors shorted the price of CEL tokens—seemingly not a bad bet when it came to a bankrupt company—others pushed back. Adopting a "short squeeze" strategy, some Celsius influencers and community members encouraged victimized investors to fight back against industry heavyweights and Celsius itself by buying more CEL tokens, thereby pushing up the price and causing losses for the short sellers. Some investors claimed that the short squeeze plan was being pushed by big CEL holders looking to dump their own tokens on the community. These warnings were generally ignored. Like doomed soldiers charging at the Somme, there were periodic short squeeze pushes that led nowhere—except to more losses and charges of market manipulation. Like many failed meme stock pushes, short squeezers weren't sticking it to the man, and they never would, as long as the game was rigged.

For Celsius and its hundreds of thousands of community members, there was no easy ending. The litigation would likely go on for years. (As always, congrats to the lawyers.) James sounded the alarm on Celsius, but few wanted to listen. Like Bernie Madoff's scam, Celsius collapsed when its internal contradictions and a number of risky decisions collided with a crashing market.

"I didn't bring it down, but I sped it up," said James, expressing some pride that he at least convinced some people to get their money out before it was too late.

James spent months studying Celsius, but it was never just about one company or its slapstick CEO. It was about fraud and deceit and solving a puzzle to reveal how people had been wronged. It was also an opportunity to show that there wasn't just one Celsius in crypto. The industry was filled with other shady actors. Celsius wasn't an outlier; it was an exemplar of how crypto operated. James sensed that, first by instinct and later confirmed through patient investigation.

I shouldn't have been surprised when James played a key role in an even more dramatic crypto crash: that of Sam Bankman-Fried and his company FTX. Even so, I still was shocked at what unfolded. Like so much in crypto, the situation was weirdly dramatic, incredibly volatile, and also very, very stupid.

CHAPTER 12

CHAPTER 11

"Capitalism without bankruptcy is like Christianity without hell." —Frank Borman

VER THE COURSE of the summer of 2022, things got squirrely with Sam Bankman-Fried's empire. On July 20, the day of my interview with Sam, Brett Harrison, president of FTX US, claimed in a Twitter thread that "direct deposits from employers to FTX US are stored in individually FDIC-insured bank accounts in the users' names" and "stocks are held in FDIC-insured and SIPC [Securities Investor Protection Corporation]-insured brokerage accounts." These statements were confusing, if not outright deceptive. Accounts on FTX US were of course *not* FDIC-insured, as FTX US is not a licensed US bank but rather a money services business, which doesn't offer customers the same protections. Only the bank accounts from which investors transferred their funds to FTX US were FDIC-insured, not their accounts on the exchange. Implying to retail traders that they would be covered by FDIC insurance was incorrect, and potentially dangerous, as the crypto markets continued their months-long decline and some of FTX's competitors and partners had already declared bankruptcy.

On August 18, the FDIC issued a cease-and-desist order claiming FTX US "made false and misleading statements, directly or by implication, concerning FTX US's deposit insurance status." The FDIC order forced FTX

to back down and delete the tweets. But then Sam Bankman-Fried took to Twitter to play damage control, and in a since-deleted Tweet, claimed to "apologize if anyone misinterpreted" FTX's previous statements. I was pissed, and responded to him, producing a testy back-and-forth. After some jousting, including another tweet he would later delete, Sam said, "I think our statement was accurate but also could have been misinterpreted, and that it would have made sense for us to have been clearer than we were to make sure that it was interpreted correctly."

Like so many interactions in crypto, it was a messy and unsatisfying affair. However, it did reinforce one thing: Sam was desperate to stage-manage his public image. The dark arts of PR were part of any actor's Hollywood education, and Sam clearly needed more lessons.

Sam decided the conversation wasn't over: He slid into my DMs. Beginning with "TOTALLY OFF THE RECORD" in all caps—going off the record is done by mutual agreement, and I never agreed—he went into a long, wonkish explanation of how FTX had essentially botched some messaging but never did anything malicious. Eventually, he said, customer accounts would qualify for FDIC insurance, but there was legalese to work out, terms of service to revise, negotiations with regulators. "Basically we think our case here was good but not a slam dunk, and it's a fool's errand to get into a public fight with a regulator, *especially* if your case isn't a slam dunk."

I told him, by implying accounts were FDIC insured, he was heaping more risk on customers. "It was dumb to tweet anything here," he admitted.

"I'm glad we can talk honestly," I said. "Very important."

He reacted with a heart emoji.

For a second I allowed myself to consider that perhaps some progress toward accountability in crypto had been made. But then . . .

The day after agreeing with me that FTX had made a mistake, Sam switched registers—"just total honesty here from me"—and warned me that he wouldn't be able to "take some of what you say seriously" as long as I appeared, at least in his eyes, to be "100% against crypto." Negativity was understandable, he said, "but 100% can't be the right amount."

Chapter 11

It was a comment I'd heard from others but never someone in a position like Sam's. It seemed borderline desperate to me. Why did he care what some actor moonlighting as a reporter thought? Regardless, I didn't forsake my principles before and I sure as hell wasn't going to for Sam Bankman-Fried. Also, I didn't need to. He was already DMing me. In my position—just trying to understand what is going on here—it was easy to be direct and honest. Sam was the one going from a public Twitter argument to some subtle private message coercion, tying himself in knots.

"All I'm looking for is the truth Sam," I said. "I'm open to whatever that is. Fwiw, I don't think you are a bad guy, and nothing (and no one) is all bad or all good. I think we can agree on that?" On the advice of my friend and ex-FBI agent Jim Harris, I wanted to draw a clear line in the sand when it came to Sam's attempt to coerce me, while maintaining an outwardly sympathetic posture to keep the lines of communication open between us. He seemed like he wanted to talk, and I was there to listen.

He reacted with another heart emoji, and then, simply: "100%."

On August 25, Sam Trabucco, co-CEO of Alameda Research, resigned. He said he wanted to spend more time with his boat, *Soak My Deck*. Typical for crypto: Even their puns sucked. "Why are journalists so excited to make my stepping down about something other than a desire to go fast over the nice water?" asked Trabucco on Twitter—the kind of innocent "who me?" tweet that catalyzed even more speculation that something was brewing.

On September 27, Brett Harrison, author of the controversial tweets, stepped down. It was a little over a month since his public drubbing by the FDIC. With top executives leaving, it seemed like something ominous was on the horizon, or perhaps was already playing out behind the scenes. The public explanation—that rich young execs were amicably departing a top crypto firm to seek new opportunities—seemed hard to believe.

Over Twitter DM, Sam spoke darkly to me of a coming conflict dividing the industry. Binance was pushing its customers to convert their stablecoins into BUSD, Binance's own dollar-pegged token. "It's the beginnings of the second great stablecoin war," he messaged me on September 5. "All the stables are gearing up for it. Taking this as a declaration of war."

Sam said that battle lines were being drawn, and Binance was trying to take him down. Binance had been one of FTX's first investors and an industry ally—while crypto was booming, at least. Now, amid mass bankruptcies and a wider economic downturn, something fundamental had changed. Sam seemed genuinely nervous. What was going on?

Alongside his colleague at FTX Ryan Salame, Sam started publicly shit-talking Binance's Changpeng Zhao. The two yukked it up over Twitter. "Been an absolute pleasure watching @cz_binance have the extremely difficult but transformative debates on twitter this past week to ensure the crypto industry moves forward in the best possible way," wrote Salame on October 29.

"Excited to see him repping the industry in DC going forward," responded SBF. "[U]h, he is allowed to go to DC, right?" It was an extremely bold move, even by crypto standards. Was Sam bragging about his government connections, which kept him safe and put Changpeng Zhao and Binance under the microscope?

The bombshell came on November 2. CoinDesk, an online crypto publication, published an article about Alameda's balance sheet, which was, officially speaking, a disaster: illiquid shitcoins, assets marked up far beyond their actual value, huge loans, sunk investments. Alameda was in precarious shape, it turned out, and it depended on a whole lot of FTT, the token created by FTX, whose value was inflated to make the company's financial position look stronger than it was. FTT was also highly illiquid—almost no one traded it, and most of it seemed to be held by Alameda/FTX.

Two days later, our friend Dirty Bubble Media, aka James Block, who helped expose the Celsius fraud, published an ominously titled post, "Is Alameda Research Insolvent?" He had gotten ahold of the Alameda balance sheet before it leaked and had time to analyze it. A few days earlier, the prospect of Alameda's collapse seemed like an absurd possibility. Alameda was supposed to be a cutting-edge trading firm, hunting everyone else's positions and using their FTX connections and market-maker status to reap huge profits. Staffed by brilliant young quants, Alameda was, according to industry rumor, subsidizing the FTX empire, making it possible for SBF to shower politicians and celebrities with money and buy the company's legitimacy. While my interview with SBF had raised many red flags—tales of his supposed genius were clearly a marketing invention—I had at least assumed that his colleagues at Alameda knew what they were doing. Even their competitors spoke of them with grudging respect, mixed with resentment.

James summed up the situation, emphasizing the role of the company's FTT token: "It's almost as if SBF found a way to hack the financial system, printing billions of dollars out of thin air against which he was able to borrow massive sums from unknown counterparties. Almost as if he discovered a financial perpetual motion machine."

That financial perpetual motion machine looked a lot like the Celsius "flywheel" concept that James had previously investigated, and that Professor Hilary Allen had warned about in February of that year. Create a token out of nothing; pump its value; put it on your balance sheet (look, you're rich!); use that loaded balance sheet to raise real dollars in investment capital; then take those dollars and buy some companies, some politicians, and naming rights to a sports stadium. Repeat the cycle—keep the flywheel spinning—until it all falls apart. Eventually it does. It has to. Alameda had enormous assets on paper, but they were mostly illiquid "assets" that couldn't be sold for real money, because no one wanted them.

Two days later, on November 6, Binance CEO CZ, who had "liked" DBM's post on the Alameda/FTX situation on Twitter, saw an opportunity to knock off an upstart rival. On Twitter, he gently announced that "due to recent revelations," Binance would liquidate any remaining FTT tokens they owned, but would "try to do so in a way that minimizes market impact," selling their lot of FTT over a period of months. Binance, which was an early investor in FTX, owned more than $500 million worth of FTT that they received when they sold their equity stake back to Alameda in 2021. At the time, FTX was eager to divest itself of its association with Binance, but in typical crypto fashion, the company didn't have enough fiat to buy out its investor. So it substituted crypto for cash, including a chunk of its own FTT token. That's the benefit of printing your own money. (The other asset FTX used to buy out Binance was more than $1 billion worth of BUSD, Binance's stablecoin.)

Now CZ was announcing his intent to sell a major quantity of an illiquid shitcoin, upon which FTX/Alameda's solvency happened to depend. The move would inevitably tank the coin's price, creating a loss for CZ and Binance, but it would be money well spent. Surely CZ knew that his announcement alone could provoke a bank run on FTX. Sam had come for CZ on Twitter, lording his citizenship and political connections over the non-American. But now CZ saw a way to take his biggest rival out. The way you start a bank run isn't by running into the bank screaming at the top of your lungs that it's insolvent. Rather, a major investor, with considerable capital and reputational weight to throw around, calmly expresses "concerns," and announces a slow exit. Other institutional players and customers, already primed by a summer of crypto company bankruptcies, rush to follow. When dealing with an insolvent company, it's wise to remember the words of Ricky Bobby in *Talledega Nights*: "If you ain't first, you're last." Voilà, bank run.

CZ played his hand well. More than a year earlier, SBF basically handed his rival the means to one day destroy him. Maybe Sam never expected CZ to sell the FTT or thought that he would do so quietly, not attracting market attention. Maybe he really believed his own hype that FTX was on a parabolic path to impossible wealth. But down here on planet Earth, Binance was still far bigger than FTX and ostensibly better capitalized. It could afford to wait. And it could afford to take a loss if it meant taking down a reckless competitor who claimed his crypto empire would one day supplant Goldman Sachs.

All hell broke loose as FTT began to slide in price. Sam and his lieutenants desperately tried to right the ship. Caroline Ellison, the CEO of Alameda Research, tweeted publicly at CZ, offering to buy all of his FTT for twenty-two dollars per token. It was a bizarre way to do business, especially when failure might mean existential peril, but for the umpteenth time I had to tell myself, *That's crypto.* It also might have been a troll, a reference to when Sam once mocked a retail trader and said he'd buy all the Solana he had, before telling the guy to fuck off. Was Caroline telling CZ to sell her his tokens and fuck off?

It didn't work. "I think we will stay in the free market," CZ wrote on Twitter. He added that his company still held a sizable amount of LUNA, which was now worthless, and included a laughing-crying emoji. Huge losses on scam tokens were apparently just part of doing business for billionaire exchange CEOs.

On the day of the midterm elections, in what seemed like the most dramatic period in crypto's short but tumultuous history, the situation shifted suddenly again. FTX announced that it was selling itself, at a fire-sale price, to Binance. Or at least, the two had signed a nonbinding "letter of intent" for such a transaction. Sam was out of money and out of options. He capitulated. CZ had won.

The letter of intent aspect was elided in a lot of news reports and tweets, and the headline became, "Binance is buying FTX." But a nonbinding letter of intent is not a commitment to do anything. CZ could back out after performing the requisite due diligence, and that is exactly what he did only twelve hours later. After reportedly examining FTX's books, CZ scotched the deal. Sorry, he told Sam, but the situation wasn't salvageable. FTX was on its own, financially adrift, facing bankruptcy. It was another cunning move by CZ. If before he had stabbed Sam in the ribs, now he was removing the knife and letting him bleed out.

At four thirty AM on November 11, under pressure from lawyers, creditors, and colleagues, Sam signed over control of FTX and more than one hundred associated companies. He resigned as CEO, handing over the company to John J. Ray III. Ray was a professional corporate cleanup artist who was brought in to manage Enron after its collapse. Twenty years later, the guy who supervised bankruptcy proceedings on behalf of one of the most spectacular frauds in corporate history declared that FTX was even worse. "Never in my career have I seen such a complete failure of corporate controls and such a complete absence of trustworthy financial information as occurred here," Ray said. He dryly noted that one of FTX's auditors, Prager Metis, boasted on its website that they were the "first-ever CPA firm to officially open its Metaverse headquarters in the metaverse platform Decentraland."

Bankruptcy filings helped fill in the picture. FTX was a shitshow. Billions had been diverted from FTX customer deposits to help bail out Alameda, only for the situation to worsen. The company had spent lavishly on celebrities, politicians, real estate, and personal loans to executives. No one knew where all the money went—especially after some $372 million in crypto flowed out of company wallets in a mysterious "hack" just hours after the bankruptcy filing. (At the time of this writing it's still unclear who was responsible, but the DOJ is investigating.) There was no risk management practice and no real accounting system—QuickBooks and Excel don't quite cut it for a multibillion-dollar firm. There wasn't even a complete roster of company employees. (Sam later disputed many of these details.)

The myth of Alameda's trading prowess and Sam's financial genius evaporated in an instant. It turned out Alameda was more of a sloppily run hedge fund than what it was often marketed as: a risk-neutral firm primarily providing market making services. Alameda had been making wild bets, and apparently it wasn't even very good at it. According to bankruptcy filings, FTX/Alameda lost $3.7 billion *before* 2022. Quite impressive to lose that much in a bull market!

How did Sam's seemingly massively profitable operation find itself so deeply in the hole? There were various theories, but the most compelling one was that it had never really been very profitable to begin with. Recall that the initial focus of Alameda Research was exploiting the Kimchi Premium, the difference in the price of Bitcoin in Korea and other Asian markets versus the United States. As lore would have it, Alameda made a killing off a simple arbitrage trade. But now others disputed that story, claiming it to be mostly a myth. In an online discussion thread on the Effective Altruism Forum, a former colleague of Sam's, Naia Bouscal, remembered it differently: "My recollection is that we made something like 10–30 million dollars," but "pretty much all of that profit had been lost to a series of bad trades and mismanagement of assets." However, Bouscal left in April 2018, and offered this disclaimer: "All of this is purely from memory," and "it could be substantially wrong in the details."

Regardless, the Kimchi Premium dried up in 2018, when South Korean authorities signaled a crackdown on cryptocurrency trading was imminent. Sam and his gang needed to find a new way to make money. The operation moved to Hong Kong, and FTX was born the following year. Via customer deposits on FTX, Sam received incoming cash to fund his operations, and Alameda Research began providing market making services on the exchange, effectively serving as a middleman between buyers and sellers. Market making can be a profitable business, but it is an extremely competitive one. According to sources cited by *Forbes*, there was suspicion among other traders that by the time crypto started its next bull run in 2020, Alameda was being beaten at its own game by other high-frequency trading firms like Jump Trading. It needed a new way to make money, so it started placing riskier bets. The head of Alameda, Caroline Ellison, tweeted in March 2021 that instead of "wasting time trying to trade back and forth for a few points of edge . . . the way to really make money is to figure out when the market is going to go up and get balls long before that." Had Alameda simply bet wrong, thinking the market would continue to explode higher, when in fact it would crash just a few months later?

In retrospect, this sort of extreme risk-taking shouldn't have come as much of a surprise. Sam Trabucco, the former cohead of Alameda, previously claimed in a Twitter thread from January 2021 that he picked up his trading strategies from those he employed at the poker and blackjack tables, even quasi-bragging about his card-counting skills. He "may or may not be banned from 3 casinos." Similarly, Caroline Ellison, the then co-CEO of Alameda, said in a podcast earlier in 2022 that "being comfortable with risk is very important." She said she could pull off her job at Alameda without her degree from Stanford: "You use very little math. You use a lot of elementary school math." In 2021, Sam explained to a podcaster how he chose the name Alameda Research to obscure the company's true nature from regulators: "If we named our company, like, Shitcoin Day Traders Inc., they'd probably just reject us. But, I mean, no one doesn't like research."

Reporting in the *New York Times* shed further light on how the speculation could easily have gotten out of control. By creating the FTT token, and incentivizing FTX customers to trade it by offering them discounts to do so, Sam and his cohorts inflated the value of FTT and other digital "assets" on Alameda's balance sheet. With Alameda serving as a market maker for the FTT token on FTX, the company was able to manipulate the price higher, giving off the appearance of profitability to outside investors. The company used the purported value of FTT as collateral to take out huge loans and then raised $2 billion from venture capital firms, allowing it to gamble with the real money it had gotten from both VCs and retail investors on FTX via the fake money (FTT) created out of thin air. The leverage employed became immense, and eventually it all collapsed in spectacular fashion as the crypto markets turned south and investors wanted their real money back.

At least $8 billion in FTX customer funds were used to bail out losses incurred from Alameda Research's wild speculation. Yet even committing that blatant act of fraud—commingling funds is illegal—was not enough to plug the hole, as Alameda had taken on even more reckless trading positions in 2022 that only deepened the firm's losses. According to Ellison, she and Sam, along with executives Gary Wang and Nishad Singh, discussed the shortfall and agreed to use customer funds to cover it. Sam denied this.

Where did the money go? According to the bankruptcy filings, Alameda loaned some $4.1 billion to "related parties." Sam loaned himself $1 billion from Alameda Research, a company he owned 90 percent of. Alameda also lent $2.3 billion to Paper Bird Inc. and Euclid Way Ltd., entities he controlled, as well as $543 million to Nishad Singh, FTX's head of engineering. He loaned $55 million to Ryan Salame, who apparently used some of that money to buy five restaurants in Lenox, Massachusetts, near where he grew up. Sam, or someone at FTX, bought a $16.4 million mansion in his parents' name in the Bahamas. Sam, his parents, and senior FTX executives purchased nearly $121 million worth of real estate on the island nation.

Poring over obscure podcast interviews and Caroline Ellison's old Tumblr posts, citizen journalists looked for clues to the company's collapse. In one post that recirculated, Ellison described the benefits of continually doubling down on risky bets, forever. The lower bound was known—you could lose everything—but the upside was infinite. Why not go for infinite?

Past comments by Sam suddenly seemed ripe for reinterpretation. Earlier in the year, in an interview with Bloomberg, he had acknowledged that DeFi staking pools were Ponzi schemes. He didn't seem to care. In a Forbes interview in June, he had said that some exchanges were "secretly insolvent." When he spoke with me in July, he said of Justin Sun and his crypto empire: "The scam is not the blockchain, the scam is the token." Was everything a confession?

Other events surrounding the company gained new context. Remember the "meme round" of investment from October 2021, in which FTX raised $420.69 million from sixty-nine investors? Juvenile humor served to obscure a more unseemly truth. Bankruptcy filings revealed that $300 million of that haul went straight to Sam, who cashed out of a portion of his personal stake in the company. At the time, Sam insisted this was a partial reimbursement of the money he'd spent to buy out Binance, but now questions swirled as to the accuracy of that claim.

In the antic breakdown of SBF Inc, the media didn't quite distinguish itself. There were excellent investigations in the *Financial Times*, the *Wall Street Journal*, and the *New York Times*. But some of these publications also embarrassed themselves by publishing soft-touch pieces bemoaning the failure of Sam's philanthropic efforts, as if it was a shame that he could no longer "save the world," or wondering how a nice, well-pedigreed young man had broken bad. Bernie Madoff also donated to charity; the problem was the money was not his to donate. It came from his investors' pockets. Sam built on a philanthropic empire—one that seemed mostly about influence peddling, not selfless giving—by allegedly stealing other people's money. There was nothing virtuous or altruistic about that; there were no lost opportunities to mourn.

But there would be plenty of time for postmortems. SBF rose to power, however ephemerally, thanks to mindless boosterism from much of the establishment: financial news channels wooing potential advertisers and conference sponsors, naive newspaper journalists who swallowed the hype, celebrities and politicians on the take, and venture capitalists whose seed money helped put the whole machine into action. Many people had something to answer for. Whether any accountability would come was an open question.

Lest we mistakenly believe Bankman-Fried was the sole bad actor in crypto, our rogues' gallery of con men once again sprang to life. During a recording of the *UpOnly* crypto podcast on November 8, Martin Shkreli—the pharma bro who epitomized corporate greed and went to jail for securities fraud—advised Do Kwon, the fugitive Terra founder, to look on the bright side of life: "Jail is not that bad," Shkreli said. Around the same time, the 3AC guys beamed in from undisclosed locations to weigh in on the con, being as they were experts in the field.

As last month's scammers came in from the cold to yuk it up on social media, the post-SBF positioning became frantic—who was to blame, who supported him, who failed to warn the public. Even us crypto skeptics got our turn in the dock—apparently our frequently repeated claims that the entire industry was built on bad economics, bad incentives, and outright fraud wasn't enough. Sam was being cast as the industry's sole villain, the obvious-in-retrospect fraudster who would become crypto's sin-eater. Anyone who had met with him—even a journalist writing a book about fraud—was due for criticism. The problem was, nearly everyone in crypto was implicated: They had all done business with Sam.

The solution was for the scammers to say they had been scammed, too. SBF—through Alameda and FTX—was the real villain. He was responsible for everything from crashing Terra to blowing up 3AC. Regardless of the veracity of these statements, the tactic behind them was clear. It was classic cooling the mark, made possible by Sam's epic fall. Even Celsius CEO Alex Mashinsky tried to rehabilitate himself, bashing Alameda as market manipulators. On Twitter, he charged that Alameda used " 'God Mode' to short coins like CEL & avoid posting collateral." It was like the Spider-Man GIF, all the crypto bros pointing at each other, shouting, "No, *he's* the bad guy."

Like some family holiday gone wrong, it became a time for the airing of grievances. Apparently, everyone in the industry hated Sam. Some claimed to have held back for fear of angering a powerful industry player. Bitcoin maximalists blamed Sam for all their problems, rightfully pointing out SBF's cozy relationship with mainstream media publications, regulators, and lawmakers (some of which he gave large sums of money). But then, as maxis are wont to do, they wandered off into wackadoodle land, painting conspiracy theories that Sam was working with Biden to send money to Ukraine via crypto. The corruption was mostly in the open: We all saw Sam meeting regularly with lawmakers, posting selfies with CFTC commissioners, and becoming one of the Democratic Party's biggest public donors. Nothing secret about that.

The crypto lobby started blubbering like a grade school kid caught with their hand in the cookie jar. With no apparent sense of shame, they did an about-face on their desire to be regulated, even blaming Gary Gensler and the SEC for not doing more to avert this disaster. The hypocrisy would only deepen. A letter from March 16, 2022, resurfaced from a group of eight congressional representatives (the Blockchain Eight), in which they had pressured Gensler to lay off crypto investigations. The group was led by Representative Tom Emmer, a Republican from Minnesota, who, the year before, had responded to SBF's congressional testimony by saying, "Sounds like you are doing a lot to make sure there is no fraud or other manipulation. Thank you, Mr. Bankman-Fried, for helping us understand the extensive guardrails a cryptocurrency exchange like FTX has in place to ensure sound crypto spot markets for investors." Rep. Emmer was hopeful that further discussions might let them proceed with legislation that would allow for a "light touch" when it came to crypto regulation. The Blockchain Eight encapsulated so much of what was wrong when it came to Washington's cozy ties to the industry. Evenly divided between Democrats and Republicans, five of the eight members received campaign donations from FTX employees. The members of the group were Tom Emmer (R-MN), Warren Davidson (R-OH), Byron Donalds (R-FL), Ted Budd (R-NC), Darren Soto (D-FL), Jake Auchincloss (D-MA), Josh Gottheimer (D-NJ), and Ritchie Torres (D-NY). The National Republican Congressional Committee, led by Emmer, got $5.5 million from FTX and its associates, helping them secure the majority in the House.

In September, crypto booster Senator Pat Toomey appeared on the *Odd Lots* podcast to bemoan regulators' "paternalistic" approach to crypto.

The senator reiterated his deep commitment to respecting the choices of American consumers, believing them to be intelligent enough to make their own decisions. A few months later, he found new talking points, issuing a half-assed mea culpa regarding Sam/FTX: "I bought the story. I bought the hype. I was impressed."

While he respected the smarts of the average American investor, the Senator himself had been too dumb to realize that crypto's figurehead might not be a brilliant visionary but rather an epic fraudster. Of course, Toomey still spoke as if Sam Bankman-Fried was the lone bad actor in crypto, and he wanted to push forward with legislation favorable to the industry before he retired in January. Tick tock, Senator. Meanwhile on the Democratic side, Senator Kirsten Gillibrand of New York responded to the revelation of the massive fraud inside crypto by hiring a former general counsel of exchange Coinbase as her new counsel for finance. The revolving door between crypto and D.C. never stopped spinning.

With the crypto industry in a tailspin, finance, media, and big tech threw themselves into a tizzy, bemoaning the corruption of a supposedly good idea. It called to mind *Casablanca*: "I'm shocked, shocked to find that gambling is going on here." You guys helped build the casino! Suddenly, establishment figures, including VCs deeply invested in the crypto economy, started bragging about how they never fell for SBF's magic.

Terry Duffy, who ran the CME group, the world's largest financial derivatives exchange, attempted a victory lap, claiming he alone saw through SBF's deception. Appearing on Tucker Carlson's TV show, he threw blame at the SEC: "I don't know where Gary Gensler was, but my regulator at the CFTC *I bribed*, I asked them, why in the world are you invoking the Commodity Exchange Act?" [emphasis mine] Oopsie!

It was a time for ritual cleansing, as hordes of business and tech reporters rushed to the sink, washing their hands of an industry they enabled for years. Legitimate technology companies like Microsoft belatedly summoned the bravery to admit that actually, when you really think about it, blockchain sorta sucked. It had no substantive use case. All the money spent to explore how maybe crypto might actually do something in the future had been wasted. Numerous other blockchain "pilot projects" quietly folded, including one by the Australian Securities Exchange.

The weirdest part of all this was that, despite facing legal liability for a monumental fuckup, Sam couldn't stop talking! He gave daily interviews, DMed with journalists (bad habit), called up crypto influencers late at night, and wrote long explanatory Twitter threads. In a conversation via Twitter Direct Messages with Kelsey Piper, a reporter at Vox, Sam talked trash about regulators ("Fuck regulators") and admitted that his effective altruism shtick was mostly nonsense. Piper: "you were really good at talking about ethics, for someone who kind of saw it all as a game with winners and losers." Sam: "ya," "hehe," "I had to be," "it's what reputations are made of, to some extent," "i feel bad for those who get fucked by it," "by this dumb game we woke westerners play where we say all the right shiboleths [*sic*] and so everyone likes us." He then rambled his way through an unconvincing story of how Alameda ended up so deep in the hole.

Sam appeared virtually at the *New York Times*' DealBook Summit on November 30, 2022, and talked for more than an hour, apologizing for his failures but claiming he never knowingly commingled funds. It was virtually impossible for that to be true. He owned 90 percent of Alameda and lived with its CEO, whom he had known—and occasionally dated—since their days at Jane Street. The once-billionaire shrugged his way through Andrew Ross Sorkin's questions. Sam said he "had a bad month," and the audience, composed of corporate types whose employers paid the $2,500 admission for them to attend, laughed at the con man who allegedly stole millions of regular Americans' money.

On a Twitter Spaces appearance, with podcaster Ran Neuner, Sam seemed to admit that some of the trades on FTX were fake. Neuner surmised, "You were just letting us buy notional tokens that actually didn't really exist. . . . That makes sense as to why there were no more Bitcoin to withdraw . . . because those Bitcoin didn't really exist." Sam concurred, "I believe that what you are saying is, in fact, part of what happened."

If that were true, Sam was running a bucket shop using customer funds. (*Bucket shops* are fake exchanges, which thrived during the late nineteenth and early twentieth centuries before being outlawed in the 1920s.) It was a disaster of a legal strategy, and not exactly a winner PR-wise either—which is perhaps why his legal team fired him and his lawyer parents rushed down to Nassau to provide assistance. In an interview, Ira Sorkin, who represented Bernie Madoff, chimed in: "Don't talk . . . You're not going to sway the public. The only people that are going to listen to what you have to say are regulators and prosecutors." He was right. Would Sam listen?

Nope! In an interview with an aggrieved Celsius customer, Tiffany Wong, Sam claimed he secretly donated as much money to the Republicans as to the Democrats, but that he had to donate to Republicans via dark money channels for PR reasons. While there was no way to verify this (dark money is dark for a reason), it might help explain why Sam refused to tell me how much he had donated politically versus charitably. Sam was caught, and decided to clam up rather than give me a hard number.

In all of his public histrionics, Sam, like every great fraudster, clung to the notion that it wasn't over. He wasn't a bad guy, he hadn't knowingly lied or swindled people, and it could still all be fixed. He said that his greatest regret, his "biggest single fuckup," was filing for Chapter 11. Late offers of emergency financing had supposedly come in (from whom, he never said). Some parts of the FTX empire were solvent, he claimed. FTX US could be restarted today, but for some reason, he said, regulators didn't want that. He accused John Ray of a power grab. He complained the law firm Sullivan & Cromwell had pressured him into signing over control of his various companies before he could salvage them. It could all be fixed, if only people would let him.

It was sad to watch, like a kid in Vegas hovering around the craps table at two AM, begging strangers to float him for one last roll of the dice. The fraud triangle was on full display: need (the losses Sam accrued gambling, if not outright stealing); opportunity (endless, given what appear to be zero internal controls and minimal regulation); and rationalization (like anyone with a gambling problem, Sam was convinced he just needed more time at the table and he could have made everything okay). It was unsettling to observe, but also infuriating. Sam the pseudo-grown-up was doing the same thing he did as a child, playing multiple games simultaneously. The only difference being these were games with other people's money.

Unlike the games Sam played as a child—or during pitch sessions with VCs—these games had consequences. As many as 1.2 million American customers of FTX lost access to their money, and 5 million worldwide. Contagion spread, with other companies failing because of their financial connections to FTX and risk proliferating throughout the system.

Things went sideways, and it was hard not to feel the industry was fumbling toward an existential reckoning. Several crypto whales died within weeks of one another, their deaths alluding to the industry's seamy underbelly. MakerDAO cofounder Nikolai Mushegian died in an apparent drowning in Puerto Rico on October 28 after tweeting a series of bizarre messages claiming the "CIA and Mossad and pedo elite" were running a sex trafficking blackmail ring.

Tiantian Kullander, 30, the founder of a once $3 billion digital asset company called Amber Group, which had a major presence in Hong Kong, died suddenly in his sleep on November 23. Soon after, Amber Group laid off 40 percent of its employees while denying rumors that it was insolvent.

Then on November 25, Russian billionaire Vyacheslav Taran perished in a helicopter crash during good weather near Monaco after departing Lausanne. He was the sole passenger. Another would-be passenger had canceled their ticket at the last minute. Ukrainian media had previously alleged that Taran, who cofounded Libertex, a trading and investment platform, as well as Forex Club, a foreign exchange trading group, had ties to Russian intelligence and laundered money.

With crypto flailing and the thieves turning on one another, attention turned once again to the Tether guys, who handled the situation with their customary levelheadedness and grace. As the *Wall Street Journal* and other publications took a look at Tether's lending activities, the stablecoin company began issuing defiant statements denouncing the media for calling Tether "sketchy" while overlooking the FTX fraud. The defensiveness was more than a touch ironic: Alameda was Tether's biggest customer, allegedly sending tens of billions of dollars in exchange for the equivalent in Tether tokens. A mystery remained: Did Alameda ever have that much money, and where did it come from?

More evidence of curious connections between Alameda and Tether came to light. On November 23, the *New York Times* reported that in March 2022, Alameda had invested $11.5 million in an entity called FBH, the parent company of one of the smallest banks in the United States. When Farmington State Bank was purchased by FBH in 2020, it had only one branch, three employees, and $5 million in net worth. The chairman of FBH was none other than Jean Chalopin, the chairman of Deltec Bank, whose most infamous client was Tether. As the *New York Times* noted, "Farmington's deposits had been steady at about $10 million for a decade. But in the third quarter this year [2022], the bank's deposits jumped nearly 600 percent to $84 million." The bank was renamed Moonstone. Its digital director was Janvier Chalopin, son of Jean.

On Friday, December 2, the DOJ called for an independent examiner to review "substantial and serious allegations of fraud, dishonesty" and "incompetence" at FTX. Criminal prosecutions and serious civil enforcement seemed like real possibilities. Sam didn't seem to care. He kept giving interviews—and kept up his *League of Legends* habit—while trying to wrest back control of a company that he thought had been taken from him prematurely.

As Sam continued his apology tour, crypto brayed for blood, hoping to sacrifice SBF on the altar of industry villainy and then move on, building through the crypto winter that had already set in. On December 12, hours after he publicly declared that he didn't expect to be arrested, SBF was arrested in the Bahamas, at the request of US authorities. That day, in a Bahamian court, SBF declared his intent to fight extradition. When the judge referred to him as a fugitive, Sam's mother, Barbara Fried, laughed. His father, Joseph Bankman, who was on the FTX payroll, plugged his ears in order not to hear what was going on. No one in the family seemed to accept the full reality—the gravity—of the situation. Or perhaps they didn't want to. Frog-marched out of the courthouse in handcuffs, Sam looked incongruous wearing a suit and sporting a five-o'clock shadow rather than his usual clean-shaven baby face. The game was over. Everything had changed.

After spending eight days in a notoriously rough Bahamian prison—albeit in the hospital wing away from the general population—Sam consented to extradition. The FBI soon picked him up and flew him to New York, where he would appear in court, beginning what could be a long legal battle.

The Southern District of New York's unsealed indictment—it had originally been filed on December 9—revealed eight charges, including wire fraud, conspiracy, and violation of campaign finance laws. Sam stood accused of funneling donations to politicians via people acting as cutouts. The criminal charges had the potential to send him to prison for the rest of his life. Prosecutor Damian Williams, the US attorney for the Southern District of New York, didn't mince words, calling it "one of the biggest financial frauds in American history."

More arrests and more charges against Sam's confederates were all but assured. On December 19, Gary Wang, cofounder of FTX, pleaded guilty to wire fraud and conspiracy to commit wire fraud, commodities fraud, and securities fraud. Caroline Ellison, the CEO of Alameda, admitted to the same crimes as well as conspiracy to commit money laundering. They agreed to cooperate in the DOJ's investigation. "Gary has accepted responsibility for his actions and takes seriously his obligations as a cooperating witness," Wang's attorney said in a statement. Some of Sam's top allies, including his former college roommate and sometime girlfriend, were ready to roll on him to save themselves.

The SEC and CFTC filed civil charges against SBF and FTX. Both alleged that Sam had actually been engaged in fraud from the start. Since FTX's creation in May 2019 until November 2022, when it fell apart, the CFTC stated that "at the direction of Bankman-Fried and at least one Alameda executive, Alameda used FTX funds, including customer funds, to trade on other digital asset exchanges and to fund a variety of high-risk digital asset industry investments."

Countless civil lawsuits bloomed from aggrieved customers and investors. The litigation would surely go on for years, generating endless billable hours. Once again, congrats to the lawyers, the true beneficiaries in all this.

There was a feeling in the air that anyone could be next, even Binance. After after a summer of bankruptcies and then FTX's epic collapse, no company seemed stable. Few crypto executives could—or at least should—be trusted to provide honest statements about the health of their business. The previous few months had shown that many, from Alex Mashinsky to Sam Bankman-Fried, would say that things were great right up until the bankruptcy filing—and maybe even afterward. Trading volume plunged to lows not seen since the current bubble began forming in the fall of 2020. According to crypto-market data provider CryptoCompare, exchange volume in December 2022 was less than it was in December 2020. All trendlines pointed further down. Having been burned once, most people weren't coming back to the crypto casino.

Binance was ascendant in terms of market share, a global Goliath. According to CryptoCompare, it accounted for two-thirds of all trading volume on centralized crypto exchanges in the last quarter of 2022. Yet it dominated a shrinking industry, and cracks started to form. On December 12, Reuters reported that federal prosecutors were considering charging Binance with violating anti-money laundering and sanctions laws, with some eager to charge CZ himself with crimes. Investors began to panic. The next day Binance processed some $1.9 billion of withdrawals in a twenty-four-hour period. (By the first week of January 2023 that number would swell to $12 billion since November.) The globe-trotting CEO, beaming in between regular meetings with heads of state, appeared in the media in an attempt to calm investors. Binance was in good financial shape, he said. In November the company hired Mazars, an auditing firm, to conduct a sort of financial inventory called a *proof of reserves*. It wasn't an audit, and it wasn't in line with standard accounting practices, but it was supposed to reassure markets that Binance was on firm footing.

On December 16, just over one week after releasing its report on Binance's holdings, Mazars announced—via Binance—that it was exiting the business of auditing crypto companies "due to concerns regarding the way these reports are understood by the public." The company deleted its website with its reports on Binance and other crypto firms. Other crypto auditors followed suit. The digital asset industry continued to argue that somehow they needed new accounting rules, or were too controversial or novel for the big prestigious firms to audit, but it was a flimsy excuse. Coinbase, after all, had been audited by Deloitte, a top firm. But Coinbase was also deep in the red and trending downward. In January 2023, it agreed to a $100 million settlement with New York state regulators to address "failures in the crypto-currency exchange's compliance program [that] made it 'vulnerable to serious criminal conduct, including, among other things, examples of fraud, possible money laundering, suspected child sexual abuse material-related activity, and potential narcotics trafficking.'"

As Mazars retreated from the crypto business, one of its former clients entered. Donald Trump, a king of schlocky endorsement deals who had called Bitcoin a scam, hyped a "major announcement." The Trump NFT collection—45,000 silly cartoonish portraits of the former prez looking cool and badass—sold out in a day at ninety-nine dollars apiece, likely netting him millions. The NFT market may have been nearly dry, but a master con man could still squeeze out a little more juice. Still, it felt like the end of something. Even some Trump fans laughed at the absurd digital cash grab. It was too much for Steve Bannon. "I can't do this anymore," he said on the *War Room* podcast. The grift got even worse; numerous online sleuths noticed Trump's collection may have relied on stolen, copyrighted images.

The crypto industry we all knew, and that some even loved, had been discredited. It wasn't just the emperor—the entire royal court was parading through town naked. Not all of them realized it yet. Some exchange executives and VCs maintained enough self-delusion (and capital on hand) to take another bite at the apple. But millions of people inside and outside crypto could see what was going on. Some of them had been left holding the bag when these same industry leaders cashed out. Now they wouldn't be made whole. And with interest rates rising, the easy money wouldn't be coming back.

In the financial crisis of 1907, J. P. Morgan and his wealthy pals saved the day by deploying their resources to backstop banks. But it became clear to the powers that be that an ad hoc intervention by the ultrarich was no way to run a modern economy. Ironically, Morgan's actions led to the creation of the Federal Reserve in 1913. In order to flourish, the country required some centralized government institutions that could coordinate on big matters of political economy. It couldn't depend on the kindness, or the self-interest, of financial elites.

That system eventually became an engine of economic inequality and political alienation. Crypto was right about that. But their solution—to create a private, trustless financial system based on code, unstable digital assets, and a new class of intermediaries—fell apart under its own contradictions, including rampant opportunities for fraud. Crypto had indeed produced something no one could trust, and Sam Bankman-Fried, their knockoff J. P. Morgan, would be remembered as one of its architects.

Bankman-Fried was no Morgan; he had more in common with Bernie Madoff. On December 11, 2008, in the midst of the subprime crisis, Madoff was arrested for running what was at the time the biggest Ponzi scheme in history: $64.8 billion. The market crash of the previous year exposed his fraud, as his clients rushed to withdraw their money only to find it wasn't there. Almost exactly fourteen years later, on December 12, 2022, Sam Bankman-Fried was charged with similar crimes after the crypto markets experienced a similarly precipitous drop, and FTX customers experienced a similar result. The similarities didn't end there: Madoff ran a legitimate market making business in addition to his fraudulent one. Did Sam Bankman-Fried's Alameda Research serve the equivalent role, or had it been a con from the beginning?

While Madoff could be depicted as an isolated villain, albeit a pretty diabolical one, Bankman-Fried's shocking demise ripped the thin veneer of respectability from crypto more broadly. Pushing the rest of the industry into crisis, it threatened to reveal an even bigger fraud beneath, perhaps ten times bigger than Madoff. Sam's fall from grace was the culmination of over a decade and a half of easy money policies that had birthed and then nurtured the fable of cryptocurrency as a magical new form of money and financial liberation. The dethroning of crypto's purported boy king left behind a kingdom in tatters. All that remained was a motley crew of crypto's major players—CZ of Binance, Justin Sun of Tron, the Tether guys—most of them safely working in faraway island jurisdictions.

Madoff defrauded some 37,000 clients, many of them quite wealthy. FTX claimed 1.2 million retail traders in the United States alone—thirty-two times larger than Bernie's scheme—and 5 million worldwide. When added to the millions of regular people who have been locked out of their accounts at places like Celsius, Voyager Digital, BlockFi, and others, the breadth of the devastation became clear. Cryptocurrency had lured in folks from all walks of life with the oldest and simplest con in the book, the get-rich-quick scheme, cloaked in the language of innovation. The hollowness of that story was now clear, but so was its power. And if we were to learn anything from crypto's wild shot across the bow of American capitalism, we needed to understand why it resonated with so many people.

CHAPTER 13

PREACHER'S FATHER

"When the capital development of a country becomes a by-product of a casino,
the job is likely to be ill-done." —John Maynard Keynes

I T'S SUNDAY, NOVEMBER 20, 2022, and I am in St. James Episcopal
Church in Hendersonville, North Carolina. It's strange to feel at
home in a place you've never been. No doubt some of it is due to
childhood memories of attending service every Sunday, steeped in the liturgy
and traditions of Episcopalianism from birth. But it also might have to do
with Indiana Jones.

From the pulpit, the Reverend David Henson begins his sermon celebrating the Feast of Christ the King by recounting a sequence from the third film
in the series, *Indiana Jones and the Last Crusade*. As undeniably cheesy as the
movie is, I adore it. (I'm a sucker for late-career Sean Connery, and this is the
one where he plays Indy's dad.) I know the scene by heart. Accompanied by a
rich American businessman and his femme fatale companion, Harrison Ford
finally reaches a secret chamber that contains the object of his quest, the Holy
Grail. In whimsical 1980s cinematic fashion, it's guarded by a 700-year-old
knight who has been kept alive by the eternal waters of the grail. But there
is a problem: hundreds of chalices are on display. Which one is the true grail,
and which are fakes? Only one offers eternal life, the others instant death.

Thankfully, the American tycoon's greed compels him to choose first. Aided by his female compatriot, he selects the most beautiful chalice of all: bejeweled, golden, gleaming. The tycoon is mesmerized. Surely this must be the cup of the King of Kings. He dips the chalice in the holy waters and drinks deeply.

We all know where this is going. The evil American's skin turns pale and then sloughs off, transforming him into a macabre skeletal freak via 1989's best practical and special effects. It's a gruesome death. But the capper is the ancient knight's understated response. Veteran character actor Robert Eddison—in a role originally intended for Laurence Olivier—lands the line of his career with pitch-perfect deadpan delivery.

"He chose . . . poorly."

The congregation of Saint James laughs heartily. A skilled storyteller, Reverend Henson uses that opening to pivot to the heart of his sermon, and a choice Jesus himself often faced during his brief time on earth. Throughout the Bible, the son of God repeatedly rejects any attempt by his followers or even his enemies to anoint him king. Instead he calls himself a servant and a shepherd of lost sheep, the bread of life to be consumed by any who so chooses. Jesus refuses power with an unshakeable humility. His aesthetics are plain, his needs practically utilitarian. When it is Indiana Jones's turn to select a chalice, he settles on the most modest one he can find: the clay cup of a carpenter. He chooses wisely.

In 1925, when the Feast of Christ the King was created, the Catholic Church had not chosen well. As Reverend Henson points out, Pope Pius XI fell in league with the fascist dictator Benito Mussolini. In exchange for the Church's allegiance, Mussolini promised to restore the beleaguered institution to its rightful prominent place in Italian society. Pius succumbed, and in so doing the Catholic Church received yet another black mark against it. On that Sunday, the reverend's message was clear. Even the institution of the Church was fallible, capable of making the same mistakes as each of us, chasing false kingdoms of wealth and power here on earth. And while Reverend Henson couldn't change history, he could at least speak truth to power in the present.

Our journey to Hendersonville started with the man in the pulpit and his willingness to talk. In the spring, David Henson sent a heartfelt message thanking us for our journalism exploring the darker side of the business of cryptocurrency. As a former reporter himself, David was glad someone was shining a light on an industry he knew was rife with scams and frauds. The reverend had seen it in his parish, but more than that it had cost his own family dearly. With courage and grace, David Henson proceeded to share with us a story about his dad, Hal.

o o o

In May 2018, the Supreme Court ruled as unconstitutional the Professional and Amateur Sports Protection Act, a law that had made most sports betting illegal—with places like Las Vegas and Atlantic City the obvious exceptions. Suddenly, a massive underground industry came into the open, as legalizing sports gambling became a decision left to the states. Unsurprisingly, most liked the idea of bringing already existent gambling into the open and collecting millions of dollars in taxes in the process. At the time of the Supreme Court decision, the *New York Times* sketched out a possible future for gambling in America, writing, "The decision seems certain to result in profound changes to the nation's relationship with sports wagering. Bettors will no longer be forced into the black market to use offshore wagering operations or illicit bookies. Placing bets will be done on mobile devices, fueled and endorsed by the lawmakers and sports officials who opposed it for so long. A trip to Las Vegas to wager on March Madness or the Super Bowl could soon seem quaint."

The *Times'* prediction came to fruition with the breakneck speed that only huge amounts of cash can inspire. Everyone—from sports leagues to casinos to software developers to smartphone makers to TV networks to colleges—saw a way to tap a new market. Their goal? To bring the casino to the people, without all the garish trappings of Vegas.

"Sports are one of the easiest, cheapest ways to reach young men," said Joey D'Urso, a journalist who's written about numerous ill-fated partnerships between European football teams and fly-by-night crypto companies. Smartphone sports betting laid the groundwork for exactly the kind of addictive gambling environment that would foster the crypto boom, which also targeted young men, with an incredibly low barrier to entry and essentially twenty-four-hour betting markets.

States, with dollar signs in their eyes, opened the floodgates to allow anyone to gamble with the swipe of a finger. Sports gambling exploded: Thirty-three states legalized it, including twenty-four that allowed online gambling. Sports betting surged from less than $5 billion a year in 2018 to more than $57 billion in 2021. By 2023, that number is projected to be $200 billion. New entrants like FanDuel and DraftKings now compete with their Vegas antecedents—Caesars, BetMGM, WynnBET—for the coveted young male demographic. Via slick marketing campaigns featuring movie stars and athletes, online sports gambling is seemingly everywhere you look. All the major leagues—MLB, the NBA, NHL, and NFL—have bought in, knowing that it's one more way to profit off of fandom.

But in late 2020 and early 2021, with the COVID pandemic still raging and many professional sports briefly on ice, a different bright shiny object appeared to be wagered on: crypto.

o o o

When David Henson thinks about his dad Hal, he can't help but smile. Harold Henson was a charismatic salesman, an evangelical preacher, and a bit of a trickster. He was the dad who was all-time QB in the neighborhood football games, the kind of guy who knew just when to throw an interception to the weakest player. David ran track from middle school through college, with a focus on hurdles and the 400-meter dash. While Hal wasn't always around, David remembers fondly the many times he'd look up after a particularly grueling practice and see his father in the stands watching. Hal never missed a meet, filming them all, rooting his son on with his trademark "GO BABY GO!" delivered with such force it shook the camera every time.

One year as David's Madison County track team was facing off against their dreaded crosstown rival Grissom High, the school received a mysterious package in the mail. The mismatched, ransom note–style lettering included a message designed to provoke a reaction. It insulted the Madison County Tigers, calling them "pussycats." His voice trembling with rage, David's track coach read the letter aloud to the team on the bus ride over to the meet. Pride challenged, Madison County defeated Grissom High for the first time since anyone could remember. Only much later did David discover that it was his father Hal who had penned the note. He even drove across town to make sure the postmark fit the rival's zip code. Hal's fatherly devotion was matched only by his dedication to pranksterism.

Harold Henson grew up poor in Alabama, but he never lacked for drive. He was the first member of his family to go to college. As a young man, he dreamed of working on Wall Street, and upon graduation he secured a coveted summer internship with a New York firm. But it didn't work out. Instead, Hal returned to Alabama and became a food sales representative, traveling the region making in-person calls to restaurant after restaurant. It was a job to which he was well-suited. A natural people person, Hal thrived in a business built on trust.

Hal's outgoing nature found another outlet as an evangelical preacher in the Churches of Christ. David recalls riding in his dad's Toyota Corolla up into northern Alabama's Sand Mountain to watch his father preach to a congregation of barely more than a dozen souls. In that intimate setting, Hal was in his element, spreading the word of God through his combination of relentless optimism and sly humor. Watching his father preach planted the seed in young David's mind that would lead him down his own spiritual path. But back then, the middle-school kid just savored any time he got to spend with his dad, who was often on the road for work. Reverend Henson still remembers the gas station Subway sandwich shop they stopped in every Sunday after church. Now and again, David will find himself compelled to order that same sandwich, a Subway Melt. "Still to this day it brings back memories," David says. "Just the smell of a Subway does that."

Harold Henson was a dreamer in the grand tradition of American men of a certain generation, believing that financial success was always just around the corner. Unfortunately, Hal wasn't always a great steward of his family's finances. He had a tendency to get sucked into multi-level marketing schemes. David recalls recoiling at the pungent odor of the tea tree oil his father purchased in bulk during one phase of a seemingly endless stream of investment schemes. Despite his considerable skill as a salesman, Hal's attempts to master

MLMs rarely worked out. That said, the MLMs always seemed to young David like more of a hobby than a serious investment. His dad's financial imagination could get away from him, but he never put in more than he could afford to lose.

Things took a turn for the worse during the subprime crisis. Hal found himself underwater on the house he purchased in Ocala, Florida, during the boom. Now dipping into his limited savings, it seemed as if he was falling further and further behind. He went through a number of job changes in a short time. Leaving Ocala for McCalla, Alabama, Hal sold his house at a significant loss. He could only afford a new home by somehow convincing the bank to give him two mortgages—a Pyrrhic victory, perhaps. Finding work as a contract salesman, he felt the toll of social isolation, and his mental health suffered.

During these years straddling the great financial crisis, David and his wife had two children, both boys. Harold Henson was now a grandfather, and he felt a pressure to provide for his lineage. Hal didn't have a lot to give his grandsons, but he did what he could. Every day when he came home from work he emptied his pockets of change, storing the loose coins in Bonne Maman jelly jars. Whenever he visited he'd bring the jars along, taking his grandsons to the toy store, where they were each allowed to purchase a small gift. At the register, Hal helped them count out the amount necessary, quarter by quarter. The boys took to calling their grandad "the patron saint of jelly jars."

Hal was down on his luck, but he figured maybe he could turn it all around. He decided to try his hand at forex trading—a vast global market for trading currencies. The forex industry is enormous—the daily global volume has been pegged at about $6.6 trillion—and in many ways represents gambling, with all of its addictive components. It's also a hugely influential market that helps determine the exchange rates for practically every currency. As with gambling, most retail forex investors lose money. I spoke to Alex Imas, an associate professor of behavioral science and economics at the University of Chicago's Booth School of Business, who studies the market. "Academic work has shown that people's behavior in the forex market is consistent with the same patterns as in the casino: They come in wanting to limit their downside, but end up doing the exact opposite—they chase their losses until the money is gone. The vast majority end up losing money because the forex market, just like a casino, has a negative expected value."

Hal quickly became obsessed with forex. Even though he had worked all his life, his retirement savings were modest. He longed for a bit more of a cushion, perhaps even an inheritance to pass down to his grandchildren. David remembers his dad even pitching it to him as a way to make a little extra money. David declined, instead becoming concerned that his father might be falling into yet another financial quagmire, only one with more serious consequences. He told his father that he didn't need to worry about his grandkids' education. David and his wife Amber, a doctor, were doing just fine.

David's concerns were well-founded: Many crypto traders start in forex before moving on to more exotic—and even riskier—financial products. Forex websites are also notorious for advertising all sorts of dubious investment ventures, whether overtly or via chat groups ostensibly set up to discuss trading strategies. These shady investment schemes and online chat groups sell a message that with the right information, a little bit of study, and perhaps some inside connections, a regular retail trader can beat the house and come away a winner. Unfortunately, the opposite is true. They never have a chance.

David can never know for sure, but he suspects that forex was how his father stumbled upon Stallion Wings, a cryptocurrency investment firm promising incredible returns.

o o o

Lin and Aaron Sternlicht run a boutique addiction services firm in New York City catering to high–net worth individuals and their families. In 2018, as the last bull market cycle of crypto ended in collapse—prices fell some 80 percent in less than a year—Lin and Aaron started to see a new kind of client: crypto addicts. They were all men under forty; some of them were Wall Street whiz kids, others upper class professionals. Lin and Aaron even treated a few teenagers, brought in by parents concerned that their kids were gambling away their minimum-wage paychecks. Initially their numbers were modest, but by the time the second bull run of crypto came around in 2021, what had been a trickle of crypto gambling addicts swelled into a tsunami.

In many respects, the people who felt compelled to trade crypto were not dissimilar from other problem gamblers the Sternlichts had treated. They were usually youngish guys chasing a dopamine high, the rush of victory. As the Sternlichts point out, "Anything that gives us pleasure can become addictive." Compulsive gambling stimulates the brain in much the same way as substance abuse, and thus is classified by the American Psychiatric Association as an addiction. But crypto appeared even more addictive than traditional gambling. In crypto, the casinos (i.e., the exchanges) never close, and finding an open seat at the poker table is always only a few clicks away. Unlike traditional stock markets, crypto trades twenty-four seven, so there is no reprieve for those who fall down the rabbit hole. Like online poker, crypto offers the illusion of control. With seemingly endless amounts of data to pore over, there's the myth of mastering the system, of being able to figure it all out. In this way, crypto trading easily morphs into compulsion and obsession. Insomnia, anxiety, and depression are commonplace. Hardcore traders self-mockingly refer to themselves as *degens*, slang for degenerate gamblers.

The volatility of crypto and the high leverage offered to retail customers add to its addictiveness. With wild swings in price, a well-placed crypto bet can be intoxicating, euphoric. Add to that leverage—essentially the ability to borrow large sums to bet with—and the highs get even higher. Recall that Binance offered regular customers 125-to-1 leverage, a ratio unheard of in regulated markets. For someone predisposed to gambling, these kinds of crypto bets are addictive in the extreme. While on a winning streak, the participant feels ecstatic, almost invincible. But if the coins collapse in price—as they often do in mere hours or even minutes in cryptoland—the losses can be soul-crushing, draining an investor's account to zero.

The Sternlichts noticed another distinction between their crypto clients and problem gamblers: Most well-heeled crypto addicts did not consider themselves gamblers, but rather investors. Their crypto-addicted clients were often otherwise sophisticated investors, deeply knowledgeable when it came to matters of finance and money. The Sternlichts were accustomed to the extreme self-confidence, if not outright arrogance, of many of their

Wall Street clients, but in crypto the attitudes were even more pronounced. Crypto addicts believed themselves to be superior investors, ahead of the curve, educated in what was surely the next phase of financial innovation. The seeming boundlessness of crypto feeds this sensation; to someone mesmerized by it, the possibilities are infinite and the egos of those under its spell swell in tandem. Crypto addicts' extreme confidence in their abilities often blinds them to their losses, opening them up to the same mistake compulsive gamblers (and most forex traders) make when it comes to money: chasing their losses until they are bled dry.

The feelings of shame associated with these losses can be overwhelming, the flip side of the extreme highs and sense of superiority corresponding to the wins. Crypto trading is usually a solitary activity, and thus the pain is mostly suffered alone. Inside crypto's hyper-masculine culture, complaining about losses is verboten, considered a sign of weakness. Remember the community's motto: DYOR—do your own research. If you lose money, you have only yourself to blame. And unlike other addictions, like substance abuse, crypto addiction is far easier to hide from friends and family. All you need is a phone and a few minutes—or even seconds—alone to feed your habit.

By the time Lin and Aaron Sternlicht get involved, the crypto gambler's addiction has usually become so severe it can no longer be hidden. A family member or spouse might discover the addict lying about his finances, or borrowing from others in order to gamble more. The loss of large quantities of money goes off like a bomb inside a family, with consequences that span generations and sunder relationships. Treatment for gambling addiction can be quite effective, but often requires stringent measures. Wresting control of all funds available to the addict may be necessary in order to eliminate his ability to relapse. And while the Sternlichts' practice has so far avoided this outcome, the most troubling fact when it comes to gambling addiction is also the simplest. It has the highest rate of suicide of any addiction.

o o o

When Hal linked up with Stallion Wings, a crypto investment group he found online, he thought he had made it. He was part of an exclusive club of savvy investors who would profit together. He had found a community. He even thought that the people who had brought him into the investment group were his friends—a degree of faith that would only deepen his troubles.

Around 2018, Hal reached out to his accountant to create a self-directed IRA. According to David, his dad believed he was investing in order to leave some inheritance to his grandkids. From the IRA, Hal would transfer funds to a Wells Fargo account and then to various LLCs that would wire the money to members of the Stallion Wings group. For a time, Hal was pleased with his choice. Via an online portal, he could see his investment surging in value. All was well.

It was when Hal tried to get his money out that the problems began. His contacts at Stallion Wings required a "tip" and "commission fees" for their services in order to release the money. That led Hal to investing more and more money until eventually he was tapped out. When Hal threatened to go to the authorities, he was told there was a "board" to which he could appeal, but his contacts at Stallion Wings pleaded with him not to do so: "I'm going to go to jail if you report me to the board." The board didn't exist, but it wasn't clear if Hal knew that. As a salesman, Hal had built his life on trusting others; now he couldn't admit he had trusted the wrong people. Even though he knew he was being extorted, Hal couldn't turn on his newfound "friends." As a mark, he had been cooled out, and there was nowhere left to go but further down the rabbit hole.

Things quickly deteriorated from there. David's maternal grandmother died in December 2019. The day of the funeral, Hal asked his wife to sign off on a home equity line of credit, basically a second mortgage on their home. She reluctantly agreed. For the next six months, Hal tapped all the sources of funds he could think of in a desperate attempt to get his original investment in Stallion Wings back. He got a loan from his employer and a loan against his life insurance policy, he borrowed against his 401K, and he maxed out his credit cards. He asked his siblings for money, as well as other relatives. He was down to his last straw.

David remembers the last time he spoke to his father, in early June 2020. It was the first time his dad had ever asked him for money. Hal needed $5,000; he was broke. He apologized to his son: "I'm sorry I'm having to do this." As a priest, David was trained in these situations. He knew he couldn't give his dad any money, that it would only feed his addiction. Instead, he offered to pay any bill he ever had, house him, give him anything except more money to give to criminals. In a rage, Hal hung up on him.

When David's mother called him on June 26, 2020, he knew what it was about before she said a word.

○ ○ ○

In the early 2000s, around the same time as the housing boom, online poker exploded. Myriad gambling websites appeared, seemingly out of nowhere, encouraging young men to fork over real money to try their hand in a game of digital cards. In 2003, a young amateur player named Chris Moneymaker gained entrance into the World Series of Poker—the pinnacle of the game—via an online satellite tournament hosted by PokerStars. Moneymaker won the whole tournament, taking in the $2.5 million pot. Millions of amateur players saw themselves in the twenty-eight-year-old from Tennessee who had suddenly hit the jackpot. The online poker boom was on.

Online poker grew from almost nothing into a multibillion-dollar business in less than a decade. A few online poker rooms in the late nineties and early aughts swelled to more than 500 by 2010. Poker tournaments were now much-hyped televised events, with online sites driving much of the advertising and the winning players becoming celebrities. The star players would often then sign lucrative endorsement deals with those sites, drawing in even more average Joes.

The Unlawful Internet Gambling Enforcement Act of 2006 laid the groundwork for the demise of the poker boom. Domestically, it meant that the people behind those websites were engaged in illegal activity and could be arrested. Some of them would be. Companies that wanted to continue to operate were forced to move overseas, setting up shop via shell corporations in the Caribbean and other friendly foreign jurisdictions.

On April 15, 2011—a date that became infamous in poker circles as Black Friday—it all came crashing down. The DOJ seized the domain names of PokerStars, Full Tilt, and Absolute Poker, as well as the funds of customers gambling on them. Full Tilt was accused of running a $300 million Ponzi scheme. PokerStars paid a $547 million fine. In this book I've repeatedly mentioned the discovery of a secret "god mode" on the site Ultimate Bet, whose parent company employed lawyers Stuart Hoegner, who went on to work for Tether, and Daniel Friedberg, who later worked for FTX. Online poker would eventually resume, and it is now legal in states like Nevada, New Jersey, Pennsylvania, Delaware, West Virginia, and Michigan. But it never recovered from the exposure of the rampant fraud at the heart of the industry.

It also didn't have to. In a few years, online poker had been replaced by something even more alluring on which young men could gamble. The original computer code that would become Bitcoin included a poker lobby, a framework from which a virtual poker game could be built. Whoever Satoshi Nakamoto was, in early 2007 they were clearly interested in methods of creating non-confiscatable digital money and how they might be used in online poker.

```
1572
... 1573   CPokerLobbyDialogBase::CPokerLobbyDialogBase(wxWindow* parent, wxWindowID id, const wxString& title, const wxPoint& pos, const '
1574   {
1575       this->SetSizeHints(wxDefaultSize, wxDefaultSize);
1576       this->SetBackgroundColour(wxSystemSettings::GetColour(wxSYS_COLOUR_BTNFACE));
1577
1578       wxBoxSizer* bSizer156;
1579       bSizer156 = new wxBoxSizer(wxHORIZONTAL);
1580
1581       m_treeCtrl = new wxTreeCtrl(this, wxID_ANY, wxDefaultPosition, wxDefaultSize, wxTR_HAS_BUTTONS|wxTR_HIDE_ROOT|wxTR_LINES_AT
```

One day we may find out Satoshi's true motivations. For now, all we know is that they were initially interested in poker. The fact that the creation of a new form of digital money coincided nearly perfectly with the impending destruction of online poker may be a historical coincidence. Then again, this is a book about money, lying, gambling, and fraud. It would only be fitting if online poker lay at the foundation of it all.

o o o

At dawn on June 26, 2020, Hal Henson was struck dead by an eighteen-wheeler on Interstate 459 in Bessemer, Alabama. In an attempt to make sense of it all, David fell back on the skills he had developed as a reporter. He found the email accounts Hal hid from his wife and with them the lengthy online correspondences between his father and other members of Stallion Wings. His dad never met anyone involved in the project in person. In retrospect, it seemed like one of many obvious red flags.

David found an address for one of the wire transfers sent to a woman's name. It was only a two-hour drive away. The man of God couldn't help it; he fantasized about driving over to her house to "let her know she killed my dad." He also knew that would do him no good; what he really wanted was to come to terms with his father's passing.

To Reverend Henson, the most pernicious part was the way Stallion Wings, and cryptocurrency more broadly, preys on people's best selves. Their desire to care for their families is turned against them, impoverishing them instead. Their longing for community and connection leaves them isolated and ashamed. David knows in his head that his father took his own life, but in his heart he feels that he was murdered.

In the last email Hal sent to Stallion Wings, the sixty-six-year-old grandfather openly discussed the depths of his financial despair. To David, his father appeared desperate for sympathy, even from those who tormented him. Maybe they were the only ones who could truly understand. But when Harold Henson confessed he was thinking about killing himself, the people who had bled him dry sent back a one-word reply:

"Bye."

The day after his father's death, David Henson went to the scene of the crime. According to David, Hal had swerved off the road in an apparent attempt to make his death look like an accident. When that didn't work, he stepped in front of an oncoming truck.

By the side of the road, in a field of Queen Anne's lace, David came upon the outline of his dad's body spray painted onto the ground. Near it lay a business card from his father's bank. On the back were the passwords to a number of credit cards Hal had set up per the instructions of Stallion Wings. The passwords Hal chose corresponded to the events David ran in track: the 300/400 meter hurdles, the 110 meter high hurdles, the 400 meter dash.

Alone in that field, David Henson screamed at the top of his lungs.

○ ○ ○

Back at St. James Episcopal Church in Hendersonville, North Carolina, David Henson concludes his sermon.

"May we have the courage to reach for the clay cup and drink from the waters of life itself. . . . May we be shepherds who stand with the most vulnerable in their most vulnerable moments, may we be servants of all people, especially those broken by the world and their own choices, may we be bread and food for a world hungry for hope, for relationship, for love."

The congregation of St. James responds in unison, "Amen."

We humans made up money, just as we made up government, religion, and all the other social constructs that wield so much power over our daily lives. We made up markets, gambling, our sense of value—all of it. As our collective creations, they are under our collective control, but our differences, and sometimes our greed, blind us to that reality.

It's intimidating to consider the daunting challenges that lay ahead, but that difficulty does not absolve us of the responsibility of doing so. As we have throughout history, we must corral the wild beast of capital and refocus its power in a way that benefits us all. If we fail to do so, today's current culture of political and criminal impunity only festers into something far worse.

Turning our nation into a casino is not the ultimate manifestation of the American dream—you, too, can be rich!—it is the perversion of it. Gambling squanders what our ancestors, when following their better angels, fought so hard to cultivate. It turns us against one another in games that are strictly competitive, further sowing the seeds of mistrust. It is an antisocial practice, built on a thin reed of lies.

Fraud is even worse, a near dead-weight loss to society. A certain low level of fraud is unavoidable, the cost of doing business in an economy as large and complicated as our own. If left unchecked, however, it erodes the rule of law to the point that no one in power is ever held to account. It becomes cynical to even think that something could be done about, say, former President Donald Trump's obvious corruption.

Capitalism itself cannot provide the answers, for it is unable to ask the questions. Left unchecked, it thirsts for expansion and consumption above all else, consequences be damned. The current iteration is killing us; capitalism is eating our democracy and destroying our planet. However, there is some good news. We made capitalism up too, which means we can alter it to our liking.

Each generation of tech and financial "innovators" promise their own form of utopia, and crypto advocates have had their turn to demonstrate theirs, with all of its attendant failings. Like so many of its Silicon Valley venture capitalist forebears, the crypto industry's vision is fundamentally a selfish one, divorced from any real sense of how the world works and what is required to bring us together rather than pull us further apart. We cannot eradicate the need for trust, and it is not just wrongheaded, but fundamentally nihilistic to aspire to do so. In the end, we have only ourselves and each other on whom we can rely.

May we choose wisely.

EPILOGUE

"INVESTMENT CONTRACTS THAT are effectively valueless are often described as Ponzi schemes, which are regulated under American law by the Securities and Exchange Commission. In my opinion, the cryptocurrency industry represents the largest Ponzi scheme in history."

I hit the red button and glanced up. Thirty feet away, on the dais above me, half a dozen senators stared back. Pat Toomey of Pennsylvania looked like he had swallowed an egg.

It was December 14, 2022. I was testifying before the Senate Banking Committee on the collapse of FTX/Alameda and what it meant for crypto, and for the millions of investors who had lost money in the process. On the other end of the panel was Professor Hilary Allen, whose February paper had anticipated crypto's collapse. Squeezed between us were Jennifer Schulp, director of financial regulation studies at the Cato Institute, and Kevin O'Leary, investor and cohost of the TV show *Shark Tank*. Professor Allen and I had been invited to describe the myriad ways in which crypto's epic collapse was entirely predictable and why the time for such shenanigans is long past. Crypto needed to grow up; lawmakers and regulators should step in and protect consumers/investors. Ms. Schulp and Mr. O'Leary were there to say we had it all wrong. They did their best.

The recent revelation by Mr. O'Leary that he had been paid $15 million by Sam Bankman-Fried's now bankrupt crypto exchange to hawk its services to the general public was slightly awkward. Mr. O'Leary's views on crypto had evolved over the years. As recently as 2019, he had called crypto "garbage," but when I was at the Bitcoin Conference (BTC) in Miami in March 2022, he assured investors that crypto's ascent to the stars was all but assured. ("The spigots of capital are going to flood into this sector, like you've never seen. So for those of us that can invest in it now—you're getting ahead of what's going to be a huge wave of interest when policy occurs.")

Now, in a fashion typical of crypto boosters caught in awkward financial arrangements with crypto companies, Mr. O'Leary claimed he too was a victim. "I lost millions as an investor in @FTX," he tweeted on November 30 while still defending SBF. A little over a week later, on December 8 on CNBC, the story changed. Now he was "at zero" when it came to his payday from the company owned by the soon-to-be-indicted Sam Bankman-Fried. He claimed he hadn't won, but he also hadn't lost. By the time he was testifying before Congress six days later, and SBF was in handcuffs, O'Leary was no longer defending the alleged fraudster. And by February 9, when appearing on Fox Business, he claimed that if Sam had pitched FTX to him on his TV show *Shark Tank*, he wouldn't have bought into the company. Apparently, the character Mr. O'Leary plays on TV is savvier than the real-life version.

Then again, things were moving quite fast in cryptoland, so it was fairly understandable that the narratives surrounding it couldn't quite keep up. On December 12, two days before the Senate hearing, Sam Bankman-Fried was arrested in the Bahamas. The next day, December 13, he was charged in the Southern District of New York (SDNY) with eight counts of criminal behavior, including fraud, conspiracy to commit money laundering, and conspiracy to commit campaign finance violations.

Sam had been invited to testify at the House Financial Services Committee hearing that day, but his arrest in the Bahamas prevented him from attending. Nevertheless, he had previously agreed to participate, and his written testimony leaked. In it, Bankman-Fried included screenshots from a chat group on the encrypted app Signal entitled "Exchange Coordination." Members of the group included Changpeng Zhao (CZ) of Binance, Paolo Ardoino of Tether, and Justin Sun of Tron. I thought back to my conversation with Bitfinex'ed from a year prior and his assertion that the supposedly multitrillion-dollar crypto industry was in fact being manipulated by only a handful of industry heavyweights operating out of (sometimes undisclosed) overseas locations. What seemed like a far-fetched theory at the time had now become entirely reasonable analysis.

There were more shoes to drop when it came to Sam and his shenanigans at the helm of FTX/Alameda. On January 13, 2023, a Delaware bankruptcy court heard that he had allegedly instructed his colleague Gary Wang to write back door code so Alameda could "borrow" billions from its customers. "Mr. Wang created this back door by inserting a single number into millions of lines of code for the exchange, creating a line of credit from FTX to Alameda, to which customers did not consent," claimed FTX lawyer Andrew Dietderich. The innovative wonders of "trustlessness" and "decentralization" were on full display. Add a single number to millions of lines of code, and voilà, one can siphon billions in "loans" from accounts held by regular folks oblivious to the swindle. Trust the code, indeed. Dietderich continued: "And we know the size of that line of credit. It was $65 billion." Bernie Madoff's Ponzi was $64.8 billion.

As he had done repeatedly before in venues such as the *New York Times'* DealBook Summit, Mr. Bankman-Fried tried to talk himself out of his troubles. He tweeted defenses and created a Substack to outline his version of events in greater detail. His attempts to rewrite history didn't stop there. Allegedly, he went so far as to contact legal counsel of FTX US ahead of the court case. According to federal prosecutors, on January 15, Bankman-Fried sent Dietderich a Signal message: "I would really love to reconnect and see if there's a way for us to have a constructive relationship, use each other as resources when possible, or at least vet things with each other." I recalled Sam's bizarre, thinly veiled attempts to influence Jacob's and my reporting the previous year. They now seemed quaint by comparison.

Not that we were unique in our experience among journalists. By then, myriad examples of SBF's attempts—however sophomoric—at altering media coverage of him had gone public. Perhaps the most egregious of these was his relationship with a purportedly independent crypto media company called The Block. On December 9, *Axios* reported that Sam had secretly loaned The Block $27 million, and its CEO, Michael McCaffrey, $16 million. McCaffrey resigned the same day. Over the course of my reporting, I'd gotten into several public Twitter spats with journalists at The Block who questioned my understanding of the industry they supposedly covered honestly. They were less voluble now.

Bankman-Fried had pursued other ways to curry favor; Capitol Hill was also a target. On February 23, prosecutors in New York added four new charges to his indictment. Among them were allegations that Sam sat at the helm of a straw donor scheme. (A *straw donor scheme* is one in which political donations are funneled through cutouts to avoid campaign finance contribution limits.) According to the SDNY, SBF and his associates made more than three hundred illegal political contributions. Documents filed in bankruptcy court asserted FTX employees had given $93 million in political donations. FTX's new bankruptcy lawyers publicly encouraged the recipients to return the money.

Sam's coconspirators were not named in the indictment, but rather referred to as CC-1 and CC-2. Allegedly, a political consultant working for Bankman-Fried told CC-1 that "in general, you being the center left face of our spending will mean you giving to a lot of woke shit for transactional purposes." Besides Sam, the two largest donors employed by FTX were its co-CEO, Ryan Salame, and Nishad Singh, one of its founders and the company's head of engineering.

On February 28, Mr. Singh pleaded guilty to charges of wire fraud, commodities fraud, and securities fraud, as well as money laundering and campaign finance violations. He became the third FTX employee to plead guilty to criminal charges and agree to cooperate with federal prosecutors in their case against their boss.

Sam was running out of friends.

o o o

On January 5, 2023, Alex Mashinsky, the CEO of crypto lending firm Celsius, was sued for fraud by New York Attorney General Letitia James. According to the lawsuit, Mashinsky defrauded hundreds of thousands of customers, including 26,000 New Yorkers, out of billions of dollars.

Information on Celsius's inner workings came to light through bankruptcy filings. On January 31, the examiner assigned in the case found that the "Celsius Network on a stand-alone basis has been insolvent since inception." It was a simple racket: Allegedly, Mashinksy and company inflated the value of the CEL token in order to enrich themselves at the expense of others. It seems that James Block, aka Dirty Bubble Media, had been right all along.

Employees of the company were ecstatic at their success. After a round of CEL purchases in September 2020, the same Celsius employees congratulated themselves on "our good work" resulting in "people thinking [the price of CEL] is going to the moon haha." They had reason to be joyous; the scam was highly lucrative for the insiders participating. According to the filing, Mashinsky walked away with $68.7 million. It wasn't a particularly sophisticated operation. Like FTX, Celsius used QuickBooks for its accounting. The mechanics of the scheme were an open secret within the company. Again, from the examiner's report: "In April 2022, Celsius's Coin Deployment Specialist described Celsius's practice of 'using customer stable coins' and 'growing short in customer coins' to buy CEL as 'very ponzi like.'" Organic (non-artificially inflated) demand for the token was extremely low, necessitating repeated manipulation: "In effect, Celsius bought every CEL token in the market at least one time and in some instances, twice."

Given the opaque and largely unregulated nature of the cryptocurrency industry, there was little stopping Celsius from engaging in what would otherwise constitute blatant fraud. While the euphoria of the crypto bubble lasted, such schemes could be concealed, leaving investors and the general public largely in the dark. But now that bubble had burst, and the pervasive criminality that formed the foundation of the industry came to light.

On January 12, the SEC charged crypto lenders Genesis and Gemini for "the unregistered offer and sale of securities to retail investors through the Gemini Earn crypto asset lending program."

On February 9, the exchange Kraken agreed to discontinue its staking program and pay a $30 million fine to the commission to settle charges against it.

On February 16, an SEC lawsuit charged Do Kwon and Terraform Labs with multibillion-dollar securities fraud. At the time of the filing, Do's whereabouts were unknown. But on March 23, 2023, he was arrested in Montenegro while allegedly attempting to board a private plane with a false passport. In an indictment by US prosecutors made public after his arrest, Do Kwon faced eight criminal charges, including securities fraud, wire fraud, and commodities fraud.

As its competitors bit the dust, attention turned to Binance, the largest overseas exchange still standing. On January 18, the DOJ announced "a significant blow to the cryptocrime ecosystem." It wasn't against Binance. Instead, the government charged the cofounder of an obscure exchange called Bitzlato with running a "money laundering engine." Anatoly Legkodymov, a Russian national living in China, was arrested for allegedly processing $700 million in illicit funds through his exchange. The initial reaction among those in the crypto industry was one of confusion, if not derision. What the hell was Bitzlato? Soon, more details emerged. Binance was one of Bitzlato's biggest counterparties. According to Reuters, Binance moved $346 million for the exchange.

On February 6, Binance abruptly announced it would stop dollar withdrawals and deposits starting February 8. On February 13, the New York State Department of Financial Services ordered Paxos, a finance and tech company based in the state, to stop issuing the Binance stablecoin, BUSD. Investors started to get the picture and headed for the exits. The market cap of BUSD was over $23 billion in November 2022. By early February 2023 it was $16 billion, and by the end of March it was below $8 billion. The real money was leaving the casino.

A bombshell came on February 16. Reuters broke the news that Binance had secretly moved $400 million from its American partner, Binance.US, to a company managed by Changpeng Zhao over the course of the first three months of 2021. Reportedly, the money was transferred from the Binance.US account at California-based Silvergate Bank to a trading firm called Merit Peak

Ltd. If that were true, the scenario appeared eerily similar to what happened with Sam and FTX/Alameda.

On March 27 the CFTC sued Binance and several related entities, as well as CZ and the exchange's former chief compliance officer, Samuel Lim, with "numerous violations of the Commodity Exchange Act (CEA) and CFTC regulations." The seventy-four-page civil action was full of juicy details. Allegedly, Binance allowed roughly three hundred "house accounts" owned either directly or indirectly by CZ to trade on its platform. According to the lawsuit, it did not enforce "any anti-fraud or anti-surveillance or controls" over those accounts. What little supervision existed over customer accounts on Binance appeared explicitly designed to give off the appearance of compliance with anti–money laundering laws without actually subjecting them to such. In reference to certain Binance customers, particularly those from Russia, Samuel Lim allegedly wrote in a February 2020 chat: "Like come on. They are here for crime."

The CFTC lawsuit included numerous references to internal communications between various Binance executives, including CZ himself, allegedly strategizing over ways to conceal that the company accepted money/cryptocurrency from dubious sources. The Binance executives also discussed how to conceal the fact that they served American customers from American law enforcement while CZ had explicitly and repeatedly denied they were doing so in the media. Yet according to internal documents, Binance's American customer base was significant; in September 2020, the mothership exchange had 2.51 million US customers. Theoretically, Binance.US (launched in September 2019) was supposed to serve those customers instead, but myriad internal communications from the CFTC lawsuit suggest this was more of a marketing strategy than the functional reality.

While the actions of the CFTC were civil in nature, it was difficult to imagine such potentially inculpatory communiqués had not been shared with officials at the Department of Justice. I recalled the leak of the "Tai Chi document" from 2018. According to *Forbes*, it consisted of an internal report delivered to CZ himself, describing a strategy of distracting law enforcement agencies by setting local legally compliant entities such as Binance.US to steer their attention away from the headquarters-less mothership of Binance itself. The *yin* of Changpeng Zhao's so-far-successful growth strategy seemed destined for a head-on collision with the *yang* of American law enforcement.

Meanwhile, on March 3, 2023, the aforementioned crypto bank Silvergate made a "risk-based decision" to shut down its crypto payments system, the Silvergate Exchange Network. In a required public filing a few days prior, it had warned investors it was on the brink of insolvency. The stock price collapsed, dropping 58 percent in a single day. Soon other banks followed. Silicon Valley Bank (SVB), another California-based lender, was declared insolvent on March 10, and the FDIC seized control of its operations. SVB was a big lender to venture capital firms that had thrived during the easy money years. Two days later, Signature Bank, headquartered in New York, was shut down by state regulators. While the bank served a wide variety of clients, from law firms to real estate developers to taxi medallion businesses, it had recently ventured into cryptocurrency. At the time of its closure, Signature held approximately $100 billion worth of assets, and $16.52 billion in digital asset–related client deposits. While the speed of the failures was alarming, I couldn't help but notice that two of the three collapsed banks had significant exposure to the volatile world of cryptocurrency, and the third (SVB) counted as clients the crypto companies Ripple, BlockFi, Circle, Avalanche, and Yuga Labs, among others. I thought back to the previous summer and how close Congress appeared to passing industry-friendly legislation that would have brought crypto far deeper into our banking system. If that had happened, things could have been a helluva lot worse.

The other major player left standing was Tether. The stablecoin company, valued at $71 billion as of March 1, 2023, had miraculously survived while the industry around it bit the dust. But there were signs that even the seemingly indestructible Tether might not persevere in the face of increased scrutiny. On February 2, 2023, the *Wall Street Journal* reported that as recently as 2018, just four men controlled some 86 percent of Tether Holdings: Giancarlo Devasini, Jean-Louis van der Velde, Stuart Hoegner, and a British businessman, who is known as Christopher Harborne in the UK and Chakrit Sakunkrit in Thailand. Mr. Harborne was a major donor to the Brexit movement, donating as much as £13.7 million ($19 million) to Nigel Farage's Reform UK party. Formerly known as the Brexit Party, Reform UK raised $25 million in total, making Mr. Harborne the party's primary donor.

On March 3, a bombshell dropped from the *WSJ*. According to emails viewed by the paper, companies behind Tether used falsified documents to obtain bank accounts in late 2018. One email cited by the *WSJ* was from an owner of Tether Holdings Ltd., Stephen Moore. According to the article, Mr. Moore argued that "it was too risky to continue using the fake sales invoices and contracts, which he had signed, and recommended they abandon the efforts to open the accounts, the emails show. 'I would not want to argue any of the above in a potential fraud/money laundering case,' he wrote."

Yet even as investigative reporters in the US and elsewhere dug deeper into Tether's murky past, the company found a new source of business in the present: El Salvador. Undaunted by crypto's recent nosedive, the country's president, Nayib Bukele, continued to push forward with various plans tying his country's fate yet closer to the volatile market. On January 11, 2023, El Salvador's legislature passed the Law on the Issuance of Digital Assets (LEAD). Among other provisions, LEAD allowed for the issuance of the long-delayed Bitcoin Bond. The Tether guys were thrilled. Per Bloomberg, "Bitfinex Chief Technology Officer Paolo Ardoino said in an interview he sees enough demand for El Salvador to issue the full $1 billion it is seeking." Where this demand would come from was anyone's guess.

While the few remaining Bitcoin maxis may have cheered the passage of the bill, the delusion of Bitcoin as an emancipatory new form of currency ran headfirst into the brick wall of reality. The only country attempting to use crypto as real money continued on its march toward totalitarianism under Bukele, imprisoning thousands. According to a January 2023 study released by Human Rights Watch, an international non-governmental organization specializing in research and advocacy, an estimated 61,000 people (including at least 1,000 children) had been arrested since Bukele administered martial law in March 2022. Given El Salvador's modest size, this represented a significant percentage of the population. To house those convicted of crimes, El Salvador built a new prison, supposedly capable of housing 40,000 inmates. At the rate "the world's coolest dictator" was going, the country's penal system would need the space. El Salvador now laid claim to the highest incarceration rate on earth.

The issuance of the Bitcoin Bond was itself fraught with consequences for the local population. Wilfredo Claros, the fisherman I visited the previous spring who lived in the hills above La Unión, would soon be forced to abandon his home and his land so the airport servicing Bitcoin City could be built. According to Wilfredo, the government offered him one-tenth the amount he had requested in exchange for his property. He was told the offer was a take it or leave it; if he wanted to argue his case in a court of law, he was free to do so. For Claros this was a cruel joke. He (and his neighbors who had been offered a similar deal) lacked the money needed to pay for lawyers, and of course, Bukele's cronies controlled the judicial system in the small country. Wilfredo was forced to accept, and his family prepared to leave and move in with his brother. No one in the government could tell them when their eviction would occur. They were left to wait.

o o o

One of the good things about writing a book instead of acting on television is a more flexible work schedule. As a result, I got to spend more time with my kids. As with most things when it comes to parenting, it was occasionally hell on earth, but there were some nice moments as well.

One night, before bed, my then six-year-old daughter, Frances, proposed playing a board game with her old man. *Monopoly Junior* is a simplified version of the original, intended for children ages five to eight. The board is smaller, there's less money involved, and only one die to roll. There are no houses or hotels to build, only properties to buy and monopolies to acquire that, once obtained, double the rent charged à la the original. The kids' game involves more luck and less skill than adult *Monopoly*, arguably making it a more accurate reflection of capitalism in practice than the version at which grown-ups play.

It also moves faster; a game of *Monopoly Junior* is designed to last less than thirty minutes. It was seven o'clock when my daughter suggested we begin. Her bedtime is eight. I checked the baby monitor. Upstairs, her brother was already fast asleep in his crib. We had a deal.

The game breezed along, sped up by the fact that there were only two players participating. Soon, all the properties had been purchased. Frances and I each held several monopolies, acquired through a combination of chance and ferocious dealmaking. We were both property-rich and cash-poor, each dancing on the knife's edge of insolvency, per the design of the brothers Parker. A conclusion loomed: The next person to land on one of the other's monopolies would go bankrupt; the game would be over. I narrowly avoided a loss with a lucky roll of the die. It was my young daughter's turn at the table.

A six landed her on the Zoo (all the properties have cute names in the kids' version), one piece of my green empire. I checked the card and announced the rent: eight dollars. I could see her cash in front of me. She only had five bucks, leaving her three short. I watched as she silently counted her bills, then grimaced. It was over.

Unless . . . Frances reached into the bank's coffers and took out the money she needed. She proudly handed over the rent. Problem solved.

"Is that allowed," I asked, a smile resting just behind my furrowed brow.

"Yes," she assured me.

"So I can do it, too?"

"Of course."

"Okay."

We continued playing. A few rolls later, I landed on one of her monopolies, necessitating my own bailout from the bank. Next it was her turn for one, and then mine again. This went on for a long while. In theory, it could have lasted all night. My daughter and I trusted each other, and there was more than enough of this paper stuff called money to go around for the both of us.

Eventually, however, it was eight o'clock. Bedtime beckoned. We agreed to a tie, shook hands, and put the box back on the shelf. The hour for games had passed.

We trudged upstairs. There was just enough time for a book and a cuddle.

ALLOW_NEGATIVE

S AM BANKMAN-FRIED ENTERED the courtroom and I did a double take. He appeared gaunt and tired. A cheap-looking gray suit perched on his shoulders; a drab purple tie hung from his neck. He twitched nervously, flicking glances around the room. The wunderkind entrepreneur and billionaire philanthropist I interviewed the year before was now a thirty-one-year-old man staring down the barrel at spending the rest of his life in jail.

It was October 6, 2023, less than three months after the publication of *Easy Money*. My suspicions regarding the California kid's improbable meteoric rise had given way to something far more serious: *The United States of America v. Samuel Bankman-Fried*. He was charged with seven crimes: six forms of fraud and conspiracy to commit fraud, as well as a charge for money laundering. The government laid out its case efficiently, relying heavily on the testimony of Sam's former colleagues. Three of them had already pleaded guilty for their participation in the scheme: Gary Wang, Nishad Singh, and Caroline Ellison. According to their testimony, the miraculous rise of Sam Bankman-Fried was predicated on a lie; Alameda Research, the trading firm Sam had founded before FTX, had been "borrowing" money from the exchange more or less since its inception. Over time things spiraled out of control.

On July 31, 2019, less than two months after FTX was founded, Sam approached Wang and Singh. Alameda was struggling; it needed money to pay bills. The firm had been on the financial ropes since the departure of key executives the year prior. According to Wang and Singh, Sam instructed them to alter the code inside of FTX's operating system so that Alameda could borrow money from FTX to pay what it owed. It was a simple change: the "allow_negative" function was enabled for Alameda, meaning it could run a negative balance on the exchange, withdrawing money from FTX in excess of what was in its trading account. Alameda was the only FTX customer that was allowed to operate this way.

The amount Alameda took from FTX was initially small, but it ballooned into tens of millions of dollars within months. The purportedly brilliant quantitative firm was in actuality terrible at trading, and its losses accumulated quickly. When questioned about the negative balance by a fellow employee, Sam responded that it was fine for Alameda to borrow as much as it needed as long as the amount stayed below FTX's total trading revenue. The limit appeared arbitrary, a way of rationalizing the fraud Sam and his cohorts were committing. Any amount of money they "borrowed" from FTX customers without their knowledge was illegal.

At the beginning of 2020, Gary Wang checked Alameda's balance: it was $200 million in the hole. FTX's total revenue was only $150 million. Alameda had blown through Sam's guardrail on borrowing in six months. Wang confronted his boss, and Sam replied that Wang had failed to account for the value of FTT on Alameda's books. FTT was the in-house illiquid shitcoin that would later contribute to FTX's demise. The notion that FTX's supply of FTT was a real liquid asset was borderline preposterous, but Wang backed down. It was easy to imagine how the situation could have gone down. FTX's principal employees were young and inexperienced. None seemed willing to confront their supremely confident boss, whose ego ironically swelled with each dollar he "borrowed" from his customers. (To offer just one example, Sam apparently believed he had a 5 percent chance of being elected President of the United States.)

Over the next two years, Alameda's negative balance mushroomed. The hundreds of millions it owed became billions. By the time it went bust in late 2022, Alameda had effective carte blanche to borrow as much as it wanted from FTX. As a student of fraud, I couldn't help but notice that the three components of the fraud triangle were all present: need, opportunity, and rationalization. A small excuse to cheat combined with the nearly unlimited ability to cheat and Sam's boundless rationalizations (via philanthropy for example) to weave a fiction that was grand in conception, but flimsy in reality.

With three of his former subordinates pleading guilty and testifying against him, the odds of Bankman-Fried being found not-guilty appeared low. His lawyers must have concurred, as he took the stand in his own defense, though Bankman-Fried did himself no favors. Under cross examination by Assistant US Attorney Danielle Sassoon, he crashed and burned. The AUSA asked the defendant a series of simple questions, often involving whether he recalled making a particular incriminating remark in the form of a tweet or during a filmed media appearance. Sam would try to duck and dodge, and Sassoon would play the evidence back for the jury to decide for themselves.

From my seat in the third row on the aisle, I had the perfect view of the witness stand, as well as the jury box. After a tense exchange during which Bankman-Fried got particularly testy with Sassoon, I saw one juror turn to another and roll her eyes in the direction of Bankman-Fried as if to say, "Can you believe this guy?" A few seconds later, another juror did the same thing. I'm no genius, but as a professional imitator of human behavior who studies the subtle art of body language, it was pretty clear that it was over.

After closing arguments, the jury took just four hours to find Sam Bankman-Fried guilty on all seven counts. On March 28, 2024, he was sentenced to twenty-five years in prison.

o o o

While Sam was self-immolating on the stand, another event portended even more trouble ahead for crypto, albeit from an unlikely source. On October 7, 2023, the fiftieth anniversary of the Yom Kippur war, militant groups associated with the Palestinian organization Hamas unleashed a vicious surprise attack on Israel. Over a thousand people were killed and hundreds of hostages were taken. The eyes of the world were drawn to the conflict, and for a moment media attention shifted away from more quotidian concerns over crypto's linkages to crime.

That soon changed. On October 10, the *Wall Street Journal* published the first in a series of articles on crypto's ties to terrorist financing and other rogue actors ("Hamas Militants Behind Israel Attack Raised Millions in Crypto"). Journalists Angus Berwick and Ian Talley noted that the Palestinian Islamic Jihad "received as much as $93 million in crypto" in the span of less than two years. Hamas and Hezbollah also received tens of millions. While crypto's true believers offered straw man arguments, or bickered over the particulars of the blockchain analytic techniques used to calculate the sums, to the public at large there was no denying the obvious: criminals love crypto because of course they do. A financial system deliberately constructed to avoid the law happened to prove extremely useful for those wishing to violate it. Articles in the *Journal* soon followed on crypto's ties to Russian gangsters and North Korean hackers.

Binance and Tether were focal points. Communications between Binance executives, cited in the March CFTC lawsuit against the company, resurfaced. Samuel Lim, the exchange's former Chief Compliance Officer, was particularly candid. Lim "explained to a colleague that terrorists usually send 'small sums' as 'large sums constitute money laundering.'" Lim's colleague joked that you "can barely buy an AK47 with 600 bucks." When it came to Binance's Russian customers, Lim was even more blunt: "Like come on. They are here for crime."

For the bad guys, Tether was the cryptocurrency of choice. The selling points were clear. In the crypto casinos, Tethers were traded 1:1 with the US dollar and instantly transferable all over the world. In other words, the perfect vehicle for money laundering. According to the *WSJ*, of the $41 million Hamas received in crypto between 2020 and 2023, more than 99 percent was in Tether. The same article noted Tether had been used for everything from compensating Chinese fentanyl suppliers to funding 50 percent of the North Korean ballistic missile system.

The constant stream of damning evidence surrounding Binance and Tether was too much to stomach for some of the most die-hard of crypto boosters. Senator Cynthia Lummis (R-WY) and congressman French Hill (R-AR), both of whom had previously attempted to push industry-friendly legislation through Congress, wrote to Attorney General Merrick Garland on October 26. They urged the DOJ "to reach a charging decision on Binace that reflects their current level of culpability and expeditiously conclude your investigation into the ongoing illicit activities involving Tether." The letter offered a rare moment of bipartisanship when it came to crypto, signifying just how far the industry's reputation had fallen in the eyes of the public.

US law enforcement finally took action. On November 21, CEO Changpeng Zhao surrendered to authorities in Seattle and pleaded guilty to money laundering. Binance pleaded guilty to violations of the Bank Secrecy Act and running an unlicensed money services business. The exchange agreed to pay a $4.3 billion fine. As such a business, Binance was required to file suspicious activity reports to the Financial Crimes Enforcement Network, but never filed a single one. According to the government, Binance deliberately failed to report more than 100,000 of these reports, "including transactions involving terrorist organizations, ransomware, child sexual exploitation material, frauds, and scams." Some Binance customers sent funds to Bitcoin wallets associated with the Islamic State of Iraq and Syria (ISIS), Hamas's Al-Qassam Brigades, Al Qaeda, and the Palestine Islamic Jihad (PIJ).

As a condition of the agreement, Binance consented to monitoring of its businesses for five years. The monitor, chosen by the government from a list provided by Binance, would have full access to the exchange's internal workings to ensure its compliance with anti-money laundering and know-your-customer laws. Importantly, the monitor was also tasked with combing through the company's records over the past five years. Any further wrongdoing uncovered could result in more charges against Binance and its executives. The US government was now inside the bowels of the largest cryptocurrency exchange on the planet, an experience that was unlikely to be pleasant for Binance's remaining employees. As former SEC official John Reed Stark put it, the agreement was the equivalent of "a 24/7, 365-days-a-year financial colonoscopy."

The Americans were done playing around. When CZ requested to return to the United Arab Emirates before his sentencing that spring—offering his entire equity stake in Binance as security—US District Judge Richard Jones denied his request. The judge cited the fact that the US has no extradition treaty with the UAE and noted that "the vast majority of the defendant's wealth is held overseas" and "he has access to hundreds of millions of dollars in accessible cryptocurrency."

Given its history, it was hard to see how Binance would continue to exist for much longer under the conditions imposed by US law enforcement. As a business, its competitive advantage appeared to be crime. The crypto industry tried to write off the capitulation of arguably its biggest player as much ado about nothing, but the facts were not on their side. Binance routinely accounted for 50 percent or more of overall trading volume in the market. Another member of the crypto cartel had been brought to its knees. CZ had every incentive to cooperate with law enforcement prior to his sentencing.

o o o

For skeptics like me, a useful heuristic in analyzing what remained of the crypto inner circle was to recall the composition of "Exchange coordination," the Signal chat group of which Sam Bankman-Fried was a member. There were five principals: Sam, CZ, Jesse Powell of exchange Kraken, crypto entrepreneur and former Grenadian ambassador to the WTO Justin Sun, and Paolo Ardoino of Tether.

Jesse Powell had resigned as CEO from Kraken the previous year. The exchange had been fined $360,000 by the Treasury Department to settle charges it had violated US sanctions. It also paid a $30 million fine to the SEC to settle charges it violated securities laws. In March, according to reporting by the New York Times, FBI agents searched Mr. Powell's home as a part of an investigation into claims he hacked and cyberstalked the Verge Center for the Arts, a nonprofit he founded. In November, the SEC sued Kraken's parent companies, Payward and Payward Ventures, for operating an unregistered online trading platform. With Powell sidelined, Sam in jail, and CZ pleading guilty, that left two members of "Exchange coordination" still standing: Justin Sun and Paolo Ardoino of Tether. And while the overall crypto market shrank, ties between the two players and their respective entities only deepened further.

Sun, his current whereabouts unknown, had been removed from his position as Grenadian WTO ambassador in March 2023, when the SEC sued him and several of his companies, including the Tron Foundation Limited. In its lawsuit, the Commission alleged that Sun manipulated the prices of coins under his control, often using celebrities to market them to the public via social media. Actress Lindsay Lohan and boxer/influencer Jake Paul were among those who agreed to settle charges for their participation in the scheme. Through a variety of legal maneuvers, Sun had thus far been able to avoid a trial. The SEC's case against him is pending, as of this writing.

In the fall of 2023, two of the exchanges associated with Sun, HTX (formerly Huobi) and Poloniex, were hacked repeatedly. In four different breaches, hackers managed to steal some $200 million from the platforms. As mentioned previously, a number of "hacks" in crypto have turned out to be inside jobs, presumably a way for insiders to siphon money from entities they control while denying responsibility for customers' losses. Given Sun's less-than-stellar reputation, the crypto rumor mill went into overdrive. Speculators wondered if Sun was trying to cash out as law enforcement circled.

There was additional evidence to support that theory. Sun was behind a relatively obscure stablecoin called TrueUSD (TUSD), which was heavily traded on the exchanges he owned, as well as on Binance. In early 2023, TUSD's market capitalization was around $1 billion, but by the fall it had skyrocketed to $3 billion. In December, just weeks after CZ's arrest and Binance's agreement with the US government was announced, Binance began encouraging customers to use a new stablecoin—First Digital (FDUSD)—by waving trading fees associated with it. Perhaps as a result, Justin Sun's TUSD plummeted, falling below $1.5 billion in a matter of months. The stablecoin became less so, with TUSD's peg to the dollar slipping to as low as ninety-seven cents in mid-January 2024. As we have seen, a depegging often precedes a stablecoin's collapse. TUSD also announced that it had engaged a new auditor, Moore Hong Kong, to provide daily attestations of its reserves. (Like the rest of its stablecoin brethren, TUSD has never been audited.) A sudden switch of auditors is another red flag when it comes to fraud.

Most bizarre of all, however, was Sun's social media feed. The Chinese-born businessman usually spoke in heavily accented English. Yet on Instagram, TikTok, and YouTube, he began posting long rambling quasi-inspirational videos while at times speaking with an elegant British accent, and at others with an American one. The videos appeared to be dubbed and digitally enhanced, and the effect was bizarre. What the hell was going on?

∘ ∘ ∘

Meanwhile, there were changes aplenty at Tether, the only other member of "Exchange coordination" left standing. On October 13, Tether announced that Paolo Ardoino would assume the role of CEO in December. The CTO had been the public face of the company for years, but now he would officially be in charge, taking over from the phantom CEO Jean-Louis van der Velde (who nonetheless remained CEO of the sister exchange Bitfinex). In honor of Paolo's promotion, I tweeted a GIF of a pirate walking the plank.

Around this time the company started printing huge quantities of new Tethers, and billions of them began trading on the crypto exchanges. Tether's market cap surged from $83 billion to $95 billion in less than three months. (The company even went so far as to print one billion new Tethers on December 25, perhaps as a Christmas present to itself.) It was yet another brazen move for the shady outfit. Apparently, those paying attention were meant to believe that legitimate companies decided to send Tether twelve billion actual US dollars at the same time that Sam Bankman-Fried was convicted, CZ pled guilty, and the war in the Middle East brought crypto's ties to terrorism to the world's attention.

Recall that Tethers are the poker chips in the crypto casino, and they are far and away the most traded coin. More Tethers are traded on any given day than the two biggest cryptocurrencies, Bitcoin and Ethereum, combined. Most Bitcoins are purchased with Tethers, not actual real money such as dollars. Little wonder then that with twelve billion new Tethers in circulation, Bitcoin's price began its magical rise once again! The OG crypto surged from $30,000 to $45,000 a coin, beginning its ascent almost as soon as Tether turned the money printer back on. Crypto advocates claimed that this was organic market demand, but that made little sense. It was also contradicted by looking at

Tether's competition: USDC. The American stablecoin was flat during that same time period, floating around $25 billion in market cap. Unlike Tether, USDC was a far safer bet for American investors, as it was required to comply with US laws. If there was genuinely new clean money that wanted exposure to crypto (a big if given the ongoing crackdown), wouldn't it want to hold USDC instead of Tether? And if there was any real money still flowing into Tether, where would it be coming from?

The relationship between Justin Sun and Tether seemed key to understanding it all. The majority of Tethers in existence had been issued on the Tron blockchain, some $50 billion in total. The amount of illegal activity they purportedly facilitated was staggering. According to a report from blockchain analytics firm Bitrace, in just one year—September 2022 to September 2023—it found "transactions totaling 17.07 billion USDT connected to underground currency exchanges, illegal commodity trades, unlawful collection and payment processes, and various criminal activities." The United Nations Office on Drugs and Crime issued a report in January 2024 entitled "Casinos, Money Laundering, Underground Banking, and Transnational Organized Crime in East and Southeast Asia: A Hidden and Accelerating Threat" finding that "USDT on the TRON blockchain has become a preferred choice for crypto money launderers in East and Southeast Asia due to its stability and the ease, anonymity, and low fees of its transactions."

The report tied together several themes of investigation, namely how the boom in online gambling had become intertwined with enormous sums of Chinese money seeking to avoid capital controls. Recall that the once-booming Chinese real estate sector had been wobbling for years under the weight of heavy debt and flagging demand. The government's draconian response to the COVID-19 pandemic inflicted further damage on the economy, as did the United States' decision to invest in domestic manufacturing. Foreign investment ebbed and the Chinese stock market tanked, falling between 40 and 50 percent from its 2021 peak. Wealthy Chinese, fearful of a collapsing economy and overbearing state, found themselves increasingly desperate to move their money overseas. One way to do so was via over-the-counter desks, where fiat currency (Chinese yuan in this case) could be exchanged for cryptocurrency. Those coins could then be instantaneously transferred all over the world via exchanges such as OKX and Binance. (Despite crypto being declared illegal in the country in 2021, OKX and Binance continued to serve millions of Chinese customers.)

When combined with a culture of online gambling, these flows of capital formed a vast underground economy perfectly suited for money laundering via cryptocurrency. According to a report from Polaris Market Research, the online gambling industry was expected to reach $205 billion by 2030. Much of that money was suspected to be dirty, the proceeds of criminal organizations. For example, in the Binance resolution, the US government noted that "Binance has directly sent and received over $1 billion with known gambling services and online casinos." The Chinese government estimated that in 2020, some five million people participated in this underground economy, amounting to $157 billion of capital outflows from the country. By wash trading cryptocurrencies using exchanges like Binance and Sun's HTX, money launderers could hide their trail. When viewed this way, the buffoonery of exchange owners like Sam, CZ, and Justin Sun made much more sense. Once celebrated as brilliant entrepreneurs, in reality they were clumsy (if briefly successful) facilitators of large-scale money laundering operations. (A source colorfully described the youthful exchange owners as the "boy band of money laundering.") The exchanges were, of course, happy to facilitate crypto gambling as well, but that was in many ways a front for obscuring what was apparently their core business: providing a platform through which criminal entities could move large sums of money while bypassing regulated banks.

The US government was beginning to take notice. Wally Adeyemo, second in command at the Treasury Department, made that abundantly clear in his remarks to the Blockchain Association Policy Summit, an industry trade group, on November 29. "While some have heeded our calls and taken steps to prevent illicit activity, the lack of action by too many firms—both large and small—represents a clear and present risk to our national security." Mr. Adeyemo described crypto's utility in financing the operations of rogue states such as North Korea, as well as funneling money to Hamas. He then went further: "We cannot allow dollar-backed stable coin providers outside the United States to have the privilege of using our currency without the responsibility of putting in place procedures to prevent terrorists from abusing their platform." This was a clear rebuke of Tether, and an unmistakable signal that the US government now had the stablecoin company in its crosshairs.

On the face of it, Tether appeared willing to comply with the powers that be, freezing wallets associated with criminal activity at the request of the DOJ, FBI, and Secret Service. By mid-December, it had frozen some $435 million. Paolo Ardoino, Tether's new CEO, boasted that Tether wanted to become a "world class partner" with the US to "expand dollar hegemony." The company "recently onboarded the US Secret Service into our platform and is in the process of doing the same" with the FBI. The irony was thick: Tether had thrived outside the reaches of American law, but it now saw the need to kiss the ring of US law enforcement and beg for mercy. Given the increasingly fragile state of what remained of crypto's inner circle, something seemed bound to give.

o o o

The printing of twelve billion Tethers in three months likely produced the 50 percent spike in Bitcoin's price, but that was not a plotline on which crypto boosters wanted to dwell. The industry desperately needed a new story to tell, ideally one that would encourage more regular folks to pay real money in exchange for potentially worthless bits of computer code. It was a hard sell. According to a Pew study from March 2023, 75 percent of Americans who had heard of cryptocurrency were "not confident that current ways to invest in, trade or use cryptocurrencies are reliable and safe." Only six percent were "very" or "extremely" confident. It's worth noting that this was a poll conducted *before* Sam Bankman-Fried's trial. The fact that the public face of the industry was facing a potential life sentence for committing one of the largest frauds in American history did not bode well for improving public sentiment.

Scouring the bleak landscape for new narratives, crypto boosters conjured hope from an ironic source: the approval of a spot Bitcoin exchange traded fund (ETF). An ETF operates much like a mutual fund. It's a publicly listed security representing ownership of a particular asset or assets—in this case, Bitcoin. An ETF is about as mainstream as it gets in the financial world. There are thousands of ETFs in everything from commodities, bonds, and equities to real estate and all manner of specialty ETFs.

Back in 2008, Satoshi Nakamoto dreamed of a "peer-to-peer currency" that would avoid all intermediaries. A decade and a half later, his radical vision of decentralized financial freedom had been pasteurized to the point where its purported salvation lay in the approval of the most pedestrian of financial products. The only way to square that circle was to admit the obvious. At the end of the day, Bitcoin boosterism was about one thing: greed. The blatant hypocrisy made me recall Robert Shiller and the observation that economic narratives, much like viruses, mutate into whatever story resonates with the public.

Up to this point, the SEC had denied the approval of an ETF tied to the spot (current) price of Bitcoin out of fears that it could be easily manipulated. For an ETF to be approved, it had to be consistent with the Securities Exchange Act of 1934, which requires that rules be designed to "prevent fraudulent and manipulative acts and practices" as well as "protect investors and the public interest." Bitcoin, and crypto more broadly, failed that test miserably.

Confusingly however, the SEC had approved multiple Bitcoin *futures* ETFs, which hold futures contracts for an asset rather than the asset itself. On August 29, 2023, in the case of *Grayscale Investments vs. the SEC*, the US Court of Appeals for the DC Circuit ruled that the SEC had acted in an "arbitrary and capricious manner" when it denied Grayscale's application to become a spot Bitcoin ETF. The Court vacated the SEC's order and granted the permission for review. The crypto crowd believed they had scored an enormous win. The spot Bitcoin ETF would soon be approved, and the glory days of crypto would return!

The hype machine cranked up again, with self-proclaimed gurus and influencers saturating social and financial media with absurd predictions. Cathie Wood, whose company ARK Invest had applied to issue its own Bitcoin

ETF, estimated her "base case" price for Bitcoin in 2030 was $650,000 a coin. The shameless crypto promoter believed $1 million per Bitcoin, or even $1.5 million was possible. Hey, you never know.

On January 9, the SEC's account on X (formerly Twitter) posted an announcement that the spot Bitcoin ETFs had been approved. The price of Bitcoin spiked immediately. Minutes later, however, SEC Chair Gary Gensler posted that the Commission's account had been hacked. Bitcoin's price briefly dropped before leveling out again. It was a fairly audacious move, even for crypto: hacking the account of the regulatory body that had denied the industry's applications for spot ETFs out of fears of market manipulation.

Amazingly enough, it didn't matter. Despite the hack, the next day the five-member body of SEC commissioners granted approval to list spot Bitcoin ETFs. In a contentious three-to-two vote, Chair Gensler cast the deciding ballot, despite his open skepticism of cryptocurrency's legitimacy. In a statement issued after the vote, Gensler described Bitcoin as "primarily a speculative, volatile asset that's also used for illicit activity including ransomware, money laundering, sanction evasion, and terrorist financing."

ETFs are publicly listed securities, and as such they are highly liquid: easy to get out of via public markets. Because crypto had been largely relegated to the fringes of the American financial system, boosters argued that the approval of a spot Bitcoin ETF would usher in a new wave of growth for what had formerly been marketed as a currency, and was now being sold as a scarce digital asset whose price could only go up. All manner of institutional investors could buy Bitcoin now! In addition, the public at large would be able to bet on crypto through their brokerage account without dealing with offshore exchanges such as FTX and Binance.

So went the story. But on January 11, 2024, when the Bitcoin ETFs began trading, the price of Bitcoin dropped. Ironically, outflows from the Grayscale Trust were largely to blame. Grayscale had sued the SEC to convert to an ETF, but once it did, investors dumped their shares in significant quantities. Six billion dollars' worth of GBTC shares were sold in the first two weeks, including nearly $1 billion from FTX's stash. Over the same time period, the net inflows to Bitcoin—the amount the new ETFs collected minus what Grayscale sold—amounted to less than $1 billion. At least initially, the approval of spot Bitcoin ETFs was hardly the game changer advertised.

Recall that the crypto market is highly illiquid and business is mainly conducted in Tethers. With the approval of spot ETFs, that illiquidity is likely to be tested. Where the price of Bitcoin will go next is of course anyone's guess, but given the number of market players who had been eliminated in the past year and a half, as well as the US government's focus on Tether's ties to illicit activity, if I were a betting man I'd take the under. In fact, I have.

o o o

My initial wager against crypto in the fall of 2021 had been an epic disaster, but by doubling down at the end of the year, when the mania was at its all-time high, I ended up turning a significant profit. Using that money, I bet against several non-crypto related frauds, and one of those bets turned out to be particularly successful. The net result was that $385,000 of capital in 2021 had grown to $1,700,000 by the beginning of 2024. Allowing for capital gains taxes due, I made more or less a million bucks betting against frauds like crypto. Better to be lucky than good, I guess. I used some of the profits to finance a documentary on money and lying.

As much fun as my time in the casino had been, I was burning out covering crypto. The "community" was often boorish and puerile, and being online 24/7 was not good for my mental health. Around the end of 2023, I told myself I was done with this crypto nonsense as soon as my obligations to the book and documentary were fulfilled.

But then, in the fall of 2023, with Tether printing billions and Bitcoin soaring once more, I detected the familiar pungent odor of crypto-hype bullshit. It was too tempting to resist. I bet roughly half a million dollars crypto would crash yet again, and soon.

I'll let you know how it turns out.

ACKNOWLEDGMENTS

To the members of the crypto skeptic community, I want to thank you for your friendship, tutelage, and guidance along the way. Unfortunately, it would be impossible to list all the skeptics who have helped me over the past two years, but I do want to thank a few of them specifically.

Thank you to David Gerard. Your wicked sense of humor and brilliant writing (often penned alongside the equally brilliant Amy Castor) helped inspire me to go down the crypto rabbit hole. I'm grateful to Cas Piancey and Bennett Tomlin for educating and entertaining me on their podcast, *Crypto Critics' Corner.* Thank you to Stephen Diehl for being as generous to fellow skeptics as he is eloquent in his deconstructions of the myths surrounding cryptocurrency. Thank you to Molly White for chronicling the absurdities of crypto and Web3 through her website web3isgoinggreat.com. I'm grateful for the work of Dr. James Block, aka Dirty Bubble Media, who's as smart as they come. Don't analyze me, Doc. Thank you to Patrick McKenzie for helping me translate the language of blockchain and public key encryption to the lay reader as simply as possible and without making a fool of myself. And I'd like to thank Bitfinex'ed, and all the other pseudonymous crypto skeptic truth-tellers I've met online who have suffered derision and harassment, for their bravery. History will be kind to you.

Thank you to Hilary Allen, Lee Reneirs, Rohan Grey, Eswar Prasad, and John Reed Stark for helping me understand American law as it relates to cryptocurrency, as well as the history of financial regulations in the US.

To Jim Harris, and all of those in the law enforcement community whom I cannot name, thank you. I have learned a lot from you.

Our reporting from El Salvador would not have been possible without the assistance of fellow journalist Nelson Rauda. I cannot wait to see what you do next, Nelson.

Thank you to Ron Chernow for your advice and counsel. I think I owe you lunch.

In a similar vein, thank you to Julian Zelizer for helping me navigate the peculiar world of publishing and publicizing a book. I appreciate the crash course, professor.

Thank you to my agent, Noah Ballard, for your stewardship of this project and your counsel along the way.

This book would not exist were it not for Jamison Stoltz, editorial director at Abrams Press. He took a chance on a TV actor with a crazy idea when no one else would. For that I am forever grateful. Thank you to Jamison and the incredible team at Abrams for all their hard work in turning my bizarre obsession into reality.

Lastly, thank you to my wife, Morena. I would never have been brave enough to try to pull this off were it not for your unwavering support and endless patience. Please let me do it again.

APPENDIX

According to the SEC's website, there are seven red flags when it comes to Ponzi schemes:

- High returns with little or no risk. Every investment carries some degree of risk, and investments yielding higher returns typically involve more risk. Be highly suspicious of any "guaranteed" investment opportunity.

- Overly consistent returns. Investments tend to go up and down over time. Be skeptical about an investment that regularly generates positive returns regardless of overall market conditions.

- Unregistered investments. Ponzi schemes typically involve investments that are not registered with the SEC or with state regulators. Registration is important because it provides investors with access to information about the company's management, products, services, and finances.

- Unlicensed sellers. Federal and state securities laws require investment professionals and firms to be licensed or registered. Most Ponzi schemes involve unlicensed individuals or unregistered firms.

- Secretive, complex strategies. Avoid investments if you don't understand them or can't get complete information about them.

- Issues with paperwork. Account statement errors may be a sign that funds are not being invested as promised.

- Difficulty receiving payments. Be suspicious if you don't receive a payment or have difficulty cashing out. Ponzi scheme promoters sometimes try to prevent participants from cashing out by offering even higher returns for staying put.

NOTES

CHAPTER 1: MONEY AND LYING

1 **Political economist:** Susan Strange, *Casino Capitalism* (Basil Blackwell, 1986).

1 **In *The General Theory*:** John Maynard Keynes, *The General Theory of Employment, Interest and Money* (Palgrave Macmillan, 1936).

2 **Golden Age of Fraud:** Harriet Agnew, "Jim Chanos: 'We are in the golden age of fraud,'" *Financial Times*, July 24, 2020.

4 **A few thousand cryptos:** CoinMarketCap, "Today's Cryptocurrency Prices by Market Cap," https://Coinmarketcap.com.

4 **An estimated forty million Americans:** Pew Research Center, November 11, 2021.

5 **In his 2019 book:** Robert Shiller, *Narrative Economics* (Princeton University Press, 2019).

6 **Between 2000 and 2003:** FRED Economic Data/St. Louis Fed, "Interest Rates, Discount Rate for United States," https://fred.stlouisfed.org/series/INTDSRUSM193N.

7 **Fed offered $700 billion:** U.S. Department of the Treasury, "Troubled Assets Relief Program (TARP)," https://home.treasury.gov/data/troubled-assets-relief-program.

7 **Fed's assets:** Board of Governors of the Federal Reserve System, "Credit and Liquidity Programs and the Balance Sheet," https://www.federalreserve.gov/monetarypolicy/bst_recenttrends.htm.

8 **Interest rates:** FRED Economic Data/St. Louis Fed, "Federal Funds Effective Rate," https://fred.stlouisfed.org/series/FEDFUNDS.

8 **Jail time:** Wikipedia, "Kareem Serageldin," last modified October, 5, 2022, https://en.wikipedia.org/wiki/Kareem_Serageldin.

8 **Bitcoin white paper:** Satoshi Yakamoto, "Bitcoin: A Peer-to-Peer Electronic Cash System," https://bitcoin.org/bitcoin.pdf.

9   **cryptographer David Chaum:** "Blind signatures for untraceable payments," Springer-Verlag, 1982, https://chaum.com/wp-content/uploads/2022/01 /Chaum-blind-signatures.pdf.

12   **DigiCash:** Wikipedia, "DigiCash," last modified March 14, 2022, https:// en.wikipedia.org/wiki/DigiCash.

12   **eGold:** Kim Zetter, "Bullion and Bandits: The Improbable Rise and Fall of E-Gold," *Wired*, June 9, 2009, https://www.wired.com/2009/06/e-gold/.

13   **Liberty Reserve:** press release, "Founder of Liberty Reserve Pleads Guilty to Laundering More Than $250 Million Through His Digital Currency Business," US Department of Justice, https://www.justice.gov/opa/pr/founder-liberty -reserve-pleads-guilty-laundering-more-250-million-through-his-digital.

13   **Bitcoins were used to pay for two pizzas:** Rufas Kamau, "What Is Bitcoin Pizza Day, and Why Does The Community Celebrate on May 22?," *Forbes*, May 9, 2022, https://www.forbes.com/sites/rufaskamau/2022/05/09/what -is-bitcoin-pizza-day-and-why-does-the-community-celebrate-on-may -22/?sh=1fab3817fd68.

14   **Silk Road:** Benjamin Weiser, "Ross Ulbricht, Creator of Silk Road Website, Is Sentenced to Life in Prison," *New York Times*, May 29, 2015.

17   **"Naturally occurring Ponzi schemes":** Robert Shiller, *Irrational Exuberance* (Princeton University Press, 2015), p. 70.

18   **Kindleberger:** Charles Kindleberger, *Manias, Panics, and Crashes: A History of Financial Crises*, 7th edition (Palgrave Macmillan, 2015), p. 29.

19   **Doesn't scale:** Kyle Croman et al., "On Scaling Decentralized Blockchains: (A Position Paper)," *Financial Cryptography and Data Security* (Springer, 2016), Lecture Notes in Computer Science, Vol. 9604, pp. 106–125.

19   **Visa:** Visa, "Security and Reliability," https://usa.visa.com/run-your-business /small-business-tools/retail.html.

19   **Argentina:** Christina Criddle, "Bitcoin consumes 'more electricity than Argentina,'" BBC.com, February 10, 2021.

22   **Dan Davies:** Dan Davies, *Lying for Money: How Legendary Frauds Reveal the Workings of the World* (Scribner, 2018), p. 260.

23   **"minor celebrity":** Shiller, *Narrative Economics*, Preface, xii.

24   **an article for the *New Republic*:** Jacob Silverman, "Even Donald Trump Knows Bitcoin Is a Scam," *New Republic*, June 7, 2021.

CHAPTER 2: WHAT COULD POSSIBLY GO WRONG?

27   **My first byline:** Ben McKenzie and Jacob Silverman, "Celebrity Crypto Shilling Is a Moral Disaster," Slate, October 7, 2021.

CHAPTER 3: MONEY PRINTER GO BRRR

32 **For our second journalistic collaboration:** Ben McKenzie and Jacob Silverman, "Untethered," Slate, October 17, 2021.

32 **director of compliance for Excapsa:** Stuart Hoegner, "Deputy GC, Director of Compliance, Excapsa, Jan 2006–Dec 2006," LinkedIn profile, https://www.linkedin.com/in/stuart-hoegner/.

34 **The Commodities Futures Trading Commission . . . had fined:** Release Number 8450-21, "CTFC Orders Tether and Bitfinex to Pay Fines Totaling $42.5 Million," October 15, 2021, https://www.cftc.gov/PressRoom/PressReleases/8450-21.

34 **the New York Attorney General had fined:** "Attorney General James Ends Virtual Currency Trading Platform Bitfinex's Illegal Activites in New York," February 23, 2021, https://ag.ny.gov/press-release/2021/attorney-general-james-ends-virtual-currency-trading-platform-bitfinexs-illegal.

34 **Pierce was living with Collins-Rector:** Joseph Menn, "Spain Arrests Fugitive in Molestation Case," *Los Angeles Times*, May 18, 2002.

34 **The fourth red flag for Tether:** Tether, "Crystal Clear Fees," https://tether.to/es/fees.

35 **"a fraud can be called a ponzi scheme . . .":** Dan Davies, *Lying for Money: How Legendary Frauds Reveal the Workings of the World* (Scribner, 2018), p. 94.

35 **multiple conflicts of interest:** Bennett Tomlin, "Tether's Executives are Deeply Conflicted," Bennett's Blog, September 13, 2021, https://bennettftomlin.com/2021/09/13/tethers-executives-are-deeply-conflicted/.

35 **Giancarlo Devasini:** Kadhim Shubber and Siddharth Venkataramakrishnan, "Tether: the former plastic surgeon behind the crypto reserve currency," *Financial Times*, July 15, 2021.

36 **The "fraud triangle" has three components:** Donald Cressey, *Other People's Money: A Study in the Social Psychology of Embezzlement* (Free Press, 1953).

37 **Razzlekhan:** Zeke Faux, "Did Razzlekhan and Dutch Pull Off History's Biggest Crypto Heist?," Bloomberg, June 29, 2022.

37 **In a scholarly paper:** John M. Griffin and Amin Shams, "Is Bitcoin Really Untethered?," *Journal of Finance* (Vol. LXXV, No. 4), August 2020.

37 **Wash trading is the practice of:** Lin William Cong et al., "Crypto Wash Trading," National Bureau of Economic Research, December 2022.

39 **calling himnself Bitfinex'ed:** Interview, October 7, 2021.

42 **A December 2021 study commissioned by Grayscale:** *Third Annual Bitcoin Investor Study*, Grayscale Research, December 2021, p. 4.

42 **Nikola, an electric vehicle company:** Jack Ewing, "Founder of Electric Truck Maker Is Convicted of Fraud," *New York Times*, October 14, 2022.

CHAPTER 4: COMMUNITY

50 **Tom Brady received 1.1 million common shares:** Jeremy Hill, "Brady, Gisele, Patriots' Bob Kraft Among FTX Shareholders Facing Wipeout," Bloomberg, January 10, 2023.

52 **42% of men:** Michelle Faverio and Navid Massarat, "46% of Americans who have invested in cryptocurrency say it's done worse than expected," Pew Research Center, August 2022.

53 **"In theory, the difference seems to be":** Amanda Montell, *Cultish: The Language of Fanaticism* (Harper Wave, 2021), pp. 160–161.

54 **Bitcoin ownership is highly concentrated:** Igor Makarov and Antoinette Schoar, "Blockchain Analysis of the Bitcoin Market," National Bureau of Economic Research, 2021.

54 **A few win, most lose:** John M. Taylor, "The Case (for and) against Multi-level Marketing," Consumer Awareness Institute, 2011.

55 **cooling out the mark:** Erving Goffman, "On Cooling the Mark Out," *Psychiatry*, 1952.

59 **"The thing that makes money money is trust":** Jacob Goldstein, *Money: The True Story of a Made-Up Thing* (Hachette Books, 2020), p. 31.

61 **no depositor has ever lost a penny:** FDIC: Federal Deposit Insurance Corporation, n.d., "History of the FDIC," https://fdic.gov/about.

62 **We tried private money . . . during the free banking era:** Arthur J. Rolnick and Warren E. Weber, "Free Banking, Wildcat Banking, and Shinplasters," *Federal Reserve Bank of Minneapolis Quarterly Review*, Fall 1982.

64 **tulip mania:** Charles Mackay, *Extraordinary Popular Delusions and the Madness of Crowds* (Richard Bentley, 1841).

66 **commitment to the gold standard . . . fraught situation:** Liaquat Ahamed, *Lords of Finance: The Bankers Who Broke the World* (The Penguin Press, 2009), p. 439.

CHAPTER 5: SXSW, THE CIA, AND THE $1.5 TRILLION THAT WASN'T THERE

74 **Axie Infinity:** Olga Kharif, "Hackers Steal About $600 Million in One of the Biggest Crypto Heists," Bloomberg, March 29, 2022.

83 **Celsius's chief financial officer had been arrested:** Dan McCrum, Kadhim Shubber, and Mehul Srivastava, "Israeli judge lifts gagging order revealing Celsius Network CFO's arrest," *Financial Times*, March 1, 2022.

83 **Mashinsky and his confederates:** Interview with Alex Mashinsky, SXSW (Austin, TX), March 13, 2022.

86 **Whinstone Bitcoin ... owned by Riot Blockchain:** Olivia Raimonde, "Crypto Miner Riot Blockchain to Buy Whinstone for $651 Million," Bloomberg, April 8, 2021.

88 **We were met by CEO Chad Harris:** Interview with Chad Harris, Whinstone executive offices (Rockdale, TX), March 14, 2022.

90 **In 2021, the greenhouse gases ... by electric vehicles globally:** Alex de Vries et al., "The true costs of digital currencies: Exploring impact beyond energy use," *One Earth*, June 18, 2021.

CHAPTER 6: THE BUSINESS OF SHOW

91 **our months-long investigation into ... Binance:** Ben McKenzie and Jacob Silverman, "Why users are pushing back against the world's largest crypto exchange," *Washington Post*, April 1, 2022.

92 **crypto took off in China ... to avoid capital controls:** Karen Yeung, "Cryptocurrencies help Chinese evade capital and currency controls in moving billions overseas," *South China Morning Post*, August 26, 2020.

92 **Binance has ... no headquarters:** Patricia Kowsmann and Caitlan Ostroff, "$76 Billion a Day: How Binance Became the World's Biggest Crypto Exchange," *Wall Street Journal*, November 11, 2021.

100 **Peter Thiel, the arch-capitalist:** Abram Brown, "Peter Thiel Pumps Bitcoin, Calls Warren Buffett A 'Sociopathic Grandpa,'" Forbes.com, April 7, 2022.

102 **"In Miami we have big balls":** Daniel Kuhn, "The Meaning of Miami's Castrated Bitcoin Bull," CoinDesk, April 8, 2022.

103 **It was Brock Pierce:** Interview with Brock Pierce, Bitcoin 2022 (Miami, FL), April 7, 2022.

106 **Eric Adams. ... in the form of Bitcoin:** Ben McKenzie and Jacob Silverman, "The Embarrassment of New York's Next Mayor Taking His Paychecks in Bitcoin," Slate, November 5, 2021.

109 **O'Leary was particularly bullish:** Adam Morgan McCarthy, "'Spigots of capital' will flood into crypto once policy and regulation are set, 'Shark Tank' investor Kevin O'Leary predicts," Markets Insider (Insider.com), April 7, 2022.

109 **Mario Gomez and Carmen Valeria Escobar:** Interviews with Mario Gomez and Carmen Escobar, Bitcoin 2022 (Miami, FL), April 9, 2022.

CHAPTER 7: THE WORLD'S COOLEST DICTATOR

114 **brash young politician named Bukele:** Gabriel Labrador, "How Bukele Crafted a Best-Selling Political Brand," *El Faro*, May 3, 2022.

119 **rollout of the government's Chivo Wallet system:** Jacob Silverman and Ben McKenzie, "Nayib Bukele's Broken Bitcoin Promise," The Intercept, July 22, 2022.

120 **a horrific spree of gang violence:** Associated Press, "El Salvador locks down prisons after wave of 87 killings over weekend," *Guardian*, March 28, 2022.

120 **Mario Garcia was one:** Interview with Mario Garcia, El Zonte (Chiltiupán, El Salvador), May 16, 2022.

122 **Bitcoin City:** Edward Ongweso Jr., "El Salvador's President Unveils Golden 'Bitcoin City' Amid Brutal Crash," Motherboard (Tech by Vice), May 10, 2022.

123 **Wilfredo Claros:** Interview with Wilfredo Claros, Condadillo (La Unión, El Salvador), May 17, 2022.

124 **admitted to having forged a secret deal:** Carlos Martínez, "Collapsed Government Talks with MS-13 Sparked Record Homicides in El Salvador, Audios Reveal," *El Faro*, May 17, 2022.

CHAPTER 8: RATS IN A SACK

129 **Do Kwon even named his daughter:** Do Kwon (@stablekwon), "My dearest creation named after my greatest invention," Twitter, April 16, 2022.

129 **The SEC subpoenaed Do:** Greg Ahlstrand, "Terra, CEO Do Kwon Ordered to Comply With SEC Subpoena Related to Mirror Protocol Investigation," CoinDesk, Feb. 17, 2022.

132 **Three Arrows Capital:** Jen Wieczner, "The Crypto Geniuses Who Vaporized a Trillion Dollars," *New York* magazine, Aug. 15, 2022.

133 **Celsius . . . paused customer withdrawls:** James Block, various articles at Dirty Bubble Media, https://dirtybubblemedia.substack.com.

136 **Celsius . . . filed for bankruptcy:** Celsius Network LLC, et al., Case Number: 22-10964 (MG), Southern District of New York, https://cases.stretto.com/celsius/.

140 **Hilary Allen . . . wrote a paper:** Hilary J. Allen, "DeFi: Shadow Banking 2.0?" *William & Mary Law Review*, 2022.

CHAPTER 9: THE EMPEROR IS BUTT-ASS NAKED

149 **He had graced the cover of *Forbes*:** Chase Peterson-Withorn and Steven Ehrlich, "The World's Richest 20-Year-Old Just Got A Lot Richer, Thanks To New FTX Funding Round," *Forbes*, October, 21, 2021.

150   **"THE NEXT WARREN BUFFET?":** Jeff John Roberts, "Excusive: 30-year-old billionaire Sam Bankman-Fried has been called the next Warren Buffett. His counterintuitive investment strategy will either build him an empire—or end in disaster," *Fortune*, August 1, 2022.

150   **a billion to bail out crypto:** Alexander Osipovich, "The 30-Year-Old Spending $1 Billion to Save Crypto," *Wall Street Journal*, August 23, 2022.

150   **plans to give away his enormous fortune:** Zeke Faux, "A 30-Year-Old Crypto Billionaire Wants to Give His Fortune Away," Bloomberg, April 3, 2022.

150   **"north of $100 million":** MacKenzie Sigalos, "FTX's Sam Bankman-Fried backs down from 'dumb quote' about giving $1 billion to political races," CNBC, October 14, 2022, www.cnbc.com/2022/10/14/sam-bankman-fried-back-tracks-from-1-billion-political-donation.html.

150   **He was everywhere . . . I dug in:** Various articles from Reuters, Bloomberg, the *New York Times*, *Forbes*, and others.

152   **Sequoia was blown away . . . during a Zoom call:** Sequoia Capital, profile on Sam Bankman-Fried from Sequoiacap.com (since removed), September 22, 2022.

156   **We began:** Ben McKenzie interview with Sam Bankman-Fried, 1 Hotel Central Park (New York, NY), July 2022.

CHAPTER 10: WHO'S IN CHARGE HERE?

180   **Elon Musk . . . promoted Dogecoin:** Eric Deggans, "Elon Musk Takes An Awkward Turn As 'Saturday Night Live' Host," NPR, May 9, 2021.

181   **President Biden . . . executive order:** White House, "Executive Order on Ensuring Responsible Development of Digital Assets," March 9, 2022, https://www.whitehouse.gov/briefing-room/presidential-actions/2022/03/09/executive-order-on-ensuring-responsible-development-of-digital-assets/.

181   **The statistics cited by the FTC:** Emma Fletcher, "Reports show scammers cashing in on crypto craze," FTC, June 3, 2022, https://www.ftc.gov/news-events/data-visualizations/data-spotlight/2022/06/reports-show-scammers-cashing-crypto-craze.

182   **The revolving door kept spinning:** Tech Transparency Project, "Crypto Industry Amasses Washington Insiders as Lobbying Blitz Intensifies," https://www.techtransparencyproject.org/articles/crypto-industry-amasses-washington-insiders-lobbying-blitz-intensifies.

186   **Mark Hays:** Ben McKenzie interview with Mark Hays, Summer 2022.

188   **The United States of America is unique:** Conversations with Lee Reiners (policy director at the Duke Financial Economics Center and a lecturing fellow at Duke Law), Summer 2022.

193 **John Reed Stark:** Ben McKenzie interview with John Reed Stark, Maryland, August 2022.

198 **Two weeks later, Kim Kardashian:** press release, "SEC Charges Kim Kardashian for Unlawfully Touting Crypto Security," U.S. Securities and Exchange Commission, October 3, 2022, https://www.sec.gov/news/press-release/2022-183.

CHAPTER 11: UNBANKRUPT YOURSELF

199 **James Block developed an interest in fraud:** Ben McKenzie and Jacob Silverman interviews with James Block, Spring and Summer 2022.

200 **Celsius stood out:** James Block, various articles at Dirty Bubble Media, https://Dirtybubblemedia.substack.com.

204 **Celsius's CFO Yaron Shalem:** Simona Weinglass, "Another 2 leading Israeli blockchain pioneers named as suspects in vast crypto scam," *Times of Israel*, March 1, 2022.

212 **KeyFi sued Celsius:** Reuters, "Lawsuit accuses troubled crypto lender Celsius Network of fraud," July 7, 2022, https://www.reuters.com/technology/lawsuit-accuses-troubled-crypto-lender-celsius-network-fraud-2022-07-08/.

CHAPTER 12: CHAPTER 11

217 **the FDIC issued a cease-and-desist order:** Ashley Capoot, "Crypto firm FTX gets warning from FDIC to stop 'misleading' consumers about deposit protection," CNBC, Aug. 19, 2022, https://www.cnbc.com/2022/08/19/crypto-firm-ftx-receives-cease-and-desist-from-fdic-about-insurance.html.

218 **He slid into my DMs:** Direct Messages between Ben McKenzie and Sam Bankman-Fried.

220 **Alameda's balance sheet:** Ian Allison, "Divisions in Sam Bankman-Fried's Crypto Empire Blur on His Trading Titan Alameda's Balance Sheet," CoinDesk, November 2, 2022, https://www.coindesk.com/business/2022/11/02/divisions-in-sam-bankman-frieds-crypto-empire-blur-on-his-trading-titan-alamedas-balance-sheet/.

220 **an ominously titled post:** James Block, "Is Alameda Research Insolvent?," Dirty Bubble Media, November 4, 2022, https://dirtybubblemedia.substack.com/p/is-alameda-research-insolvent.

223 **Sam signed over control:** MacKenzie Sigalos, "Sam Bankman-Fried steps down as FTX CEO as his crypto exchange files for bankruptcy," CNBC,

November 11, 2022, https://www.cnbc.com/2022/11/11/sam-bankman-frieds
-cryptocurrency-exchange-ftx-files-for-bankruptcy.html.

228 **"'God Mode' to short coins..."**: Alex Mashinsky (@Mashinsky), Twitter,
December 3, 2022, https://twitter.com/mashinsky/with_replies.

229 **the Blockchain Eight:** David Dayen, "Congressmembers Tried to Stop the
SEC's Inquiry Into FTX," *The American Prospect*, November 23, 2022, https://
prospect.org/power/congressmembers-tried-to-stop-secs-inquiry-into-ftx/.

229 **the year before:** Tom Emmer (@GOPMajorityWhip), Twitter, December 8,
2021, https://twitter.com/GOPMajorityWhip/status/1468698269391880192.

230 **a former general counsel:** Jarod Facundo, "Sen. Gillibrand Hires Former
Crypto Lawyer," *The American Prospect*, December 2, 2022, https://prospect.
org/power/sen-gillibrand-hires-former-crypto-lawyer/.

234 **Alameda had invested $11.5 million:** Stephen Gandel, "Crypto Firm FTX's
Ownership of a U.S. Bank Raises Questions," *New York Times*, November 23,
2022, https://www.nytimes.com/2022/11/23/business/ftx-cryptocurrency
-bank.html.

234 **SBF was arrested in the Bahamas:** CFTC complaint against FTX, United
States District Court (Southern District of New York), December 21, 2022,
https://www.cftc.gov/media/8021/enfftxtradingcomplaint122122/download.

237 **In January 2023:** Giulia Heyward, "Cryptocurrency giant Coinbase strikes a $100 million deal with New York regulators," NPR, Janu-
ary 4, 2023, https://www.npr.org/2023/01/04/1146915338/coinbase-
settlement-cryptocurrency-exchange-new-york-dfs.

CHAPTER 13: PREACHER'S FATHER

243 **a story about his dad, Hal:** Multiple interviews with David Henson in 2022;
reporting trip to Henson family and church in Hendersonville, North Carolina,
November 2022; screenshots, texts, bank statements, and other documents
about Hal Henson's crypto purchases provided by David Henson.

247 **addiction services:** Interview with Lin and Aaron Sternlicht, Fall 2022.

EPILOGUE

257 **I was testifying before the Senate Banking Committee:** December 14, 2022.

258 **"The spigots of capital..."**: Kevin O'Leary, Bitcoin Conference (Miami,
FL), 2022, https://www.youtube.com/watch?v=UgoZGn6Y74g.

258 **his written testimony leaked:** https://s.wsj.net/public/resources/documents
/SBFwrittentestimonynotes12122022.pdf.

259 **Back door code:** Pete Syme, "Sam Bankman-Fried's secret 'backdoor' discovered, FTX lawyer says," Insider, January 13, 2023.

260 **The Block:** Sara Fischer, "Exclusive: SBF secretly funded crypto news site," Axios December 9, 2022.

260 **straw donor scheme:** USA superseding indictment, United States District Court (Southern District of New York), February 23, 2023, https://storage.courtlistener.com/recap/gov.uscourts.nysd.590940/gov.uscourts.nysd.590940.80.0.pdf.

260 **Mr. Singh pleaded guilty:** David Jaffe-Bellany and Matthew Goldstein, "Third Top FTX Executive Pleads Guilty in Fraud Investigation," *New York Times*, February 28, 2023.

260 **Alex Mashinsky . . . was sued for fraud:** press release, "Attorney General James Sues Former CEO of Celsius Cryptocurrency Platform for Defrauding Investors," NY Attorney General, January 5, 2023, https://ag.ny.gov/press-release/2023/attorney-general-james-sues-former-ceo-celsius-cryptocurrency -platform-defrauding.

261 **Information on Celsius's inner workings:** Final Report of Shoba Pillay, Examiner, United States Bankruptcy Court (Southern District of New York), January 30, 2023, https://cases.stretto.com/public/x191/11749 /PLEADINGS/1174901312380000000039.pdf.

261 **Binance was one of Bitzlato's biggest counterparties:** Tom Wilson and Angus Berwick, "Exclusive: Binance moved $346 mln for seized crypto exchange Bitzlato," Reuters, January 24, 2023.

261 **the New York State Department of Financial Services:** Patricia Kowsmann and Caitlin Ostroff, "Regulator Orders Crypto Firm Paxos to Stop Issuing Binance Stablecoin," *Wall Street Journal*, February 13, 2023.

262 **the government charged . . . Bitzlato:** press release, "Founder and Majority Owner of Bitzlato, a Cryptocurrency Exchange, Charged with Unlicensed Money Transmitting," US Attorney's Office (Eastern District of New York), https://www.justice.gov/usao-edny/pr/founder-and-majority-owner-bitzlato -cryptocurrency-exchange-charged-unlicensed-money.

264 **Silvergate made a "risk based decision":** Rachel Louise Ensign, "Crypto Bank Silvergate to Shut Down, Repay Deposits," *Wall Street Journal*, March 8, 2023.

264 **four men . . . Tether holdings:** Ben Foldy, Ada Hui, and Peter Rudegeair, "The Unusual Crew Behind Tether, Crypto's Pre-eminent Stablecoin," *Wall Street Journal*, February 2, 2023.

264 **who is known as Christopher Harborne:** Protos, "Brexit's top donor outed as Bitfinex, Tether parent shareholder," April 23, 2021, https://protos.com /bitfinex-tether-digfinex-shareholder-harborne-brexit-bankroller/.

265 **issuance of the long-delayed Bitcoin Bond:** Michael D. McDonald, "El Salvador Passes Law Allowing Bitcoin Bond Issuance," Bloomberg, January 11, 2023.

INDEX